Literature and Lives

Literature and Lives

A Response-Based, Cultural Studies Approach to Teaching English

Allen Carey-Webb
Western Michigan University

National Council of Teachers of English
1111 W. Kenyon Road, Urbana, Illinois 61801-1096

Staff Editor: Tom Tiller

Interior Design: Doug Burnett

Cover Design: Barbara Yale-Read

NCTE Stock Number: 29641-3050

It is the policy of NCTE in its journals and other publications to provide a forum for the open discussion of ideas concerning the content and the teaching of English and the language arts. Publicity accorded to any particular point of view does not imply endorsement by the Executive Committee, the Board of Directors, or the membership at large, except in announcements of policy, where such endorsement is clearly specified.

Although every attempt is made to ensure accuracy at the time of publication, NCTE cannot guarantee that all published addresses for electronic mail or Web sites are current.

Library of Congress Cataloging-in-Publication Data

Carey-Webb, Allen, 1957–
      Literature and lives : a response-based, cultural studies approach to
   teaching English/Allen Carey-Webb.
            p.   cm.
      Includes bibliographical references and index.
      ISBN 0-8141-2964-1 (pbk.)
      1. Literature—Study and teaching—United States. 2. Pluralism (Social
   sciences) in literature—Study and teaching—United States. 3. English
   language—Study and teaching—Social aspects—United States. 4. Reader-
   response criticism—United States. I. Title.

   LB1631 .C39 2000
   820'.71'073—dc21   00-053293

Teaching is an act of love, and thus an act of courage.
Paulo Freire, *Pedagogy of the Oppressed*

Contents

Acknowledgments

This book emerges from twenty-five years of teaching and scholarship, and my debts are great and to many people.

First, to those who guided me or collaborated with me in the teaching described in these pages—Diana Golden, David Hartleroad, Andrea Doxtader, Missy Deer, Tisha Pankop, Eva Kendrick, Melinda Dobson, Rigoberta Menchú, and Jackie Johnson—thank you for making this book possible.

I have learned so much from my high school and college students in Oregon and Michigan and have mentioned only a few by name. Yet over and over again, all of my students have facilitated my growth as a person and as a teacher. My thanks especially to students at Western Michigan University, aspiring and practicing English teachers themselves, who read and made suggestions on drafts of this manuscript; this would be a lesser book without their help.

So many of my teachers have shaped the ideas that guide this book. Robert Beery and Gene Persha at Jefferson Junior High School in Minneapolis made social issues important to me. Laura Perko at Lincoln High School in Portland, Oregon, inspired me to make literature part of my life. Harold Pagliaro, Susan Snyder, and Craig Williamson at Swarthmore College developed my passion for literary scholarship. Ken Sharp, Chuck Beitz, and Linda Lim made political theory meaningful. At Lewis and Clark College, Paul Magnussen taught me about writing and helped me make it through student teaching. Vernon Jones and Dan Duke sensitized me to classroom interactions. Susan Kirschner introduced me to women's literature. Deborah Lockwood and Steve Beckham offered encouragement and directed me toward doctoral study. Rick Hardt has been a professional mentor for twenty-five years. At Lakeridge High School, Jo Wollen supervised a rank beginner. At the University of Oregon, Steve Rendall introduced me to literary theory, and Barbara Guetti, Irving Wolfarth, Wolf Solich, Linda Kintz, Elizabeth Davis, and Tres Pyle deepened my understanding. Bill Strange directed me to English education and modeled a Euro-American teacher who walked the walk in minority literature. Suzanne Clark reminded me that *how* I teach tells more than *what* I teach. Alan Wolfe nurtured me, supported my interest in postcolonial literature, and offered a model of engaged thematic curriculum—I miss him.

I could not have survived in the teaching profession, or written this book, without fine colleagues all along the way. At Swarthmore College, Jean Sternlight, Ari Gabinet, and Immanuel Jinich befriended and supported a kid from the West Coast. At West Linn High School, fellow teachers Bob Hamm, Ward Lewis, Greg Stephens, Dave Holmberg, Anna Druse, Pat Cole, and Larry Hunt helped me come through the early years and, eventually, thrive in the classroom. At the University of Oregon, fellow graduate students Yue Gang, Marilyn Miller, Lifongo Vitende, Anuncia Escala, Paul Semonin, Tugrul Ilter, and Ken Johnson created a remarkable intellectual community. At Western Michigan University, John Cooley, Gwen Raaberg, Ellen Brinkley, Connie Weaver, Jil Larson, Paul Farber, Gunilla Holm, Susan Edgerton, Joe Kretovics, Peter Walker, Mike Jayne, and Debbie LaCroix provided a personally and intellectually supportive environment in which to work and learn. Mark Richardson, Jil Larson, Daneen Wardrop, Grace Tiffany, and Scott

Dykstra offered a reading of the first three chapters and reminded me not to dismiss the contributions of the New Critics too lightly. At the University of Cantabria, Gonzalo Martinez Camino, Juan Cuesta, Ed Dalley, and Javier Diaz Lopez welcomed me into another culture.

As both a high school teacher and as a college professor, I have been fortunate to have outstanding chairs and administrators who upheld my teaching and fostered experimenting. I greatly appreciate the support of Grace Herr, Dick Sagor, Ken Hill, Bob Kane, Shirley Scott, Arnie Johnston, and Elise Jorgens. Other teachers should be so lucky.

Thank you to Western Michigan University for the precious sabbatical during the academic year 1998–99 that allowed me to finish the first draft of this book.

Dawn Boyer, Michael Greer, and Peter Feely, my developmental editors at NCTE, offered unflagging encouragement over the years during which this book was in process. Tom Tiller at NCTE did an excellent close reading of the manuscript.

Cathy Lewis, Holly Zimmerman, and Emily Roberts at Western Michigan University gave me a hand searching the Internet. Meg Dupuis helped with illustration and permissions.

Many ideas have been tried out on audiences at conventions held by NCTE and the Michigan Council of Teachers of English. I prize these conferences, those who organize them, and those who give feedback to presenters.

This book's extensive bibliography barely begins to capture my many intellectual debts; yet I take full credit for mistakes, omissions, and shortcomings.

Literature and Lives has most certainly been a family effort. I cherish the support, ideas, and welcome distractions provided by Jill, Nathan, and Jessica.

Permissions

Grateful acknowledgment is made to Afeni Shakur and Amaru Entertainment, Inc., for permission to reprint material from "Trapped" by Tupac Shakur.

In addition, portions of this book have been drawn from previously published essays:

Material in Chapter 2, "Teaching about Homelessness," was previously published in "Homelessness and Language Arts: Contexts and Connections" in *English Journal* 80.7 (1991), pp. 22–28.

Material in Chapter 3, "Genderizing the Curriculum: A Personal Journey," was previously published in "Women's Writing and the Literature Curriculum at Y2K" in *Oregon English Journal* 22.1 (2000), pp. 43–50.

Material in Chapter 4, "Addressing the Youth Violence Crisis," was previously published in somewhat different form in "Youth Violence and the Language Arts: A Topic for the Classroom" in *English Journal* 84.5 (1995), pp. 29–37. Selected portions also appeared in "Prison, Race, and Social Justice: Teaching to the Contemporary Crisis" in *College Literature* 22.3 (1995), pp. 1–16.

Material in Chapter 5, "Shakespeare and the New Multicultural British and World Literatures," was previously published in "A Multicultural Tempest: Shakespeare for the 1990s" in *English Journal* 82.4 (1993), pp. 30–35.

Material in Chapter 6, "*Huckleberry Finn* and the Issue of Race in Today's Classroom," was previously published in "Racism and *Huckleberry Finn:* Censorship, Dialogue, and Change" in *English Journal* 82.7 (1993), pp. 22–31.

Material in Appendix A, "Letter Exchange with a First-Year Teacher," was previously published in "Sometimes Things Just Don't Work Out" in *English Journal* 88.6 (1999), pp. 19–22.

A longer and somewhat different version of the material included in Appendix B, "A Note to Teachers on the Truth of Rigoberta Menchú's Testimonial," is slated for publication as "Teaching, Testimony, and Truth: Rigoberta Menchú's Credibility in the North American Classroom" in *The Rigoberta Menchú Controversy,* edited by Arturio Arias (forthcoming from the University of Minnesota Press).

Introduction

I have found teaching to be like writing—a rich and recursive undertaking. Starting a new class is like beginning a rough draft. At the outset I am anxious that the class will "work." As the semester goes forward I have surges of energy, sometimes productive and sometimes not, an occasional good passage surrounded by other places that need work. Teaching the course a second time, like rewriting, involves reorganizing, cutting the extraneous, expanding the good stuff, and moving toward a more polished product. As I gain experience, I know better where I want to focus, and it becomes easier to clarify the main ideas.

In teaching, as in writing, main ideas need revision. What I continue to learn brings new insights and directions. As my confidence as a teacher develops, I have found it easier to listen to my students, to weave their responses into the curriculum, and to rewrite the drafts of my courses by attending to their lives and experiences. In so doing, I find myself in a dynamic interchange that never fixes itself as a final draft.

This book shares some of my "rough drafts," stories from my classroom where the main ideas emerge from new approaches that we now call "cultural studies." I try to show how these main ideas undergo revision as I interact with and learn from students in a "response-based" environment. My students have ranged from troubled teenagers to advanced graduate scholars, from suburban ninth graders to inner-city African Americans, from high schoolers with "senioritis" to highly motivated aspiring and practicing teachers. As this book puts forward visions of response-based cultural studies teaching, I will, at times, propose ideas I am working on but have not yet "proven." Drawing on the classes I have taught, I am also trying to imagine what my next draft might look like. Often I come to questions, not final answers. In this sense, though you now have in your hands a "finished" book, it is a book that, like my own teaching, is still being "written."

On my teaching journey I have found that literary scholarship and theory can make the connections between literature and our students' lives stronger, better, and, as the kids now say, "fresher" than ever. This view may astonish some of my colleagues who think of literary scholarship as stuffy and obscure or of literary theory as dry and esoteric. Many may be surprised that I think literary theory or scholarship has any relevance whatsoever to middle school, high school, or even undergraduate English teaching. Yet, as I have learned through my own experience, the way that we teach literature is now and has always been governed by particular literary theories and schools of literary scholarship—whether or not we understand or acknowledge them.

The more I have been able to learn about the philosophies that shape the academic study of literature, the better I understand what I actually do as I teach English, and the better I can explain my teaching practices to my colleagues, to administrators, and, above all, to my students. To understand and go beyond the training we have received, to explain what we currently do, to bridge to new possibilities, and to help us make the best choices for our students—for all of these aims, theory has great potential. Yet literary theory in particular can be obscure, especially when it is removed from the context of the world in which we live and teach. Thus, I will approach theory through the stories I tell about my own classroom. My goal is to put the power of theory where it will be of most use: in the hands of teachers.

Tracing my own growth and evolution, each chapter of this book focuses in turn on a class I have taught and, often, on the classrooms of other teachers I am working with as we address related themes and issues. At the same time, each chapter explores my development of a thematic and theoretically informed cultural studies approach to teaching. In so doing, each chapter includes brief introductions to literary theories, scholarly approaches, or literature teaching issues relevant to and emerging from my classroom experiences. Since these introductions are set off from the text, they can be read or studied separately, and, taken together, they provide a sort of teacher's guide to literary scholarship and theory.

The first chapter, while telling a story from one of my early years as a teacher, introduces reader response and cultural studies. Each of the theories addressed in subsequent chapters offers yet another angle on the teaching of literature and, at the same time, demonstrates, either by illustration or counter example, the potential of the emerging field of cultural studies for the classroom. In the sixth chapter, I address two issues vital to classroom teachers: the formation of the literary canon and the problem of censorship. In the chapter before the conclusion I talk about an experimental class I have taught for aspiring English teachers, and here I also address some of the latest literary theories, including postmodernism and deconstruction.

Through the years, my classes have been influenced by nearly all of the new theories and approaches to literary scholarship, yet my personal experience cannot begin to represent the wonderful variety and possibility of English teaching. Even though I have taught in several schools and universities, I have always worked, like all teachers, within the constraints of particular teaching assignments, classrooms, budgets, and institutions. This explains, for example, why the chapters on the youth violence crisis and on censorship tend to focus on texts and issues that arose as I taught introductory courses in African American literature. Had I been teaching other courses at the time, the texts, discussion, and focus would, of course, have been different.

New teachers at all levels face staggering demands, including the high-speed and high-stakes effort to master classroom exchanges and relationships, as well as the challenge of acquiring suitable teaching ideas and materials. (New teachers might want to skip straight away to Appendix A, which presents an e-mail exchange about how to survive the first year.) As we gain experience we find ourselves going beyond the textbooks and anthologies we are provided with and beyond the training we have received. I have found theoretically informed English teaching to be a risk, an adventure, and an opportunity to engage students that I can't reconcile with canned or cookbook approaches.

Yet, for everything they have to offer, the theories and methods I want to bring forward here are not "silver bullets," and, in teaching, as my own classroom frequently reminds me, there are no guarantees. I make a case for a reader response–based cultural studies approach to teaching literature because this approach has opened up relevant possibilities for my classroom. I am confident that many of the materials and methods I describe can be adapted to a wide range of students and settings.

Thus, with every chapter, you will also find modest annotated bibliographies of materials I have used and suggestions for continued professional reading. Given the demands on teacher time, I know carefully selective lists can be helpful, yet I also believe that the most important reading and classroom materials are ones we find for ourselves. They are specific to the moment, to our particular students, courses, and situations. Libraries, bookstores, the Internet, conferences, fellow teachers, and our students—all are brimming with materials, possibilities, and ideas that will evolve our teaching and greatly enrich our classrooms. The secret is not to repeat someone else's list or experience, but to begin your own looking, listening, researching, exploring, and experimenting.

In this book, I shuttle between secondary school and college classrooms. Living in both worlds, so to speak, I am aware of a profound communication gap. Public school language arts teachers and college English professors have far too little contact, and there can be misunderstanding, even suspicion and lack of respect, between us.

As I hope every chapter in this book illustrates, middle school, high school, and college teachers have a great deal to learn from each other. We teach the same students, often the same works of literature, and share backgrounds, methods, and goals. College professors depend on public school teachers to provide them skilled students excited about literature study. Public schools depend on college teachers to take the interest and needs of aspiring and practicing teachers seriously. It is true that college professors need to get off their campuses, visit public school classrooms, and enter into dialogue and professional exchange with public school teachers. It is also true that public school teachers need to continue their literature educations and open themselves up to theoretical perspectives on their teaching and curriculum. I hope that *Literature and Lives* helps bridge the gaps between secondary school and college English teaching. Working together is eminently to our mutual benefit and very much in the interest of our students.

Currently, as a professor of English education and postcolonial literature, I find myself more committed than ever to language arts and literature teaching. Classes of aspiring new teachers thrust me into the exciting ferment that is going on in our profession. New materials are constantly at hand. The idealism of rookie teachers rejuvenates me, and the skill and openness of seasoned veterans inspires me.

Wherever you are in the profession, I hope *Literature and Lives* fires your imagination, generates questions, and opens possibilities that you and your students find meaningful. I see this book as a moment in a conversation, a conversation between theory, scholarship, curriculum, and classroom realities, between students and the world we all live in, and between you and me as reader and writer. Experiment with what you find here, and share your results with others. Let me know where these experiments take you and your students.

1 A Course in Contemporary World Literature

Contemporary World Literature" was not a subject that I knew much about. I had never taught the class before. I didn't have a textbook. I didn't have any prepared curriculum. Yet in a few days, streaming in to meet me in room 12C would be a rowdy group of twenty-nine high school kids. In this mixed lower-track course for sophomores who weren't taking a writing class and seniors who were avoiding British Literature, student reading levels would range from fourth-grade to college.

Three years earlier I had entered the profession with an English degree and a teaching credential, but otherwise poorly prepared to deal with the students and courses for which I was responsible. My training was primarily in British literature, with an emphasis on the tradition of Chaucer, Shakespeare, and the Romantic poets. In my college classes we had attempted to understand the unity of form and meaning in imaginative works of art and contemplated the supposed "eternal truths" that literature revealed to us. How such literature or such truths might be understood by teenagers as significant to their lives was not a subject that, as far as I can tell, crossed the mind of my professors. Even by the restricted standards of the 1970s, my college courses were narrowly focused. The only literature by a woman writer that I was asked to read during those four years were a few short stories by Flannery O'Connor. I never encountered—in fact I wonder now if at that time I had ever heard of—any writing by American minority authors. I had never been asked to read a book published within the last fifty years or written by an author outside of the British-American tradition. In other words, I had never taken a class or even been assigned a text that might be called "world" or even "contemporary" literature.

I learned from the former World Literature teacher that copies of *Old Yeller* were available. I am not especially proud of the fact that to this day I haven't read *Old Yeller*. Maybe by the time you read this I will have remedied my ignorance. For all I know this presumably heartwarming story about a boy and his dog is the ideal classroom text. At the time, however, *Old Yeller* seemed so far from the exciting promise of "Contemporary World Literature" that I couldn't envision handing it out.

Instead, I headed to our school's book room to see what else, if anything, I could find that was not yet reserved by another teacher—all of them senior to me. Unfortunately our ready-to-retire book room warden was convinced that the fewer books on her shelves, the less work she would have to do, and she consigned unused titles to the flames. Those that remained she was reluctant to let escape. In other words, beyond *Old Yeller,* precious little was available. The only thing I could break away with that might possibly fit the definition of "Contemporary World Literature" was a dusty class set of Elie Wiesel's autobiography, *Night.* So with this book the semester began.

Those who have taught *Night* have some idea what my students and I were in for. Wiesel tells the story of the Jewish Holocaust from his own experience as a fourteen-year-old deported to Auschwitz and separated from his mother and sisters. Desperate to keep his father alive, Elie constantly risks his own well-being in a futile struggle that shakes his faith in God and humanity. Written in a simple and direct testimonial prose, the book allowed students of different reading abilities to enter into the discussion. Their responses and questions varied and included many that I could not answer: How could this have happened? What would I have done if these things happened to me and my family? Why didn't the Jews fight back? (Did they fight back?) Are there things like this happening today that we don't know about? How could we find out? What could we do? Students were responding in an intense and personal way to a story that seemed to be far from their own experience. Moreover, their behavior was unlike that of the other "low-track" high school students I had been teaching. These students were reading ahead, doing the homework, listening to each other in class. They were caring deeply about—and feeling troubled by—what they were learning.

I tried to create a variety of ways for them to turn this interest into a fuller response. In addition to small- and large-group discussions, students also wrote letters to Mr. Wiesel, illustrated scenes that seemed important to them, and created monologues for a number of characters. Several students became involved in research on various aspects of the Holocaust, trying to find answers to questions that arose in the discussion. Through their research and my own, we began to find other materials that would enrich our understanding of Nazi racism. We read a selection from William Shirer's *The Rise and Fall of the Third Reich* that showed how Hitler created youth movements, influenced schools, controlled the media, and "Nazified" German culture. We watched a re-creation (and translation into English) of one of Hitler's speeches from the video of Albert Speer's controversial *Inside the Third Reich.* (See the list toward the end of this chapter for additional materials for teaching about the Holocaust.) As we learned more about cultural and historical contexts, the Holocaust began to seem less like an abstracted evil and more like a real event in history—

it began to seem, in other words, not so distant from the present day. This sense significantly increased with the next class event.

Inspired by the impact of *Night* and the interest it kindled in the students, I contacted the Holocaust Resource Center at our local synagogue. From their librarian I learned that some extermination camp survivors were still alive and living in our area. With a measure of uncertainty, I phoned the number the librarian had given me and asked Diana Golden if she would be willing to speak with my class. Mrs. Golden told me that for forty years following World War II, she had not spoken about her experiences, not even sharing them with her own children. Yet, because a few historians had begun claiming that the Holocaust had never taken place, she was determined that the truth must be told. She said she had been seventeen years old when she was taken to Auschwitz, about the same age, she supposed, as many of my students. "Yes," she said. "I will come to your class."

Nearing seventy, Mrs. Golden was confident and resolute, yet it was clearly difficult for her to talk to us, and, at times, her courageous poise gave way to tears. Rounding up, train cars, Auschwitz in the middle of the night, selection, loss of family, desperate struggle for survival: as my students listened to Mrs. Golden speak, these were no longer events in a book but something that had happened to a real person we were coming to know. The students listened intently, and the questions they had been asking came up again with even greater urgency. I had talked to the class about treating Mrs. Golden respectfully; therefore, I felt a bit uncomfortable when, as time for questions was nearing an end, Sherrie, one of the "low-achieving" sophomores, asked if she could touch the numbers that had been tattooed on Mrs. Golden's arm in the concentration camp.

In response, Mrs. Golden pulled up the sleeve of her dress and rolled over her hand to expose the inside of her forearm. First Sherrie, and then the other students, stepping tentatively out of their desks and across the room, reached out and touched the clearly visible blue numbers marked on Diana Golden's skin.

Mrs. Golden's visit to my World Literature class was an event that I believe none of us will forget. Looking back on it eighteen years later, I recognize that her visit and the teaching of a Holocaust unit also touched something in me that began to enlarge my vision of English teaching. Starting off Contemporary World Literature with *Night*, the Holocaust, and Diana Golden's visit, my students and I were immersed in discussion, writing, questions, and feelings that went beyond the boundaries of English literature study—at least as I, until then, had experienced it. We weren't addressing literary genres or terminology. We weren't climbing a list of great writers simply "because they were there." We weren't learning writing skills merely to satisfy the academic requirements of the competency test or the next grade level. Instead we were vitally concerned about real people in the real world, about what had happened to them, and about what these events meant to us. We were reading, writing, and learning intensely, about history, literature, culture, racism, and how they intertwined. Above all, and at Sherrie's instigation, students were being touched, and touching others, in ways that I hadn't expected.

As that Holocaust unit drew to a close, I found myself, as usual, rushing to consider what the class would be doing next. Although I didn't understand exactly how things would be different, I realized I had a new level of intensity, involvement, and meaning to aim for. Trying to identify possible materials, I went from our school to bookstores and to the public library. I wanted to build on the themes and issues we had started with, and I hoped to extend them into a broader consideration of "Contemporary World Literature" relevant in some measure to my students and their questions about what was happening *today*. In the 1980s, Cold War tensions were still high. Threat of nuclear war was a subtle given in our lives, something there but rarely brought to the surface. The word *Holocaust* provided a link, I thought, and I came across several collections of contemporary Russian short stories. Photocopying like mad, I made these stories the focus of my next unit, one that allowed us to look at our "enemies" in the "Evil Empire" and discover a human face. We watched the film *Doctor Zhivago,* and students did research projects on Russian life and culture. My library and bookstore forays also led me to read contemporary works from India and Africa written in English, as well as works from Latin America in translation. Literary works, films, essays, photographs, speakers, research, library trips: they all began piling up on each other and extending our curriculum and analysis in many directions. As I feverishly sought ways to teach that could develop the kinds of human connection that were encouraged by *Night,* new worlds of literature, experience, and supplementary materials were opening up.

My journey into more effective teaching included plenty of bumps and potholes, as my experience with Contemporary World Literature illustrates. In an effort to develop a more careful step-by-step scope and sequence for our students, integrate writing and reading into the same courses, and reduce tracking, our English department decided to drop its remaining elective classes in favor of a sequence of grade-level-based, full-year survey courses. Thus, the year after I started teaching Contemporary World Literature, the course was no longer in existence. Although individual teachers could vary what they were doing, the content in the new courses was organized by the nationally standardized textbooks with which we were provided. The new understandings and approaches generated from the Holocaust unit did not have an opportunity to mature in a second draft of the course. Nonetheless, teaching Contemporary World Literature showed me ways that my teaching could center on sensitizing students to the experiences of others, help them communicate from heart and mind together, and connect them to pressing social issues.

I allowed what I was learning from Contemporary World Literature to spill over into my other classes. My department chair agreed to purchase a class set of Alan Paton's *Cry, the Beloved Country*, and I introduced it into my British literature class. We watched movies about South Africa and read history and contemporary essays. As with *Night* I realized I needed to respect my students' responses and allow their questions and interests to set directions for where our discussion and reading would take us. The divestment debate (did U.S. companies need to leave South Africa in order to fight apartheid?) was going on in Congress, and the class expressed an interest in the issue. Thus we read newspaper articles and magazine essays and debated what stand the United States should take on the issue. While I had an opinion, in this discussion it was important for me to hold it back, to let students explore the complexities and make up their own minds. We didn't come to a consensus on divestment, but their reading of *Cry, the Beloved Country* was becoming all the more compelling and relevant. And, as they learned about apartheid keeping White and Black people ignorant of each other in South Africa, my suburban middle-class White students began to ask about the segregation that was still evident in our community.

In a hallway closet I found an out-of-use class set of John Hersey's book, *Hiroshima,* and started using it in Freshman Language Arts along with a variety of essays, speakers, and films that addressed what we could do today about the nuclear threat. As I expanded the kinds of texts that were read in my classes, addressed present-day issues, and developed integrated thematic units, my teaching was moving away from a narrow emphasis on the literature I had read in high school and college. The more I strayed from the textbooks, the more risks I took, the more I found material in which the students could develop a passionate interest, the greater excitement and relevance my courses seemed to take on—and the more my students were willing to read, write, and work.

Still I felt a reluctance to let go of traditional curriculum and approaches. My own high school experience, my undergraduate education, and the weighty and authoritative organization of the textbooks I was given made me doubt the innovations I was making. Had I strayed from what literature classes were supposed to be? Were students learning the "right stuff"? I still valued the classics, but how could I integrate the new worlds of literature I had glimpsed? What changes could I make? How far should, or could, I go? What was the content of language arts classes *supposed* to be, anyway? Who had decided? Why?

Contemporary World Literature and the experimentation I was doing in other classes made it plain that all students, and especially those struggling in school, needed to discover that everyone, even the most persecuted or oppressed, has a voice that can and should be heard and respected. I saw that for the White and relatively affluent American young people in my upper-track courses, comparing their experiences with people different from themselves was a revelation. Somehow the media and the insulation of their suburban community led many to believe that their experience was "normal," that everyone else in the world was either like them—or wanted to be like them. Although it was preliminary and haphazard, Contemporary World Literature also convinced me of the value of focusing on the content of literature and of carefully linking materials together in historically meaningful ways, ways that would generate student interest and make possible a wide variety of responses. This approach helped me better connect reading, writing, and speaking. It helped me make my teaching simultaneously relevant to issues in the contemporary world and respectful of my students' independent and critical thinking.

Although at the time I didn't have a name for the kind of teaching I was beginning to do, today I would call it a form of "response-based cultural studies," one that draws on both the "reader response" work pioneered many years ago by Louise Rosenblatt and the emerging "cultural studies" approaches rapidly affecting literature and cultural study around the world. My first experiments with response-based cultural studies were almost chance events, but, as I have learned more about literary theory and history, reader response and cultural studies have come increasingly to provide a base for careful thinking about English teaching—both the way I have been trained and the teaching I am trying to do.

Reader Response

Although they may not recognize themselves as enacting a literary theory, teachers who encourage students to develop and explore their personal re-

▶

sponses to literature are putting the "reader response" theory into practice. Rather than lecture, recitation, or the discovery of some predetermined meaning, reader response teachers favor small- and large-group discussions, literature circles, creative writing, and dramatic and artistic activities that help students engage actively with what they read and express their individual responses and understandings—just the kind of activities my students became involved in with *Night*. First set forward as a coherent theory of reading by Louise Rosenblatt in the now-famous book *Literature as Exploration* (1938), reader response emphasizes that the way a work of literature is understood depends upon the interaction between reader and text and upon the presumably unique personal meaning that readers create for themselves.

Because this approach respects student reactions and insights and focuses on the interactive process of their learning, reader response is an important theory for teachers to know about. Rosenblatt herself emphasized teaching contemporary literature more likely to engage student interest and passion. She also understood that the more reader-response teachers can draw student experiences into the classroom—the more self-aware students become—the better readers they are likely to be. As a movement for the reform of English teaching, reader response has helped teachers move away from telling students what to think or herding them all to the same "correct" interpretation.

At the same time, however, an exclusively reader-response approach does have limitations. Rosenblatt's followers have tended to romanticize both the effect of literature and the individual uniqueness of student response. Because of the focus on reader rather than text, reader response tends not to be very helpful when it comes to thinking about content for English courses, about how we choose among "great" works, about why we might prefer the literary canon to popular texts or vice versa. Indeed, some reader-response-based classrooms, such as the one described by Nancie Atwell in the first edition of her fabulous book *In the Middle*, focus entirely on students as independent readers with no common texts for analysis and discussion. By itself, then, a knowledge of reader-response theory would not have provided answers to the questions I was having about curriculum after teaching Contemporary World Literature. Reader response doesn't facilitate our thinking about how we define "cultural literacy," how and why we should select literature for study, nor even what "literature" is and how our definitions have changed over time. Yet, as reader response takes us into the interaction between reader and text, it opens the door to a variety of approaches that further and more compellingly elaborate the connection between literature and lives.

Cultural Studies

The very limitations of reader response are precisely the strengths of a cultural studies approach. Cultural studies emphasizes the integration of literary works, even the most canonical, with the whole range of cultural expression. In the classroom, cultural studies calls for up-to-date and engaging thematic curriculums where culture, social structures, and historical circumstances are explored side by side with a particular emphasis on how those issues touch real people in the present day. While it draws on the insights and interests of "multiculturalism," cultural studies is both broader in its inclusion of issues of social class, women's studies, and popular culture, and more critical in its emphasis on social change. Thus the cultural studies movement explores not only the high literary culture that has been the traditional domain of English teaching, but also the lives of people whose voices, perspectives, and experiences are seen as the very stuff of which culture is made. As I came to learn about cultural studies, I began to realize that I had already started doing it in Contemporary World Literature and my other courses.

In exploring a particular issue or theme, a cultural studies approach might involve doing a close and careful reading of one or more literary works, along with studying a television program, doing library research, and reading prose essays. Research papers can be combined with literary analysis, personal reflection, and argumentation. A cultural studies approach might lead us to compare traditional canonical authors with contemporary popular materials, including the mass media. Cultural studies invites a wide variety of new and potentially invigorating writing into teaching, such as interviews, ethnography, testimonials, surveys, film, and media analysis. It urges us to be self-reflective but not cavalier about the disciplines we work in. While mixing genres and crossing disciplinary boundaries, cultural studies spurs us also to consider how the establishment of genres and disciplines has functioned historically.

Thus cultural studies fosters critical thinking and activism as it wrestles with how we see ourselves and others in the process of understanding and acting in society. The perspectives of "marginal" groups such as women, ethnic minorities, and working-class people are important in cultural studies. Valuable in themselves, they also help us better understand dominant ways of seeing. Thus cultural studies is interested in ethical, moral, and social questions. Emerging from British social theory, studies of American popular culture (such as television and film), and new forms of literary scholarship (such as multicultural studies, gender studies, and postcolonial studies), cultural studies is increasingly shaping the university-level study of literature, generating academic conferences, publications, and new ways of

▶

thinking about the job of English teaching. Cultural studies serves as an umbrella category inclusive of many of the new theories and approaches we will examine in this book.

Yet cultural studies also needs reader response if it is to avoid the danger of "political correctness"—when teachers dictate, legislate, or otherwise pressure students to hold particular opinions rather than respecting their insights, experiences, ideas, and perspectives. As we further explore the concept of cultural studies in subsequent chapters, I hope to show that bringing reader response and cultural studies approaches together offers exciting possibilities for the language arts teaching of the future.

Many teachers have already begun to integrate reader response and cultural studies approaches. I have found that an understanding of response-based cultural studies has enhanced my sensitivity and openness to students, increased my range of freedom and choice, and inspired me to become a more aware and a braver teacher. It has helped me carefully and systematically build on the kind of teaching I began in the Holocaust unit mainly by a stroke of luck. Those of us who have been teaching for any length of time have seen dramatic changes inspired by the new research in composition studies and the widespread integration of a writing process approach. A response-based cultural studies approach to English teaching is at least equally important and has the potential to transform our curriculum and purpose.

A couple of years after teaching Contemporary World Literature, I had a conversation with a stranger that led me to take the next step on my journey toward integrating these new approaches into the world of my students. This encounter, and its implications, provide the focus for Chapter 2.

Resources for Teaching about the Holocaust

There is an enormous body of fine materials for teaching about the Holocaust. Here is a short list of high-quality and frequently used resources.

Print Materials

- *The Diary of a Young Girl* by Anne Frank tells the true story of a sensitive and talented Jewish girl hiding out with her family in Amsterdam before her capture and death in Bergen-Belsen.
- *I Never Saw Another Butterfly,* edited by Hana Volavková, is a moving collection of drawings and poems by children in the Terezín Concentration Camp.

- Art Spiegelman's *Maus: A Survivor's Tale* is a Pulitzer Prize–winning exploration of the experience of a survivor and his son, written in a mature comic book format.

- *Night* by Elie Wiesel is the testimony of a teenager transported with his family to Auschwitz and Buchenwald.

- *The Rise and Fall of the Third Reich* by William L. Shirer offers a readable, comprehensive history of the Nazi regime written by an American correspondent who lived in Germany in the 1930s. My students read the sections "The Nazification of Culture," "The Control of Press, Radio, Films," and "Education in the Third Reich" (241–56).

- Primo Levi's *Survival in Auschwitz* is one of the best-known and most powerful survivor testimonies.

- Todd Strasser's novel *The Wave: The Classroom Experiment That Went Too Far,* and the film made from it, demonstrate to American students that fascism can happen in America in a school like theirs.

Films

- *Anne Frank Remembered* interviews Anne's friends, family, and protectors to depict her life before hiding, in the annex, her capture, the Auschwitz camp, and her death in Bergen-Belsen.

- *Night and Fog* by Alain Resnais is an overpowering, unrelenting, and unforgettable short film that uses extensive documentary footage. If you show this film you may want to make viewing optional.

- Steven Spielberg's *Schindler's List* is a Hollywood historical recreation that finds a hero amidst the Holocaust story.

- *Shoah* by Claude Lanzmann includes more than four hours of interviews with survivors and others; an abridged version is also available.

Web Sites for Teaching about the Holocaust

- The "Auschwitz Alphabet" Web site provided by Jonathan Blumen has clear and specific information about the camp and how it functioned: http://www.spectacle.org/695/ausch.html.

- Al Filreis, professor of English at the University of Pennsylvania, maintains a "Literature of the Holocaust" site that offers a rich list of resources, including materials from other genocides in addition to that of the Jews during the Nazi period: http://www.english.upenn.edu/~afilreis/Holocaust/holhome.html.

- The Florida Center for Instructional Technology offers "A Teacher's Guide to the Holocaust" at http://fcit.coedu.usf.edu/Holocaust/.

- The Fortunoff Video Archive for Holocaust Testimonies is maintained by the Yale University Library, and portions of testimonies can be downloaded. See http://www.library.yale.edu/testimonies/homepage.html.The Nizkor Project has a collection of Holocaust materials, including videos. See the project's Web site at http://www.nizkor.org/.

- The Simon Wiesenthal Center's Web site includes a page where questions can be submitted to Holocaust survivors. The site can be found at http://www.wiesenthal.com/.

- The United States Holocaust Memorial Museum has extensive online materials for teachers and students: http://www.ushmm.org/. They offer summer programs and internships for teachers.

Readings in Reader Response

- *How Porcupines Make Love III* by Alan C. Purves, Theresa Rogers, and Anna O. Soter is a theoretical and practical guide to reader response approaches to literature teaching for secondary teachers.

- *Literature as Exploration* by Louise Rosenblatt still makes excellent reading and is the classic text in American reader response.

- *Literature for Democracy: Reading as a Social Act* by Gordon Pradl explores the democratic possibilities of reader response teaching.

- *A Teacher's Introduction to Reader-Response Theories* by Richard Beach is one of a series of books published by NCTE to acquaint teachers with literary theory.

- *"You Gotta BE the Book": Teaching Engaged and Reflective Reading with Adolescents* by Jeffrey D. Wilhelm shows how a passionate middle school teacher can turn on even the most reluctant readers.

Readings in Cultural Studies

- *Crusoe's Footprints: Cultural Studies in Britain and America* by Patrick Brantlinger offers an example of cultural studies scholarship in British literature.

- *Cultural Studies,* edited by Lawrence Grossberg, Cary Nelson, and Paula Treichler, is an enormous and influential collection of academic cultural studies essays that has something for everyone.

- *Cultural Studies in the English Classroom,* edited by James Berlin and Michael J. Vivion, is a collection of essays by English professors about how to integrate cultural studies approaches into their departments and courses. It includes essays on cultural studies teaching in composition and literature courses, including Shakespeare.

- Antony Easthope's *Literary into Cultural Studies* draws on British cultural theory to make a clear argument that literary studies needs to become cultural studies.

- *Media Culture: Cultural Studies, Identity, and Politics between the Modern and the Postmodern* by Douglas Kellner is a good introduction to cultural studies as it is practiced and theorized by academics. Examples of the media culture that Kellner analyzes include *Rambo, Beavis and Butt-Head,* the Gulf War, Spike Lee films, advertising in general, and the cultural phenomenon generated by Madonna.

- *Redrawing the Boundaries: The Transformation of English and American Literary Studies,* edited by Stephen Greenblatt and Giles Gunn, is a collection of approachable essays by leading practitioners of the major schools of literary scholarship and theory.

- *Reshaping High School English* by Bruce Pirie examines the potential impact of new literary theory for high school teaching and is a good lead-in to a cultural studies approach.

- In *Translating the Curriculum: Multiculturalism into Cultural Studies,* Susan Huddleston Edgerton elucidates the theoretical background of cultural studies and draws on her own classroom experiences to address how educators can develop meaningful approaches to teaching literature and autobiography.

2 Teaching about Homelessness

On an October evening, while walking on the wooded hill behind my house, I was startled and a bit frightened to come across a large, bearded man about my age living under a plastic tarp. Perhaps because I was frightened—or maybe just because I am an English teacher—I started talking rapidly to him, telling him about myself and asking questions. John explained that he preferred to camp by himself, away from the dangers of being "rolled" either under the freeway bridge or near the railway tracks. He didn't want to be around the "winos" downtown, the "proselytizing" of the mission, or the unfriendly looks and remarks of passersby. As a single man he didn't qualify for the family shelters. He told me he could make more money at odd jobs than he could by spending the same time chasing welfare or food stamps. Even though he was healthy, a high school graduate, experienced in mechanical work, it was hard to get work without an address, car, phone number, driver's license, ID, or good clothes.

Under his tarp John had a small battery-operated television set. When he learned I lived just down below him he wondered if he could charge his batteries on our porch socket. Over the next few months I saw John and spoke with him often. I began to notice him trudging back and forth to town. In the midst of Oregon's December rains, I noticed his soaking tennis shoes and I bought him an inexpensive pair of work boots, an "early Christmas present." When a couple of odd jobs fell through one week, he borrowed ten dollars to buy food. Over the next month he paid me back, quarter by quarter.

Before I met John I knew we had a "homeless problem" in the United States. After I got to know John, it was as if my antennae were better attuned. I zeroed in on newspaper articles on the subject: homeless parents and children turned away from overcrowded shelters, bulldozed shanties in New York, marches in Washington, D.C. I started to *see* more people on the streets, older people, panhandlers, so-called "crazies," young people, even high school students like the ones I had been teaching for the last seven years. I read Jonathan Kozol's book *Rachel and Her Children: Homeless Families in America.* I saw a film called *Streetwise* about homeless teenagers in Seattle. As I thought of the international scope of the problem, images came to me of the enormous shantytowns I had seen a year earlier in Mexico City.

Through my reading, I learned that there were multiple and complex reasons for the homelessness increasingly affecting a variety of populations. Changes over the past twenty years have included: decreased federal spending on low-income housing; conversion and loss of existing subsidized and low-income housing; destruction and "gentrification" of single-room occupancy hotels; export and elimination of manufacturing jobs, along with increases in low-paying service jobs; rapidly rising rent and utility costs; cutbacks in drug and alcohol treatment; loss of institutional services for persons with mental illness; and, an insufficient and ineffective government "safety net." In short, the most basic cause of homelessness was not an increase in laziness, poor education, or promiscuity, but a loss of jobs and services, and, above all, a shortage of affordable housing.

As my awareness grew I began to realize that I needed to tie the issue of homelessness into my teaching. Inspired by what I was learning in my high school classes, I had taken a year's leave from my high school classroom to start a graduate degree focusing on world literature, and my fellowship called for teaching an introductory college English course in nineteenth- and twentieth-century fiction. Building on the approaches I had started with in Contemporary World Literature and on what I was beginning to learn more formally about cultural studies, I decided to focus the whole literature class on the topic of homelessness and bring in some of the contemporary world literature I was now, finally, reading. This meant not using the literature anthology that was standard fare for the class, but, instead, creating my own reading list.

We began our cultural studies–based investigation of the problem of homelessness by reading Jonathan Kozol's social essay *Rachel and Her Children*, viewing the documentary film *Streetwise*, and having the director of our town's emergency housing program speak to the class. Although this was probably not the way that students had expected their class in nineteenth- and twentieth-century literature to spend its first two weeks, most seemed to go along, becoming involved right away in discussion about the homelessness problem.

The easy part was to sympathize with the plight of the families in the homeless shelters in New York City or the teenagers on the street in Seattle. It was actually harder to come to terms with the issue when it was closer to us. A street about two blocks from our classroom was frequently populated by disheveled people asking for spare change. Many students walked down this street on their way to my class. When the topic of "Thirteenth

Street" came up, a heated discussion ensued. Sean wanted to know if the students should give these people money. Jared doubted that they really even were "homeless." Ray argued that panhandlers and homeless people were not the same. Anessa thought that the people she saw were "lazy." Heather and Lisa didn't feel safe walking down the street when they were there. Jordan said that he was going to school to get an education; why weren't those guys?

It was evident from our discussion that the problem of homelessness was not only close at hand, but also something students had strong feelings about. I sensed that exploring the issues the students were raising would take us deeper, engaging us in new kinds of critical thinking about the world and our places in it.

Drawing on a cultural studies "main idea" like homelessness, a vital dialogue was beginning to emerge between issues in the world and the experiences and knowledge that my students were bringing to class. The reading, film, speaker, and discussion on the topic of homelessness at the beginning of the course created a context for the literature and other materials that we looked at through the rest of the semester. It was within this context that we began reading *Oliver Twist; Down and Out in Paris and London; Cry, the Beloved Country; Nectar in a Sieve,* from India; *Joys of Motherhood,* from Nigeria; and *One Day of Life,* from El Salvador (see the list at the end of the chapter for additional reading suggestions on the topic of homelessness). Our focus on poverty and homelessness gave us something specific to watch for as we read the literary works, and what we learned from one text we could bring to the reading of the next. Using "homelessness" very self-consciously as the guiding principle for this class helped me to recognize that the way I introduce, order, connect, thematize, and conclude my teaching establishes some kind of framework that will inevitably direct what and how students learn. This was equally true, I realized, in the courses I had taught that were organized by literary genres, where we focused on literary structures and terms, or in courses organized along national traditions, where we focused on the relations between authors and periods and how works defined a supposed "national character."

In this class the first literary work we read was the novel *Oliver Twist,* about an orphan in a nineteenth-century English poorhouse who runs away to London and ends up part of a gang of street hoodlums thieving for an evil old man named Fagin. This classic work by Charles Dickens provided us an opportunity to consider the problem of homelessness in a historical context. While Dickens clearly criticizes the hypocrisy of the poorhouse and its failure to meet even minimal standards in helping the poor, the sentimental ending of the novel—where Oliver is rescued by the wealthy and good-hearted Mr. Brownlow—seemed to my students to romanticize solutions to the problem of poverty and homelessness.

As we read the book, I brought another problem to my students' attention: the novel's anti-Semitism. I shared with the students some anti-Semitic political cartoons from Dickens's day that displayed racial stereotypes clearly repeated in *Oliver Twist*. We also looked at letters written to Dickens by his Jewish contemporaries who were highly critical of the Fagin character. Dickens promised his critics he would create a more favorable Jewish character; his novel *Martin Chuzzlewit* was the result. Nonetheless, anti-Semitic portraits exist elsewhere in Dickens and in British literature.

Textbook editors have censored the anti-Semitic scenes from *Great Expectations*—a novel included in all ninth-grade textbooks. (Note Dickens's stereotypical portrayal of "Habraham Latharuth" in the full version of the text.) While understandable, perhaps this censorship is unfortunate. If examining anti-Semitism helps students think about the Holocaust, it is also, unfortunately, relevant in our own day to ongoing anti-Semitism and its subtle variations such as the global conspiracy theories of the far-right militia movement. When I taught *Great Expectations* to ninth graders, they found it enlightening to do close reading of the anti-Semitic scenes. Awareness of the Jewish stereotype led one student in the class to ask us, weeks later, if the obviously humorous "Aged Parent" at the end of the novel might not also be a stereotyped depiction of older people. (Students could also examine other problematic anti-Semitic works or works with anti-Semitic characters from British literature, including, for example, Chaucer's "The Prioress's Tale," Shakespeare's *The Merchant of Venice*, George Eliot's *Daniel Deronda,* and selected poetry of Ezra Pound and T. S. Eliot.)

In my class focused on homelessness, students not only were enabled to think critically about the stereotyping of Fagin, but also they began to see how Jewish stereotypes connected to our study of the homelessness problem. Through discussion, we began to see how the stereotypical treatment of Fagan not only misrepresents Jews but also casts the evil of the social situation onto a particular, flawed individual. Reading Dickens and discussing his novel through a cultural studies perspective removed the halo that can place great writers beyond criticism and helped my students become more sophisticated readers and thinkers.

The next book we read was Stephen Crane's *Maggie: A Girl of the Streets,* a novel frequently taught in high school and college courses not to focus on issues of poverty but to illustrate the literary style of naturalism or realism. Crane was also a journalist, and along with *Maggie* we read several of his "New York City Sketches", in which he described spending alternating days with poor and rich New Yorkers. Contrasting the Dickens and Crane novels allowed my students to make some of the traditional comparisons between sentimentality and realism, and, with the cultural studies approach we were using, this difference had real significance to the questions that students had asked at the outset of the course. Realism suggested that environmental factors needed to be accounted for in explaining human behavior. It was easier in reading Dickens to "blame" the poor for their condition, whereas with Crane there seemed to be an indictment of the social order itself. Several students wrote papers comparing Dickens's portrayal of the prostitute Nancy with Stephen Crane's presentation of Maggie. This comparison allowed the students to consider the effect that differential standards of morality can have on women. Even traditional distinctions between literary periods, such as that between romanticism and naturalism, made more sense to students when they were grounded in the kind of real-world issues that a cultural studies approach was making possible.

We also read George Orwell's *Down and Out in Paris and London*, a work that is part reportage, part autobiography, and part testimony (see Chapter 7 for more discussion of "testimonials"). Like Dickens and Crane, Orwell challenged the middle-class view of the poor as "lazy" or "undeserving" and turned our attention to broader social causes. As we read books by multiple authors, all exploring a common theme, the works shed light on each other. Comparing *Maggie: A Girl of the Streets* with *Down and Out in Paris and London* and *Rachel and Her Children* raised questions about the realism of Crane's naturalism, the filtering of Orwell's reporting, and the selections and organization of the testimony gathered by Kozol. In short, regardless of the genre, we were not hearing the unmediated voice or voices of homeless people themselves; rather, each text was, in its own way, a representation. Putting these texts next to one another undercut any one text's claim to truth, and all the texts, in differing ways, needed to be read as "fiction."

In this class we were still studying Dickens, Crane, and Orwell, but we were thinking about them in historical, social, and political contexts, developing thematic connections that put the classic authors and works into dialogue with popular culture and common experience. I was discovering that a cultural studies approach could be inclusive of authors from the traditional "canon" and that terms like "fiction" could be explored in an English class as not merely a generic category; instead, we were looking at various social "fictions" woven into the literature and shaping our own way of seeing and understanding the world. Students were also becoming better critical readers, more aware of the ways in which texts were socially and historically located and how these works influenced their own views.

Recently I learned about an exercise that Bruce Pirie does with his students to help them gain further perspective on themselves and their social positions as readers:

> When my senior students read a set of essays about social conventions (articles about homelessness and menial labor), I ask them to write "personal" responses, but *not* as themselves. Rather, they react in assigned roles as labor leaders, business owners, homeless people, ultraconservative politicians, feminists, and so on. They then gather in mixed groups to discuss, still in role, these responses. After reflecting on this process, students are in better positions to understand their own participation as an audience—their readings and uses of texts. (Pirie 30)

In my class on homelessness the three "Third World" novels we read allowed the students to draw parallels and make connections with societies we usually mischaracterize as "exotic" or "other" and to think about the problem of homelessness from a more global point of view. The vision in the Indian and African novels of industrial development displacing rural communities, aggregating large impoverished populations in the cities, and assaulting family and community ties was, looking back, familiar from Dickens, Crane, and Orwell. A film like *Roger and Me* (detailing the effects of the movement of automobile plants from Michigan to Mexico) allowed students to draw direct connections between First and Third World homelessness. Some students gained a sense of personal relationship with people very different from themselves. One young woman wrote a moving paper showing similarities between the experience of her own mother and Nnu Ego, the overworked, impoverished Ibo heroine of the ironic Nigerian novel *Joys of Motherhood* by Buchi Emecheta.

The Third World literature we read also suggested differences between homelessness in U.S. cities and in other parts of the world, thus adding to our understanding of the experiences of homeless people. The hardships imposed by colonial and neocolonial relationships were unprecedented in the earlier reading in the course. Manlio Argueta's *One Day of Life,* treating the brutal experience of peasants at the beginning of the revolution in El Salvador, raised tough questions about U.S. foreign policy in the region, about what we might even describe as an active policy of creating homelessness. *One Day of Life* focuses on a systematic repression, a culture of violence and terror that differs both in kind and degree from the other texts we read. Yet, in depicting a resistant and revolutionary consciousness, it raises questions about the factors that inhibit such a consciousness in North America. In order to understand homelessness in Africa and Latin America, a critique of industrial development was not enough; rather, a complex understanding of race and gender relations, international politics, and differing cultural contexts evolved out of our reading. And didn't we need this more complex understanding to think critically about homelessness in America as well?

The thematic cultural studies orientation and the seriousness of the homelessness problem in our immediate community prompted students to attempt a wide variety of forms of research, writing, and direct involvement. Students interviewed community members, including shelter operators, ministers, homeless people, government officials, and even school principals: *How does the problem of homeless children affect your school? How could homeless children be better served by school systems?* A number of students attended community meetings and volunteered in homeless shelters. They talked about their experiences in the class and urged other class members to become more involved. Understanding the various causes of homelessness in Eugene, Oregon, suggested activities that could be undertaken to address our local problem.

When I have taught about serious, difficult, or potentially overwhelming issues like the Holocaust, apartheid, or homelessness, I know that my students stand to gain vital cultural knowledge and significant academic benefit, but I find that I worry about how such heavy topics will affect them emotionally. I have wondered whether or not examining such topics will support or undermine their interest in participating in the world. When such units are over I usually feel positive about the result, and discover yet again that careful reading, discussion, and writing about powerful subjects increases rather than numbs my students' human sensitivity. And I know that they can't wisely participate in the world unless they clearly understand it.

What this course demonstrated to me, then, was that when students recognized the possibility of affecting the homeless crisis in our own community, they were able to become involved and, most important, develop hope for the future. As our class discussions followed the news, students became aware of concerned citizens, political activists, homeless advocates, and homeless people themselves taking various actions across the country; they could see their own activity as not only local but also part of an inclusive social movement involving people of all political parties and from different walks of life. Making these connections, I realized, is a significant part of what reader response and cultural studies teaching is all about.

Reading and discussing the portrayal of homelessness in literary works provided students with critical tools for their cultural studies analysis of real-world people and institutions. Students not only developed sensitivity to others, they also questioned a perfunctory charity. They understood more clearly Hoch and Slayton's point that "a politics of compassion that identifies the vulnerability of the homeless as the cause of their predicament too easily overlooks the social and economic history of the urban working poor and their struggle for affordable shelter" (7–8). If involvement with real-world issues and events developed consciousness, it also led to better written projects, extended and deepened reading, and provided a basis for passionate oral reports and intense class discussion. The course was not a complete break with the conventions of literature study. Students did write "literary analysis" papers, looked in interesting ways at an author's treatment of themes and language, and compared two or more works; yet, as students had a more precise historical and social understanding of the texts, these traditional papers were sharper than usual.

Many students were somewhat surprised by a literature course that focused on homelessness, and the appropriateness of the topic was something that, at times, I debated in my own mind. Teaching the course as a graduate student, I was not sure what the regular faculty would think of my focus on homelessness, how it might affect my future teaching opportunities in the department or my letters of recommendation. I was a bit worried at the end of the second week when one student (I had a class of fifty) told me he was going to drop the class because it was not what he had expected. After I raised the issue in discussion, several others indicated that they felt a literature class should focus on "characters and plot." As the term went on and we read more literature, the students found our initial reading and discussion of the homelessness problem more and more useful to their analyses of the texts. By the middle of the semester I noticed a real enthusiasm, not so much for solving the problem of homelessness— I saw this from the beginning—but for thinking about the social, historical, and thematic content of the literature we were reading. The end-of-term evaluations of the course were almost unanimously positive about focusing on homelessness.

The process of designing and teaching the class raised questions for me about priorities in teaching literature, and it was invigorating to see students begin to ask questions about the purpose and content of what they were studying, even when those questions challenged my own long-held assumptions. For years I had taught in the same way I was trained, emphasizing discussion of plot, character development, and literary language. The historical context of literary works, the political manipulation of language, and the relevance of social issues in the present day were there, but in the back seat. Now, as a graduate student, I was learning about the influence of New Criticism, with its emphasis on the closed and the literary quality of texts as works of art, and thus I was coming to understand more clearly the training I had received in literary study.

New Criticism

Arising in the 1930s and 1940s, New Criticism emphasized the artistic or "aesthetic" aspect of literature, where metaphor, irony, and poetic devices are interpreted so as to come together to create an "organic unity" of form and meaning. Attracted to the beauty of poetic language, New Critics celebrated the complexities of individual literary works. Reacting against historical and political approaches, the New Critics argued that literary works were best understood separately from the lives of their authors or the historical period in which they were written. They returned to the text to justify their interpretations and fostered "close readings" that could escape what they saw as stifling and pedantic academic traditions.

Yet as New Criticism itself became an institutionalized tradition during the conservative 1950s, it was structured into standardized textbooks and reduced to a safe, mechanical method for teaching literature. Just as grammar books (such as Warriners) became the way to teach writing, so literary terms and skills textbooks organized by literary genre became—and still are—the way to teach literature, especially at the secondary level. Controversial issues need not enter literature textbooks—the texts could focus on literary artistry and be adopted without objection in large states like Texas or California. One textbook I used (and it is still one of the sales leaders) emphasized, among others, terms like: alexandrine, apostrophe, caesura, consonance, dénouement, epode, iambic pentameter, kenning, metonymy, ottava rima, Spenserian stanza, sprung rhythm, terza rima, trochee, and villanelle. While such terms may be more definable and "testable" than the varied interpretations made possible by literature, they are difficult to retain or make relevant. For how many of our students do these terms help make literature more beautiful or enjoyable—or relevant?

A cultural studies approach recognizes that there is complexity in all forms of cultural expression; however, the particular kind of complexity that the New Critics were interested in biased them in favor of certain literary works from the high Western canonical tradition, for instance Metaphysical poetry. It was hard for the New Critics to appreciate other kinds of complexity found in various genres or traditions, and as a result the supposedly unbiased technical approach of New Criticism often ends up fostering a rigidly

▶

conservative orientation to the literary canon. Moreover, the subject that a work of literature addresses, what its significance might be to the reader, or what it could tell us either historically or for our own time—none of these vital considerations for good teaching are given much weight in New Criticism.

The contribution of the New Critics was to focus on close reading, on rigorous attention to the words on the page. Teaching students to read carefully is one of the most important things we do. Yet a meaningful approach to close reading needs to build on the strengths of the New Critics and go beyond their narrow literary values. Meaningful English teaching needs to be historically involved, better connected to the real world, and it needs to foster students' appreciation of and critical thinking about the whole range of cultural expression.

As I have moved between different levels in the educational system, I have seen a New Critical emphasis on literary artistry get reduced in junior high, high school, and college classrooms to lectures and quizzes on literary terms, genres, the structure of sonnets, and so on. Well-meaning English teachers, year after year, blame teachers at "lower" levels for failing to teach literary vocabulary—vocabulary that I know for a fact the teachers have, indeed, made strenuous efforts to teach. Memorizing complex and technical vocabulary, however, is not the same thing as mastering a skill or a subject—a truth that most of us have learned about teaching grammar but that we seem less willing to understand about teaching literature.

Over time I have also learned about the alternatives to a New Critical approach, many of which can be understood under the cultural studies umbrella. Teaching a class on homelessness and literature, I began to see more clearly how theoretical views about the nature and function of literature really do influence our everyday teaching, whether or not we recognize it.

When I began teaching, I thought that what went on in my classroom was unique. I used textbooks but usually supplemented and modified them. Yes, I reproduced with my college and high school students some of the same discussions that I had had when I was a student—but there were important differences. I tried to work within the scope and sequence set forward by my department, but there was always significant room for individual variation. In short, my teaching was, as I saw it, my own creation. It wasn't until I went back to graduate school and really began to study literary theory and the history of literature teaching that I began to realize how, even without my knowing it, the values, norms, interests, texts, and purposes of particular schools of literary criticism—especially New Criticism and certain traditional historical approaches—were playing themselves out in my own classroom whether I willed it or not.

I had always told my students that sometimes one has to get out of the world one is living in before he or she can see it clearly, but it was surprising for me to discover that I was the fish that didn't know that it was living in the water—until I was hooked and hoisted into the air. Looking back at the water, so to speak, I came to recognize that traditional literary theory and approaches had created the lake I was swimming in. I had been repeating my own literary training without knowing there were other options. Now I was discovering new literary theories, especially those that fall under the heading "cultural studies," that advocated, supported, and extended the teaching I was experimenting with and finding so successful. Theory was helping me understand and justify doing more in my classroom than simply repeating the way I had been taught.

Historical Criticism

Before, during, and after the rise of New Criticism, at least three alternative historical approaches to literature have been influential: biographical criticism, literary tradition criticism, and political criticism. (Historical approaches evolved from a long tradition of literary study called "philology"; see Appendix C for a discussion of this tradition.)

In biographical criticism, literature is read by examining its relationship to the author's life. A knowledge of the life and struggles of an author gives students a clearer sense of the varied purposes of writing, allowing them to make connections between themselves and well-known artists. Biographical approaches are especially important for teaching some of the "new" literature by women and by minority and Third World authors. Unfortunately many textbook accounts of authors' lives are incomplete or boring—that which might generate the most discussion is absent. For instance, we would not likely learn from a textbook or anthology that Willa Cather was a lesbian, that James Baldwin was gay, that Helen Keller was a radical socialist, or that Forrest Carter was a member of the Ku Klux Klan.

In literary tradition criticism, what matters is not the life of the author, but the relation of his or her work to "great literature" both before and after. Awareness of a literary tradition can help students as they seek to understand the methods, forms, and concerns of writers, and effective teachers

▶

have been able to find connections between literary traditions, history, and students' lives. Yet reading within supposed "literary traditions" may isolate literature from the deeper and more interesting histories it can tell. Uncovering a relationship between, for example, Twain's irony in *Huckleberry Finn* and Crane's naturalism in *Maggie: A Girl of the Streets* may be of less value than comparing their treatment of ethical choices, poverty, public charity, family life, gender roles, and so on. Even the best English teachers face serious hurdles in exciting their students about rarefied "literary traditions." Among the experts, literary traditions, periods, and relationships are notoriously difficult to define; such esoteric disagreements may be difficult for secondary or college students to enter into.

Political criticism is an approach that has been influential in some university courses but less so in high school or middle school. Political criticism has a long history, often tied to social change and revolutionary movements—Leon Trotsky, for instance, wrote *Literature and Revolution* in 1924 while he was directing the Red army from a train car. Socialist criticism was especially popular in the United States during the 1930s. Political critics explore the relationship of literature to social classes and examine the dynamics of power and domination, poverty and racism, resistance and liberty—issues important to Americans from the Revolution to the present. Political critics consider the treatment of social classes in traditional literary works while including literature by and about working-class people, as well as those who are poor and disenfranchised. Yet working-class literature and even the "political" works of familiar authors—such as Stephen Crane's "New York City Sketches," John Steinbeck's *In Dubious Battle,* or Langston Hughes's radical poetry—are too often eliminated from the curriculum. A passion for social change inspired many authors we customarily teach, yet to avoid "controversy" we focus on their literary artistry. (I see my course on homelessness as being in the tradition of political criticism—precisely the tradition the New Critics worked against.)

The students' course evaluations for the class on homelessness encouraged me in the social justice and cultural studies approach we were exploring. In the anonymous final evaluations for the course, a first-year student wrote, "Although the course is a literature class, the instructor dealt more with the issues presented in the books that we read. I found this to be very interesting and very informative." A junior commented, "Most other [English] classes just talked about characters and irony, etc. This class made me think about the world, and how little/lot we've changed our attitudes, our thoughts, and what we've learned from our past history." Another first-year student said, "Theme of the class 'homelessness' a shock at first, but wonderful! I learned more in this class in one term than any other writing or literature class I've ever taken." From a senior English major: "I have benefited tremendously from this class. I was delighted to have a teacher who approached what is generally a 'survey' type class as an intense study of a very important world situation. The reading list was excellent and well chosen."

I realize that an entire course on homelessness and literature may not be feasible or even desirable, as valuable as such a course might be. There is the literature anthology, the textbook, the curriculum guide, the need to coordinate syllabi, shortages of time, and, in high school and middle school at least, the issue of money for purchasing materials. Yet a great deal can be accomplished on a small scale, using works, anthologies, or authors we already teach, and adding or augmenting with one or two new texts, packets, films, or speakers. I think we should recognize that homelessness and poverty have long been important themes in literature and that these themes are often ignored or put to the side in scholarship, textbooks, standardized tests, and teaching. Don't some of our most frequently taught stories—widely treasured works such as "A Modest Proposal," *Huckleberry Finn, The Grapes of Wrath,* or *Of Mice and Men*—address homelessness and the value of the perspectives of homeless people? I believe that taking seriously many of the writers we care about means paying attention to the social dimensions of their work, in relation to both their time and ours. A key to cultural studies teaching, then, is helping students make connections between the literature they read in the classroom and the life experience of people in their community and around the world.

Perhaps it is obvious that the topic of homelessness is only one approach that English teachers can take to help their students make such connections. From a cultural studies viewpoint, there are any number of relevant thematic approaches. Of course, literary texts are interesting to us precisely because they can be appreciated from a variety of perspectives. Meaningful cultural studies themes emerge out of social and historical realities and they challenge us to identify or forge authentic connections between the present and other time periods, and between our cultures and those of other people. As with the topics of homelessness and the Holocaust, cultural studies themes help young people explore their roles and responsibilities as community members and global citizens. The safe, superficial themes often foregrounded in anthologies and school text-books do not usually lead us into authentic forms of cultural studies unless ways are found to engage the realities of the historical and cultural contexts in which we live. Potentially relevant topics such as family, friendship, and love become more meaningful when their cultural diversity, socioeconomic aspects, and significance to present-day realities are addressed. As an English teacher, I found that this course on homelessness allowed me to self-consciously develop curriculum beyond New Critical and safe historical approaches.

Cultural studies does not confine English classes to merely sober or depressing subjects such as the Holocaust or poverty, as important as these issues are. Good teaching should also be joyful, optimistic, and hopeful. Cultural studies allows us to examine issues in the lives of our students and connect them with questions as deep as that of their own identity. Taken together, cultural studies and reader response approaches help students examine, understand, and creatively speak back to the social categories, images, and roles that tell us who we are. At least that is my ambition in the teaching described in the next chapter.

Resources for Teaching about Homelessness

Studies of Homelessness

- *American Refugees* by Jim Hubbard provides photographic documentation of homeless Americans often accompanied by description and personal testimony. An excellent classroom resource for reading, writing, and discussion.

- *The Faces of Homelessness* by Marjorie Hope and James Young is a readable and thorough overview of the homelessness problem with excellent chapters on the deinstitutionalization of mentally ill persons and approaches to working with homeless people.

- *Homeless Youth* by Jan van der Ploeg and Evert Scholte both examines the causes of homelessness among youth and suggests solutions in the form of prevention and intervention programs. A good complement to the film *Streetwise*.

- *London Labour and the London Poor* by Henry Mayhew includes extensive nineteenth-century interviews with poor people in London; the book was drawn on by Charles Dickens for many of his novels. Excerpts from this pioneering work are still fascinating and add to a reading of Dickens or any nineteenth-century literary works treating poverty or homelessness.

- *Rachel and Her Children: Homeless Families in America* by Jonathan Kozol overviews the homeless crisis and challenges readers to rethink their attitudes toward homeless people. Very readable and compelling.

- *Songs from the Alley* by Kathleen Hirsch counterposes a history of homelessness and social policy with the story of contemporary homeless women and the women who work with them.

- *Street Lives: An Oral History of Homeless Americans* by Steven VanderStaay has a wide cross section of short oral histories, many with photographs, that could easily supplement classroom reading.

- *Twenty Years at Hull House* is Jane Addams's famous and inspiring account of her pioneering social work with immigrants in a settlement home in Chicago in the late nineteenth century.

- *What You Can Do To Help the Homeless,* a booklet by Thomas Kenyon and Justin Blau, will interest students with its thirty-two simple and direct strategies for individuals, families, and organizations.

Films Treating Homelessness

- *Down and Out in America* explores the processes that produce and perpetuate homelessness by gathering the testimony of homeless people in New York, Los Angeles, and rural Minnesota. Relevant to any discussion of homelessness, the film includes a segment on the family farm that would tie in well with *The Grapes of Wrath.* There is also footage of some of the locations and individuals mentioned in Kozol's *Rachel and Her Children.* Winner of an Academy Award for Best Documentary in 1986.

- *Home Less Home* is a documentary that contrasts interviews with homeless people with stereotypical images of the homeless as they are depicted in the mass media and in American culture as a whole. Director Bill Brand says, "We're so accustomed to homeless people as victims that when they speak, we no longer believe they are homeless."

- *Modern Times,* directed by Charlie Chaplin in 1936, is a classic silent comedy addressing the impact of industrialization. One can consider it also to be about homelessness.

- *Promises to Keep* was nominated for an academy award. Narrated by Martin Sheen, this film describes the life of Mitch Snyder, empowering homeless activist. The documentary contains footage from the making of the made-for-television film about Snyder, *The Samaritan.*

- *Roger and Me,* directed by Michael Moore, is a quirky documentary assembling testimony about the effects of the closing of General Motors plants in Flint, Michigan. A great discussion starter, it will allow students to hear a variety of perspectives.

- *Salaam Bombay!,* directed by Mira Nair, is a sensitive and insightful portrayal of the lives of homeless children in India, filmed on location and without professional actors.

- *Streetwise* is a documentary about street youth in Seattle in which high school students will recognize themselves and be highly motivated to discuss and write about homelessness.

- *Sugar Cane Alley,* directed by Euzhan Palcy, tells the story of poor sugarcane workers in Martinique in the 1920s from the perspective of a young boy—an effective way to introduce Third World material into the classroom. In French with English subtitles.

- *Takeover* is a provocative documentary about a movement organizing homeless people to take over vacant homes in middle-class neighborhoods.

Literary Works Addressing Homelessness

- *One Day of Life* by Manlio Argueta was written during the El Salvadoran civil war in the 1980s and tells the story of peasants forced out of their homes and communities.

- Charles Baudelaire wrote two disturbing and interesting prose poems, "Beat Up the Poor" and "Eyes of the Poor," that stage encounters between street people and the wealthy in nineteenth-century Paris.

- William Blake's *Songs of Innocence and Experience* are sophisticated and subtle poems speaking of abandoned children, chimney sweeps, and London poverty in the late eighteenth century, as well as the threat this experience poses to an outlook that would attempt to remain innocent.

- Stephen Crane's *Maggie: A Girl of the Streets* tells the story of a working-class girl who is taken advantage of and turned out by her family before she turns finally to the streets. Crane's "New York City" sketches explore his interest in the difference between wealth and poverty.

- *Oliver Twist* by Charles Dickens criticizes the Poor Law and explores the street life and underworld of London.

- In *Joys of Motherhood* by Buchi Emecheta, Nnu Ego must leave her tribal life and find a way to support herself and her children in the slums of modernizing Lagos, Nigeria. Despite the pride Nigerian women are supposed to take in motherhood, Nnu Ego finds it a thankless experience.

- *The Beggars' Strike, Or, The Dregs of Society,* Aminata Sow Fall's ironic novel from Senegal, asks, "What would happen if street people went on strike?"

- *Life Among the Piutes* by Sarah Winnemucca Hopkins chronicles the displacement of her people and their struggle to find a new home after the arrival of the first White people in Nevada.

- *Nectar in a Sieve* by Kamala Markandaya is a touching and deceptively simple novel that depicts the way a family of peasant farmers in rural India is forced from its land and ends up homeless in the city.

- *Kaffir Boy* by Mark Mathabane tells the story of a Black South African tennis star who documents Apartheid's assault on the homes and lives of black people.

- Rigoberta Menchú's *I, Rigoberta Menchú* is a powerful and highly readable testimonial of an Indian woman whose family is forced off their land and terrorized by the Guatemalan military. (See Chapter 7 for a fuller discussion of this book and of testimonials as a genre.)

- *Down and Out in Paris and London* by George Orwell gives an account of his experience in the 1930s washing dishes in Paris and tramping across England in an effort to learn about the lives of the poor.

- *Cry, the Beloved Country,* Alan Paton's classic novel of South Africa, is still effective in depicting the experience of poverty and homelessness in a South African township. Rather than no longer teaching it, I suggest continuing to use it along with contemporary and Black sources, such as *Kaffir Boy* (see separate entry in this list), and inviting students to explore conditions in South Africa in transition.

- *This Migrant Earth* (also titled *And the Earth Did Not Devour Him*) by Tomás Rivera is a fascinating collection of short pieces addressing the experience of migrant Mexican American farm workers in the Midwest.

- Upton Sinclair's *The Jungle*, a classic study of the meatpacking industry, is also a look at homelessness among European immigrants in the nineteenth-century American city.

Web Sites for Teaching about Homelessness

- The Bay Area Homeless Program site offers information and links, as well as the "Homeless Education Kit," which looks like a good activity resource for teachers. Go to: http://thecity.sfsu.edu/~stewartd/.

- Communications for a Sustainable Future (CSF), located at the University of Colorado at Boulder, maintains the HOMELESS Web site, which contains links to over five hundred Internet sites (in several countries) that provide information on homelessness. From this page you can also access the discussion list about homelessness: http://csf.colorado.edu/homeless/.

- Habitat for Humanity invites people of all backgrounds to build houses in partnership with families in need. Their Web site can link students to events, affiliates, and housing projects across the country and around the world: http://www.habitat.org/.

- The Iowa Department of Education offers an online version of a pamphlet to help schools and teachers better respond to the educational needs of homeless children: http://www.wmpenn.edu/pennweb/LTP/DOEMat/LEHC1.html.

- The Web site of the National Alliance to End Homelessness includes profiles of homeless citizens, background and statistics, policy and legislation, and a list of practical ideas about how individuals can join in the effort to end homelessness. Includes fact sheets for students at different grade levels. The site is located at: http://www.naeh.org/.

- The National Coalition for the Homeless is an advocacy network committed to ending homelessness. Its Web site contains information, testimonials, legislative materials, links, and publications: http://nch.ari.net/.

Readings in New Criticism

- *Practical Criticism* (1929) by I. A. Richards inspired a generation of American literature teachers to focus on the self-contained meaning of poetry and the way that the preconceptions of student readers distracted them from the words on the page. Richards's study was an important precursor to both New Criticism and American reader response.

- *Seven Types of Ambiguity* by William Empson is an early (1930s) and illuminating example of a brilliant critic making close readings of canonical English poets.

- *Understanding Poetry* (1938), co-authored by Cleanth Brooks and Robert Penn Warren, rapidly became the standard textbook for the teaching of literature. Addressing only poetry, and canonical White male British and American poetry at that—of more than 150 authors represented, 3 are women—Brooks and Warren argued that "literature should be studied as literature." Reissued in 1951 and 1960, *Understanding Poetry* institutionalized New Critical priorities in both university and high school teaching.

- *The Well-Wrought Urn* (1947) is Cleanth Brooks's collection of essays on paradox in Shakespeare, Pope, Gray, Wordsworth, Keats, Tennyson, and Yeats. It captures the spirit of New Criticism where scholars were explicitly "not critical relativists, not cultural historians, not sociologists, but makers of normative judgment" (251).

Resources for Historical Criticism

Biographical

There are hundreds of fascinating literary biographies and autobiographies on almost any canonical writer of your choosing. Here are a few that I or my colleagues have found especially interesting.

■ *Frost: A Literary Life Reconsidered* by William Pritchard is a concise and sympathetic account of Frost's life. He is interested in drawing Frost's ideas out of his letters and poetry.

■ *Henry Thoreau: A Life of the Mind* by Robert D. Richardson is a well-written volume that explores the evolution of the writer's thought in a social context. The same is true of Richardson's *Emerson: The Mind on Fire.*

■ *James Joyce* by Richard Ellman is considered one of the best biographies of the twentieth century.

■ *The Life of Charlotte Brontë,* Elizabeth Gaskell's classically Victorian biography, is full of Brontë's letters and offers a sympathetic account by another woman novelist of the same era. For a modern treatment, Lyndall Gordon's biography, *Charlotte Brontë: A Passionate Life,* sympathetically takes you inside the author's life and temperament.

■ *Lives of the Poets,* written between 1777 and 1781 by Samuel Johnson and available in many editions, offers a picture of the literary life of the eighteenth century and includes biographical accounts of Milton, Swift, Addison, Pope, Gray, and many others.

■ *Recollections of the English Lake Poets* by Thomas De Quincey focuses on Wordsworth's personal experiences and gossip, and is a charming nineteenth century biographical work.

■ *Walt Whitman's America: A Cultural Biography* by David Reynolds examines Whitman in the context of nineteenth-century American social and cultural development. Includes a frank and balanced account of Whitman's sexuality.

■ *The Life of Langston Hughes* by Arnold Rampersad offers a rich portrait of the "Shakespeare of Harlem." Don't miss Hughes's own autobiographies; *The Big Sea* is a delight to teach.

Literary Tradition

■ *The Cambridge History of American Literature,* edited by Sacvan Bercovitch, is a more recent and inspirational resource for American literature teachers. Several volumes include a series of extended essays by top scholars reading the literary tradition from a variety of historical and cultural perspectives.

■ *Literary History of the United States,* edited by Robert Spiller et al., is an example of the kind of comprehensive reference compendium that examines writers within a literary tradition (in this case, Euro-American). The first volume is over 1500 pages.

■ T. S. Eliot's *Selected Essays 1917–1932* includes essays on Marlowe, Shakespeare, Dante, and the Metaphysical Poets, along with the famous piece "Tradition and the Individual Talent."

■ *The Short Oxford History of English Literature* by Andrew Sanders.

There are any number of literary histories of England spanning a broad range of perspectives and periods. This one caught my attention as apparently well done and self-reflective, though at 676 pages it is not exactly "short."

Socialist

- *The Communist Manifesto,* written by Marx and Engels in 1854, is as good a place as any to start with socialist thought.

- *Culture and Society 1780–1950* by Raymond Williams provides a good starting point for studying one of the most influential of the Marxist literary critics. Also appropriate would be Williams's *Marxism and Literature.*

- M. M. Bakhtin's *The Dialogic Imagination* is an intriguing example of a socialist approach to literature. Highly regarded in the current literary scholarship, this book examines the history of the novel form and its unique use of a diversity of language practices from different levels of society.

- Granville Hicks's *The Great Tradition: An Interpretation of American Literature Since the Civil War* is a classic socialist study from the 1930s.

- Vernon L. Parrington's *Main Currents in American Thought: An Interpretation of American Literature from Beginnings to 1920* is a classic socialist study from the 1920s.

- *Marx for Beginners* by the Chilean Rius uses a cartoon format to make this difficult thinker more broadly comprehensible and would appeal to high school or college students.

- Terry Eagleton's *Marxism and Literary Criticism* is a short and clear introduction to Marxist criticism. Also useful is his book *Ideology,* which lucidly explores the meaning of this key term by synthesizing and building on a wide range of scholarship.

- Alfred Kazin's *On Native Ground: An Interpretation of American Prose Literature* is a classic socialist study from the 1940s.

- *The Profession of Authorship in America 1800–1870* by William Charvat may not be explicitly socialist in orientation, but it offers an illuminating historical approach to literature, examining the book as a market commodity as well as the effects of the publishing business on literature. This work addresses Cooper, Poe, Longfellow, Melville, and others.

- See also the list of recommended readings on post-Marxism at the end of Chapter 7.

3 Genderizing the Curriculum: A Personal Journey

Not long after teaching Contemporary World Literature, I was taking graduate courses to renew my teaching certificate, and one night a week I engaged in conversation about literature and teaching with other adults. Even if a particular class was dull, I could "zone out" in the back of the room and reflect on the challenges I was facing with my own students. One semester, without thinking much about the topic, I signed up for a graduate class titled Women in Literature.

As the students and the professor took their seats around a long table and began to introduce themselves that first evening, an awareness came over me: I was going to be the only guy in the classroom, the only male in a Women in Literature seminar.

On the syllabus were books by authors I had heard of but never read, such as Virginia Woolf and Alice Walker, and many others completely new to me. As I have said, I had in the past been assigned very little literature by or about women; nevertheless, I reminded myself, I didn't need to be worried. I was an English teacher. I had lots of academic preparation. Why should this literature class be different from any other? Certainly, I was for equal rights and equal pay for women—didn't that mean I was a feminist? With these thoughts in mind, I decided, I should try to appear as nonchalant and as at ease as possible in my minority of one. Still, telling myself "I can handle this" was not enough to end a certain sense of vulnerability.

As my classmates introduced themselves—many were also high school teachers—I was struck by their enthusiasm. They knew some of the books already and "couldn't wait to get into the rest of the reading." They had been "waiting for years for a course like this." A teacher named Shelly pointed out that we were in the 1980s and it was "about time for this class to be offered at our college." The feeling continued that this course might be unlike others I had taken.

As the course unfolded, students made reports about the lives of the authors we were reading, and these reports played a significant role in our discussion of the literature. Our conversation found connections between the struggles of the heroines of the novels and the lives of the authors who had created them, and these relationships made the literary works all the more interesting. Moreover, my classmates were frequently making connections between characters in the novels and women they knew— their mothers, grandmothers, sisters, aunts, even themselves. Trained as I was in New Critical approaches, these connections between personal histories and literature were, at first, confusing. I found myself wondering about the appropriateness of family histories in a literature course. Yet, when we read Virginia Woolf's *A Room of One's Own* and discussed the attempts of the main character to obtain a university education in England in the 1920s, I found myself talking about the challenges my grandmother faced in trying to attend college in St. Louis at about the same time period.

In this nearly all-female class taught by a female professor and focused on women's literature, I noticed that the women students were more assertive about their ideas than in most courses I had taken before. Not that anyone wouldn't let me speak, or in any way cut me off, it was just that my female classmates were comfortable challenging and disagreeing in a way I was not accustomed to hearing from women students in literature classes focused on male authors. Was I beginning to understand that there was something inhibiting for women in traditional male-centered literature classes?

This was the class where I first encountered Buchi Emecheta's ironic Nigerian novel *Joys of Motherhood,* and I remember just how unusual the book seemed. Not only was the topic unfamiliar, but the writing itself appeared to me somehow unnatural, contorted. It seemed to me as if this book lacked the literary quality of the British classics to which I was accustomed. On the other hand, my classmates loved it and I didn't quite understand why. In the seminar I ventured to ask, "Don't some of you find the prose of this book uneven or poorly worded?"

"Could you give us an example?" the professor asked.

Although I suggested a couple of paragraphs, when we looked more closely at the text I realized that I was unable to justify my point very clearly—to my classmates the passages seemed fine, and the closer we looked, the harder it was to put my finger on inadequacies.

I realize now that this course in women's literature was introducing me to new materials, new approaches to reading literature—especially reader response and biographical approaches—and challenging the New Critical and canonical literary values I had been educated in. Even if I didn't fully understand it at the time, the seminar was causing me to reflect on my own teaching and on the literature I was assigning to my students in my high school classes. My first reaction to the new ideas and approaches had been to see them as somehow "lowering standards"; on this point, my view began to evolve.

Several years later I was able to realize how far this evolution had taken me, when, for a different course, I read *Joys of Motherhood* a second time. Now, after taking graduate courses in African literature and reading more literature written by women writers on my own, I could better recognize Buchi Emecheta's treatment of her themes and her commentary on the experiences of Nigerian women. This time the prose seemed compelling. Later still, teaching the same book in my own class on homelessness made it completely clear to me that my initial difficulties with *Joys of Motherhood* were not so much the result of the text itself, but of my inexperience as a reader and the narrowness of my academic training.

This Women in Literature seminar, along with teaching about the Holocaust and my encounter with a homeless man, were experiences that influenced my development as a teacher, and as a person. Translating these moments and experiences into my own teaching, making connections with students, and reworking my goals and methods—all of this is precisely what keeps me excited about being in the classroom. Yet the process has not always been smooth or as successful as I would like.

After Women in Literature, I began, awkwardly, to include more writing by women and more treatment of "women's issues" into my courses. My British Literature class for college-bound twelfth graders was just the place to start. Why had it not concerned me that I was teaching a yearlong literature course meeting five days a week without a single novel, play, short story, or even poem written by a woman author? My first experiment was going to be a direct borrowing from my graduate class; my department chair supported my request to order a class set of Virginia Woolf's *A Room of One's Own*.

The experiment didn't turn out particularly well. If I was every bit the converted teacher armed with what I thought was a wonderful new book, the students were reluctant. Despite the connection I had been able to make with my grandmother, the book didn't make a personal impact on them. They got the main point that it was hard for women to write fiction if they didn't have any resources or time—or, as Woolf puts it, "a room of one's own"—yet neither the young men nor the young women in my class saw the issues raised by the book as still relevant. "Today women can do anything they want," Jennifer pointed out. "If women want to go to college or become writers, there is nothing stopping them," Nathan said.

If students had a hard time connecting the book to the present day, they were more open to thinking about what Woolf was saying about the past. Perhaps our best discussion developed from Woolf's examination of just how far Shakespeare's hypothetical sister (a woman with her brother's talent and love of language) might have gone in Shakespeare's day.

> Any woman born with a great gift in the sixteenth century would certainly have gone crazed, shot herself, or ended her days in some lonely cottage outside the village, half witch, half wizard, feared and mocked at. (*Room* 51)

Of course, Virginia Woolf is notoriously difficult to read, and much of the subtlety, playfulness, and irony of the essay was pretty tough sailing for most students, even with the best study questions and discussion leading I could muster.

If I didn't succeed in making the essay relevant to my students, teaching *A Room of One's Own* was still an education for me. As I taught the book and entered into dialogue about why I liked it, I began to understand it better myself. I could see how it was revolutionary for Woolf to develop the argument of her essay through the daily experience of her female characters, so that, in her hands, the academic essay form began to merge in intriguing ways with personal narrative. Writing in this way, Woolf validated the experience of women in the absence of their academic representation, in their exclusion, in her day, from participation in elite all-male universities, such as (in the book) "Oxbridge."

While teaching *A Room of One's Own* was educating me about women and fiction, it was also showing me some of the challenges of attempting feminist teaching. It was hard, at least at first, for the sixteen-and seventeen-year-old women and men I was teaching to see ways that feminist writers might have meaning for them. They were right—at least in part—that roles for women had changed since Virginia Woolf's day and that the issues in Woolf's essay, at least as I had presented it, were distant from their own experience.

I had somewhat more success addressing women's experience with my students the following year, when I taught the more romantic *Jane Eyre*. Although the students were aware of the nineteenth-century time period of the book, they could sympathize with the abuse Jane suffered from her adoptive mother, the harsh conditions of her education at the Lowood school, the importance of her friendship with Helen Burns, and the narrow range of choices open to Jane when her education was finished. These students were interested in the fact that Brontë had written under a man's name, and they (and I) found some of the passages in the novel thought-provoking:

> Millions are condemned to a stiller doom than mine, and millions are in silent revolt against their lot. Nobody knows how many

rebellions besides political rebellions ferment in the masses of life which people earth. Women are supposed to be very calm generally: but women feel just as men feel; they need exercise for their faculties, and a field for their efforts as much as their brothers do; they suffer from too rigid a constraint, too absolute a stagnation, precisely as men would suffer; and it is narrowed-minded in their more privileged fellow-creatures to say that they ought to confine themselves to making puddings and knitting stockings, to playing on the piano and embroidering bags. It is thoughtless to condemn them, or laugh at them, if they seek to do more or learn more than custom has pronounced necessary for their sex. (112–13)

The debate we had in class about whether or not Charlotte Brontë should have had Jane marry Rochester began to raise issues that my students were able to identify with—they had definite ideas about equality and fairness in relationships and marriages.

As the topic of women's experience entered my British Literature course, I saw myself and my students move from looking at how women were represented in literature to a wide variety of gender issues. I began connecting literature to historical and contemporary subjects in more of the texts I was teaching, not only in those written by or about women. Teaching *Macbeth*, for example, I began to see that not only was the representation of Lady Macbeth not exactly complimentary to women, but also the whole code of manhood that Macbeth adopts serves to limit and trap him. Indeed, the theme of manhood seemed to run throughout the play. We found it in Macbeth's violence, in his "vaulting ambition," in his determination to disprove Lady Macbeth's challenge to his masculine pride, and in the contrast between Macbeth and Macduff in their willingness to experience feelings of pain and loss. Thus, exploring gender roles in *Macbeth* provided an opportunity to connect the issue of gender expectations to the young men in the class as well as to the young women. Now I see this focus on gender issues in Shakespeare's plays and other works of literature as a vital part of a historically grounded cultural studies that can connect to students in the present day. I have since read Katherine Usher Henderson and Barbara F. McManus's *Half Humankind: Contexts and Texts of the Controversy about Women in England, 1540–1640,* a collection of street pamphlets from Shakespeare's day that richly illuminates gender issues in his plays and could easily be taught along with them. (For more discussion of cultural studies approaches to Shakespeare, see Chapter 5.)

Although I continue to take steps toward addressing gender issues in my classes, much of what I have been learning recently has come from the new teachers I have been working with. Many of them have read Whaley and Dodge's *Weaving in the Women: Transforming the High*

School English Curriculum. Offering a wealth of new works and curricular ideas, this book helps us think more critically about the curriculum that is already in place. It puts forward a student-centered, reader response, and explicitly feminist pedagogy for English teaching. The authors declare:

> We believe that all English teachers can and should work toward including more literature by and about women and toward a more feminist approach to teaching, empowering both young women and young men and opening up English to something more exciting and more interesting, ultimately leading students to take charge of their own learning. (2)

Weaving in the Women demonstrates how movements for social change coupled with new kinds of scholarship are actively changing both the texts we teach and the ways in which we teach them.

Women's and Gender Studies

One of the most powerful forces in the transformation of English teaching at both the secondary school and university levels has been the women's movement and associated feminist criticism and scholarship. While I realize that for many a "backlash" may have given the term "feminist" negative connotations, all of us recognize the contribution that the women's movement has made—and continues to make—toward addressing gender inequality and increasing the choices available to both women and men. Of course, the teenage years constitute a vital time in the establishment of self-esteem and in the shaping of gender roles and identities. Imitating television programs and music and sports stars, being bombarded by advertising, and participating in school events and on football teams and cheerleading squads—even in chess clubs and literary magazines—teenagers and young adults are immersed in a world where gender roles are supercharged. Unfortunately, young people typically have few opportunities to carefully examine gender codes, roles, and expectations. The work of women's studies and gender studies thus becomes particularly relevant to English teachers and forms one of the most important approaches under the cultural studies umbrella.

Women like Virginia Woolf, Simone de Beauvoir, Adrienne Rich, Tillie Olsen, Kate Millet, Julia Kristeva, Hélène Cixous, Barbara Christian, Paula Gunn Allen, Gayatri Spivak and many others have recovered and validated writing by women, raised questions about gender equality in the traditionally male literary canon, and explored gender questions across cultures. Their efforts have helped us recognize the quantity, quality, and value of writing by women. Consciousness-raising movements, women's studies programs and feminist scholarship have forged a history of women-centered teaching and learning, making connections between people's lives and the literature curriculum, connections relevant to both women and men.

Part of this feminist tradition consists of gender studies, an effort not so much to look at biological determinants of sexual difference or sexual orientation, but instead to examine the way that roles for men and women—and for heterosexuals as well as for gay, lesbian, bisexual, and transgendered persons—have developed historically and culturally, and how these roles continue to be made and contested in the present day. The distinction between "gender," as created in a particular culture, and "sex," as a biological inheritance, is central to the work of many feminists who point out that being a man or a woman is more than a physical characteristic. Indeed, scholars like Michel Foucault have shown that, rather than being "natural," gender concepts and categories have changed dramatically over time. Such an insight makes it more difficult—and perhaps more interesting—to read literature from different cultures and historical periods. Like multicultural studies, gender studies urges us to become more sensitive to the way we think about and understand ourselves and others.

Feminist and gender studies have opened up awareness and created a justification for thinking of gender issues as a fundamental part of English as an academic subject. Roles for men and women, equal treatment and opportunity, family and love relationships, sexual assault and abuse, school and workplace equity—all are topics that feminist writers and scholars have legitimated for literature and language arts classrooms. Bringing feminist and gender studies into the classroom encourages teachers to take that which is vital in the lives of young people and make it intellectually meaningful to the literature we read and teach. Further, feminist scholarship provides teachers and students alike with the critical tools they need to analyze themselves and the world.

Before reading *Weaving in the Women* in my class, Andrea Doxtader says, her interest in women's studies was "already sparked." Just as I was, Andrea was influenced by a course she had taken in women's studies. Responsible for eleventh-grade American literature in a small town in rural Michigan, she organizes her teaching around the theme of civil rights, and women's experience is an important part of the curriculum. After reading American Indian literature and African American slave narratives, Andrea engages her students in a unit on women's history and literature. I observed a class that had just finished "The Story of an Hour" by Kate Chopin and was exploring issues in women's history before reading "A Jury of Her Peers" by Susan Glaspell.

Student groups were reading short pieces from a variety of sources, many gleaned from Andrea's women's history course. The articles included a brief history of the legal status of women from the eighteenth century to the present, a speech by educator and activist M. Carey Thomas titled the "Desire of Women for Higher Education," a speech by Mary C. Vaughan about the goals of the temperance movement, an essay by Margaret Sanger about the importance to women of birth control, and a short essay on the issue of unequal treatment of women in employment. In jigsaw fashion, one group would report on their article to the rest of the class. I observed a discussion where the students talked about the difficulties women faced in trying to go to college. I quote this discussion here not only to show how much better Andrea was able to raise these issues than I was when I taught *A Room of One's Own*, but also to show how the essays that Andrea chose created a cultural studies context that made the literature she was teaching more meaningful to her students. As you read the conversation, notice how students connect their reading about history to their experience in the present.

Sharon:	"In those days only boys went to school. Young women prayed to God to be able to learn."
Jessica:	"Why didn't they go?"
Sharon:	"It was thought to be 'bad for a woman's health.'"
Robert:	"Home Ec was probably the only class they would let girls take in those days."
Teacher:	"Are there any students in this class who kind of like math or chemistry or biology?"
Shelly:	"Yes, I do—I like math. I like chemistry."
Teacher:	"What difference would it make if you couldn't study those subjects?"
Martha:	"It seems like they tried to protect us. They thought they would protect us. Think of how dumb you would be sitting home every day."
Andrew:	"The reason more women started going to college was that nowadays you need more education to get the same job."
Jessica:	"We need to be able to support ourselves. Women have to go to college to be able to get a job."
Abbey:	"You can't always count on other people to take care of you."
Shelly:	"My goal is to get married in order to be happy, not to take care of someone."

Robert: "Nowadays you can't depend on just one income. We couldn't live on just my dad's wages."

Janelle: "Now it is pretty equal. You can't discriminate like you used to. So I can't get worried about what happened in the past."

Brittany: "It is totally different nowadays. Now everything is pretty much equal. It is all in the past."

Robert: "I think discrimination still goes on. At my mom's work everyone but her got the same raise, yet she works harder. It's a Japanese company and they treat their women workers differently. We got a new truck and that five thousand dollars would have been the down payment. I think discrimination still goes on today."

Sharon: "In the 1600s women had no legal rights. They couldn't own property or engage in business. A married woman had no rights except through her husband. Anything she earned went to the husband, not her."

Crystal: "Nowadays we can be just as active as we want to be. Back then women were treated like children."

Pete: "What this is all about is how the past and present connect."

Mark: "In those days they finally made it a misdemeanor to beat your wife, but that was all."

Teacher: "Many women believed the problem was alcohol, the 'demon rum.'"

Martha: "It isn't that bad today. I don't think the majority of people are beating their wives because of liquor."

Jessica: "Yeah, but I have seen commercials on TV about the danger of wife beating."

Abbey: "Anybody heard of times when people drink too much and then do things they don't intend to do?"

Robert: "Does it say why they [the women] took it? Or did they organize?"

Kate: "Yeah, they formed this Temperance Movement."

Sharon: "Women got sick of not being able to do a lot of things and so they started to speak out."

This discussion shows students learning about women's history, information that, within a cultural studies perspective, will be very helpful as they read women's literature. The discussion also shows students attempting to make sense out of new information by processing it with what they already know. In reader response fashion, the same texts generate differing thoughts and reactions depending greatly on what students bring to the work. In this discussion, students are testing ideas, disagreeing, learning from each other, and not simply accepting any supposedly "politically correct" viewpoint as they examine the relevance of women's history to their experience and that of their families. Andrea explained to me after class:

> Some of the guys were worried that in this unit we were just going to do male bashing—but I want us to look at the reasons people in the eras we are studying had the beliefs that they did. They were raised to think certain ways and that is something we are going to look at.

Reader response and cultural studies approaches ought to generate disagreement and controversy; that very tension serves as a stimulus to learning. This approach requires, as in Andrea's room, the creation of trust and an openness to the full range of viewpoints students bring to the class. In this regard the modeling done by the teacher is especially important.

———————

The creative use of controversy was also a theme in another class I visited that focused on connecting gender studies to literature. Teaching an upper-track literature course to college-bound seniors, Missy Deer planned a unit where her students could explore the various perspectives of men and women by comparing Richard Wright's autobiography *Black Boy*—about his experience growing up in the South—with Zora Neale Hurston's novel *Their Eyes Were Watching God,* which describes a young Black woman's struggle to find equal relationships in rural Georgia and Florida. The comparison Missy established is a rich one: critics such as Henry Louis Gates Jr. have seen both novels as central to African American writing and have posited the creative differences between Wright and Hurston as relevant to divergent viewpoints between succeeding generations of male and female African American writers.

The students read *Black Boy* first. In his autobiography, Richard Wright talks about how he longed to cast down the burdens of Blackness in the Jim Crow South. Analyzing the novel, students wrote about the burdens that Wright carried and the injustices and discrimination he suffered in the public world of the playground, the street, the library, and the workplace. In *Their Eyes Were Watching God*, Hurston's emphasis is not on Black/White relations but on the challenges facing African American women who seek independence, love, and respect within their own communities. Describing their dual oppression, Hurston repeatedly refers to Black women as "de mule uh de world."

After reading both books, the students tried to compare the portrayal of men and women. Like many of the critics at the time the novels were written, students found *Black Boy* to be a more effective exploration of the inequalities of Jim Crow than *Their Eyes Were Watching God*. In teaching *Their Eyes Were Watching God,* Missy found it was difficult for students, even her African American women students, to identify with Janie, the main character. Even though Janie was kept at home and forced to chop wood by Logan Killicks, her first husband, students were suspicious of her leaving him. "What did she expect? To sit there all high and mighty?" These sixteen- and seventeen-year-old students living in a generation when many parents have divorced considered Janie's running away to be unacceptable even if life with Killicks tore her away from all of the things she loved.

Yet as the students probed farther into the texts and continued to compare them, new insights came to light. They noticed that it was hard to find positive female characters in Wright's book. Many students were disturbed by the corporal discipline meted out to Richard by his mother and aunts, and they wondered how the story might have been told differently if it were written from a woman's point of view. With these observations students began to better understand the oppression of women that Hurston addresses. By the end of the unit, Kristin wrote the following:

> After Jody dies, she finally has a taste of freedom that lasts only temporarily for Tea Cake comes into her life. Though his smiles and laughs were lighter than a feather, he too took her over as his own. All three men ultimately display their possession through physical abuse by hitting her. . . . Janie led a difficult and ever-changing life. The burdens that she carried not only made her feel like a puppet, but a beautiful woman who was beaten by a society that restrained her from doing what she desired most.

As Kristin describes, Janie's persecutions took place within the context of personal relations; they were more "private" than the "public" segregation described in *Black Boy*. Yet the student's examination of these two books demonstrates that the private sphere is also a place for power relationships, that, as the women's movement argues, the personal is political. Students began to recognize how unequal power relationships are supported in the society Janie lives in. Janie's grandmother had told her that, after all, "love comes a mere second to security and protection"—a position many of Missy's students would seem to agree with.

Missy discovered some of the possibilities and challenges of helping students to appreciate women's experience in literature as she explored the complexities that arise when issues of gender and race come together. Increasingly, gender studies attends to a wide variety of complications, not only addressing the different histories of men and women but, indeed, rethinking the very categories of *male* and *female*, and exploring issues of gender identity and sexual orientation.

It started the day Butch Carrigan decided I was interested in jumping his bones.

"You little fruit," he snarled. "I'll teach you to look at *me*."

A moment or two later he had given me my lesson.

I was still laying face down in the puddle into which Butch had slammed me as the culminating exercise of my learning experience when I heard a clear voice exclaim, "Oh my dear! That *was* nasty. Are you all right, Vince?"

Turning my head to my left, I saw a pair of brown Docksiders, topped by khaki pants. Given the muddy condition of the sidewalks, pants and shoes were both ridiculously clean.

I rolled onto my side and looked up. The loafers belonged to a tall, slender man. He had dark hair, a neat mustache, and a sweater slung over his shoulders. He was kind of handsome—almost pretty. He wore a gold ring in his left ear. He looked to be about thirty.

"Who are you?" I asked suspiciously.

"Your fairy godfather. My name is Melvin. Come on, stand up and let's see if we can't do something with you."

So begins Bruce Covill's playful tale "Am I Blue?" the title story of a collection of short pieces by well-known contemporary young adult fiction writers, all, in one way or another, addressing the theme of gay and lesbian experience. Realism gives way to magic as a stereotypically effeminate "fairy godfather" appears granting three wishes. When Vince wishes that all gay and lesbian people should turn blue, he is surprised to discover people in varying shades of blue everywhere he looks—TV newscasters, football players, grocery clerks, teachers, even the school bully who pushed Vince in the mud.

One of my former students currently teaching low-track high school sophomores in an ethnically mixed inner-city school experimented with an innovative method of teaching "Am I Blue?" during a short story unit focused on the theme of fear.

Tisha Pankop always greets her students at the door; on this day, without explanation, as students came into the room she handed out to more than half of them a blue triangle with a circle of tape. Some students said, "Hey, give me one!" Others barely noticed what their teacher was doing. Seeing the blue triangles but not knowing their purpose, two boys often at the center of class attention went into action before the period even began. Tony took several blue triangles from other students and began sticking them on himself. Jamal, with a triangle on his back, danced around the room singing repeatedly to an upbeat rhythm, "I'm blue. . . . I'm blue . . . . I'm blue. . . . I'm blue. . . . "

Tisha began class with a brief discussion of the question: What does it feel like for those of you who do not have blue triangles like the rest of the students? One said, "It doesn't matter." Another, "I really wanted one." Another asked, "Why didn't I get one?" Next, the students sat on the carpet, Tisha passed out "Am I Blue?" and they took turns reading it aloud. David Martinez did an excellent job reading the part of the fairy godfather, and his swishy voice inspired some laughter. At the moment in the story when it was revealed what the color blue means, several triangles went flying across the room and landed in the center of the circle. Other triangles stayed where they had been taped. A couple of students stated: "You tricked us." "You got us." Several young women students sat with triangles on and didn't say anything.

Tisha asked, "Why did some of you throw your triangles off?"

"I'm not gay. I don't want anybody to think I am."

"It's OK for girls to be gay, but not guys."

Caprice, a girl who had her boyfriend's initials painted on her face commented, "It's fine with me if they are gay, I just don't want to know."

Marcy, one of the most outspoken—and often contrary—students, said, "I have an uncle who is gay. Don't you have someone in your family who is gay?" Several students who were Catholic explained that in their religion homosexuality is considered sinful. The topic of their unit came up—"fear"—and the students began to talk about fears of homosexuality and about the fears that a homosexual young person might face. One student pointed out that the fear in "Am I Blue?" was like the fear of Olaf in the story "Big Black Man," a fear that was made worse because it couldn't be openly discussed.

The students didn't come to any final conclusion except that it was "sad about the way the kid in the story was treated." Tisha says that some students may have had a hard time with moments in the discussion, yet more careful listening seemed to take place in class that day than previously. Views were shared, different perspectives were accepted, and students were pretty much respectful of each other. As the class was ending, Langston asked if Tisha herself was gay and the class became very quiet.

Tisha responded, "Does it matter to you?"

"No, no."

Tisha explained to me that because she is not gay she felt safe leaving her answer to this personal question a mystery. "Straight teachers have to be there to make a stand because the teachers who are not, in a district that might not support them, are really at risk." Teachers who "just keep quiet" on this topic are, in Tisha's view,

> helping their gay/lesbian students find their way to suicide—the four students who have come out to me in the last few years have all had those thoughts on their mind. Using a story like "Am I Blue?" means a lot to those kids. I have seen kids make a dramatic change for the better in their whole experience in school when they feel there is even just one safe person they can talk or write to.

While utilizing controversy and exploring differing points of view are part and parcel of cultural studies teaching, the topic of homosexuality remains particularly sensitive. Hoping for tenure in the coming year, Tisha noted that after teaching this story she did not get any calls or contacts from parents, though some of the students in her other classes heard about the story and asked to borrow copies. Tisha says that if she were to teach the story in an environment where parents were more critical about what was happening at the school, then it might be a good idea to clear her plan with one of the vice principals. Developing a reputation as a good teacher, informing administrators and parents, inviting diverse views into the class, creating alternative assignments, developing policies, appealing to fundamental principles of democracy and free speech—all of these are ways that teachers can create the freedom to do important teaching in addressing issues such as gender and sexual orientation. (See further discussion in the "Censorship and Teacher Freedom" section of Chapter 6.)

As we shall see, controversy and contrasting points of view are also central to the next chapter, where I explore teaching about the violence in our culture and in our students' lives.

Gay and Lesbian Studies

Almost all of us who work in secondary schools find ourselves in overtly homophobic environments. At the college level there may be more freedom, but similar prejudices and curricular exclusions exist. In either setting it may be uncomfortable for us to connect our teaching to the outpouring of literature with gay and lesbian themes, or to academic scholarship, conferences, and journals focused on issues of sexual orientation. Of course many

▶

of the great authors that we do regularly teach in public school and college literature classes were or may have been "homosexual" or "bisexual," including not only Plato, Sappho, and Shakespeare, but also Walt Whitman, Emily Dickinson, Willa Cather, A. E. Housman, Virginia Woolf, E. M. Forster, Tennessee Williams, Oscar Wilde, Langston Hughes, and James Baldwin. Many of these authors directly address homosexuality in their creative work, though those works are usually censored from our reading lists. While I recognize the difficulties we face in our buildings and communities—and the challenges involved in looking at homophobia within as well as without—I have found that discussing issues of sexual orientation is vital and important. Given the high rates of depression and suicide for gay and lesbian youth, such teaching may even be lifesaving. Moreover, exploring the scholarship in gender studies can help all students better understand gender issues, recognize and address sexism and homophobia, and break down rigid gender roles for men and women.

Like gender studies, gay and lesbian studies (sometimes called "queer studies" by its practitioners) emphasizes the social construction of sexual identity and sexual orientation. It concerns itself with much more than sexual acts or activities; it also addresses the whole constellation of feelings, relationships, and identity. Being "gay," "straight," "bisexual," or "transgendered" means different things in different cultures and different moments in history. If Greeks and Romans viewed same-sex attraction as the highest form of love (see Plato's *Symposium* for example), early Christian philosophers such as Plutarch (see his *Essay on Love*) tried to argue for the supremacy of heterosexual attraction (a topic explored in Foucault's *The History of Sexuality*). The fixed and binary classification of people as "homosexual" or "heterosexual" is a relatively new development, scholars in this field argue, taking place in medical, psychological, and social discourse only during the last decades of the nineteenth century and the first decades of the twentieth. The categorization of certain behaviors or attitudes as "masculine" or "homosexual" simultaneously defines and circumscribes "heterosexual" or "feminine" behavior and vice versa.

Like feminist and multicultural studies, gay and lesbian studies is also tied to broader social movements and events. The modern gay liberation movement dates from the Stonewall protest against police harassment of gay men at a bar in New York in 1969. Yet scholars of gay and lesbian studies do not confine their thinking to a sexual minority but instead see their work as important to the lives of people across the spectrum of sexuality. The literary scholar Eve Kosofsky Sedgwick, in her award-winning book *Epistemology of the Closet,* explores homoerotic desire in canonical literature by writers such as Herman Melville, Oscar Wilde, Henry James, and Marcel Proust. Others investigate the burgeoning new creative literature with gay and lesbian characters and themes. As gay and lesbian scholarship, often influenced by feminist thought, explores the panoply of sexual, identity, and relational differences between people, there remain differences and disagreements about the nature of identity and sexuality, about strategies for addressing homophobia, and about approaches to examining sexuality in literature.

The Women's Literature Canon

Gender issues are present in all literature. I list here a handful of literary works that English teachers have found particularly fruitful in their treatment of the perspective of women. There are many other more complete lists of works appropriate for teaching about gender; see, for example, Whaley and Dodge's *Weaving in the Women.*

- *The Awakening* by Kate Chopin tells the story of a woman in nineteenth-century New Orleans who finds the narrowness of her married life unbearable.

- *The Bell Jar* by Sylvia Plath is an autobiographical novel tracing the breakdown and suicide of a brilliant woman writer.

- *The Golden Notebook* by Doris Lessing is about a woman passing through a breakdown to a greater sense of wholeness. It is an ambitious and frank novel divided into four different notebooks that express different aspects of the character's personality.

- *Jane Eyre* by Charlotte Brontë is more than a gothic romance; it is also the story of an intelligent woman who must make her own living. She confronts the challenge of maintaining her independence and self-respect.

- *A Room of One's Own* is an extended essay by Virginia Woolf exploring the issue of women and fiction from a variety of perspectives and is an important work in the English feminist literary tradition. *Three Guineas* extends Woolf's reflections to the issue of women and education.

- *Surfacing,* by the Canadian writer Margaret Atwood, is about an artistic woman who has had an abortion. She deals with the repressed memory and pain, seeks her father in the Canadian woods and, in confronting his death, becomes able to face her past.

- Shakespeare's *The Taming of the Shrew,* like many of his comedies, offers a strong and fascinating female character. This play focuses on questions of mastery in male/female relationships and its ambiguous ending creates lots of room for discussion.

- Tillie Olson's *Tell Me a Riddle* is a collection of short pieces exploring women's perspectives. The best-known story is "I Stand Here Ironing."

- "The Wife of Bath's Tale" in Chaucer's *The Canterbury Tales* is told by one of early English literature's most independent-minded female characters. Her prologue offers a repudiation of classical and medieval misogynist tracts, and her tale explores the question, "What is it that women most want?"

- *The Yellow Wallpaper*, a turn-of-the-century novella by Charlotte Perkins Gilman, addresses the experience of a woman confined by her husband and driven to the brink of madness. In a more lighthearted vein, Gilman's *Herland* presents a fascinating utopian world run by women.

Multicultural Additions to the Women's Literature Canon

Here are my suggestions for a few multicultural possibilities that could be added to the curriculum to address the experiences of women of color.

- *Brown Girl, Brownstones* by Paule Marshall is a sensitive story about the growing-up of the daughter of immigrants from Barbados.

- *Efuru* by Flora Nwapa explores from a woman's perspective the life of the Ibo people of Nigeria before colonialism.

- *Gorilla My Love* by Toni Cade Bambara is a collection of stories about African American girls growing up in New York City.

- *The House on Mango Street* by Sandra Cisneros is a collection of prose poems telling the story of a Chicana girl growing up in Chicago.

- *I Know Why the Caged Bird Sings* is the first volume of Maya Angelou's wonderful autobiography. Addresses the topic of sexual abuse.

- *The Line of the Sun* by Judith Ortiz Cofer tells the story of a Puerto Rican family moving to New Jersey.

- *The Norton Anthology of Literature by Women* edited by Sandra Gilbert and Susan Gubar is a rich and useful anthology that considerably extends the canon of women's writers. It includes, for instance, the entire text of Toni Morrison's *The Bluest Eye*.

- *Second-Class Citizen* by Buchi Emecheta is an autobiographical novel about the experience of African immigrants in London.

- *Spider Woman's Granddaughters,* edited by Paula Gunn Allen, is a collection of short stories by Native American writers.

- *Sunlight on a Broken Column* by Attia Hosain is a novel addressing the experience of Muslim women in India.

- *Their Eyes Were Watching God* by Zora Neale Hurston is a classic of African American women's writing that tells the story of a woman seeking equality in love relationships and freedom in her personal life.
- *Waterlily* by Ella Cara Deloria is a touching Native American novel about a Sioux woman in the nineteenth century.

Works for Teaching about Sexual Orientation

- *Am I Blue? Coming Out From the Silence,* edited by Marion Bauer, is a collection of short stories with gay or lesbian themes by well-known young adult fiction writers.
- *Anne on My Mind* by Nancy Garden is a tender young adult novel about two high school senior women who fall in love.
- *The Celluloid Closet,* co-directed by Rob Epstein and Jeffrey Friedman, is a mind-opening historical documentary film (based on the book of the same title by Vito Russo) about the portrayal of gay and lesbian characters in classic Hollywood films. It demonstrates, among other things, that various communities of people view and interpret film in strikingly different ways.
- *The Drowning of Stephan Jones* by Bette Greene is a young adult novel exploring homophobia and violence against gay men.
- *In Your Face: Stories from the Lives of Queer Youth* by Mary Gray presents the thoughts of fifteen gay and lesbian teenagers on their experiences of coming out, fitting in at school, and getting along with friends and family.
- *Jack* by A. M. Homes is a young adult novel about the experience of a high school basketball player whose father is gay.
- *Ruby* by Rosa Guy describes the experience of a young West Indian black woman growing up in New York City whose attraction to a self-confident, intellectual girl inspires her ambition.

Readings in Feminist Criticism and Gender Studies

- Judith Butler's *Gender Trouble: Feminism and the Subversion of Identity* is a highly theorized challenge to the distinction between gender (as socially constructed) and sex (as biologically given).
- "Genderizing the Curriculum" is the focus of the January 1999 issue of *English Journal* (88.3). Carol Gilligan's *In a Different Voice: Psychological Theory and Women's Development* argues that women tend to base their morality in relationships with others, whereas traditional male moral philosophers have valued disembodied right and ideals.

- *The History of Sexuality, Volume 1: An Introduction* by Michel Foucault examines the construction of gender identity in European history.

- Elaine Showalter's *A Literature of Their Own: British Women Novelists from Brontë to Lessing* is an acclaimed study of nineteenth- and twentieth-century women writers.

- *The Madwoman in the Attic: The Woman Writer and the Nineteenth-Century Literary Imagination* by Sandra Gilbert and Susan Gubar is a readable, iconoclastic landmark in the study of women's literature. It includes discussion of Austen, the Brontës, Mary Shelley, George Eliot, and Emily Dickinson in the context of nineteenth-century beliefs about women.

- *On Lies, Secrets, and Silence: Selected Prose, 1966–1978* by Adrienne Rich is a fine and influential collection of essays on women, literature, and education.

- *Reviving Ophelia: Saving the Selves of Adolescent Girls* by Mary Pipher makes the case that current social values and practices undermine the confidence of girls during their early teenage years, which are crucial to the emotional and intellectual development of young women.

- *This Bridge Called My Back: Writings by Radical Women of Color* by Cherríe Moraga and Gloria Anzaldúa collects outspoken poetry and essays that challenge Eurocentric and middle-class-biased perspectives in feminist thought.

- *Weaving in the Women: Transforming the High School English Curriculum* by Liz Whaley and Liz Dodge is a terrific resource for secondary teachers—discussed in the text of this chapter.

- *Women's Ways of Knowing: The Development of Self, Voice, and Mind* by Mary Belenky is based on interviews with more than one hundred women and addresses how they feel silenced in families and schools.

Readings in Gay and Lesbian Studies

- *Epistemology of the Closet* by Eve Kosofsky Sedgwick examines gay identity in modern culture and literature.

- *The Last Closet: The Real Lives of Lesbian and Gay Teachers* by Rita Kissen explores the experience of gay and lesbian teachers and the roles that their straight colleagues can play in addressing homophobia.

- *The Lesbian and Gay Studies Reader,* edited by Henry Abelove, Michèle Barale, and David Halperin, is a collection of pathbreaking academic essays.

- *Queer Kids: The Challenges and Promise for Lesbian, Gay, and Bisexual Youth* by Robert Owens Jr. is a useful resource guide to the experiences and needs of young adults in the sexual minority.

Web Sites to Support Gay and Lesbian Teens

- The Cool Page for Queer Teens provides good information for teens and for their parents: http://www.pe.net/~bidstrup/cool.htm.

- ELIGHT is an online community for gay, lesbian, bisexual, and transgendered youth and young adults that provides a safe forum for people to speak out, share, and find others like themselves: http://www.elight.org.

- Financial aid information for gay and lesbian youth is available at http://www.finaid.org/otheraid/gay.phtml.

- The Gay/Lesbian/Bisexual/Transgendered youth resource directory can be found at http://www.youthresource.com/.

- InsideOut Magazine is an electronic publication for gay/lesbian youth: http://www.iomag.com/.

- The National Coalition for Gay, Lesbian, Bisexual, and Transgendered Youth offers a Web site that includes an archive of coming-out stories, information about community role models, resources for schools, bulletin boards for teens, links to other sites, and more: http://www.outproud.org/.

- Oasis is an online Webzine written by and about queer and questioning youth: http://www.oasismag.com/.

- The organization Parents and Friends of Lesbians and Gays offers support, information, and advocacy. The site features news on national issues, family stories, and other resources. See http://www.pflag.com/.

- Project YES is an educational organization that encourages the healthy development of all youth, including gay, lesbian, bisexual, and transgendered youth. Includes outreach information for clergy and congregations. See http://www.projectyes.org/.

- The Youth Assistance Organization provides information and a safe place online to engage in dialogue with others: http://www.youth.org/.

4 Addressing the Youth Violence Crisis

I came to the corner and looked down the street and I saw a little boy about eight years old with a gun in his hand pointed at someone, and that made me realize that the streets aren't a safe place anymore and that you always have to watch your back wherever you go and whatever you do.

Cindy (fifteen years old)

Alienated from faltering families, schools, and neighborhoods, young people in all parts of our country are becoming increasingly violent, turning to gangs and militia movements, becoming involved with deadly weapons, the drug economy, and still more heinous forms of criminal behavior. All of us read about it in the news; for many of us it is an immediate issue in our classrooms. We learn of drive-by shootings, of weapons found in school, neo-Nazi sympathies, of violence on campuses, and of assaults and even murders committed by children barely (or not even) in their teens. The 1999 tragedy at Columbine High School in Colorado riveted the nation's attention on the deadly mixture of alienated youth, guns, and school violence. While drugs, alienation, and violence are not new, perhaps it no longer shocks us to learn that more teenagers are killed by firearms than by all natural causes combined, that three times as many African American young men die in homicides than in automobile accidents, and that more and more children in rural as well as urban areas admit to carrying handguns.

As crime has become a major political issue, a national outcry has arisen for increased policing, more prisons, mandatory sentencing, and treating juvenile offenders as adults. But these "easy" answers are shortsighted and ineffective, as law enforcement officials themselves point out. While the number of Americans in prison doubled between 1980 and 1990, violence, especially among the young, increased during the same period. Our country has far and away the world's highest incarceration rate; for Black men in America it is five times higher than in South Africa under apartheid. What is truly unfortunate about the lives of these young people is that their antisocial behavior is often a desperate if misdirected attempt to secure their most basic human needs, to establish for themselves safety, respect, and belonging.

I have found that in order to comprehend this fundamental irony of the youth violence crisis, it is useful to enter into the experiences and perspectives of many of our young people and to explore the ways in which intersecting lines of alienation, poverty, racism, and shattered family life condition their lives. In this chapter I propose that such an investigation can and should be part of a response-based cultural studies curriculum relevant to many different language arts and literature courses. By examining pertinent literature, films, essays, and even music lyrics, and by listening closely to each other, my students come to better comprehend and begin to address the violence in our country and in our lives.

To begin, I will describe the experience my students and I had in a lower-division college survey course in African American literature focused on an exploration of the violence crisis, particularly among African American youth. Despite my emphasis in this class on violence and racism, it is clear that issues of violence, alienation, gangs, and availability of weapons and drugs affect all racial groups and touch all Americans. (The bibliography at the end of the chapter suggests materials teachers can use to address issues of violence from a variety of perspectives and cultures.)

Focusing an African American literature course on a cultural studies theme such as youth violence meant transforming a class that typically celebrated the artistic contributions of African American writers and, instead, drawing on those artistic works to investigate a pressing, real-world issue in the African American community. Attempting to keep the course response-based entailed actively involving my students and using the reading as a springboard for discussion, writing, and class activities. High school teachers with whom I have been collaborating are also integrating these materials and themes into their teaching, and the second part of this chapter describes their efforts.

My experiment took place in a class with an equal mix of African American and White students from Detroit and small towns in Michigan; the students ranged from first to senior year. Since this was an African American literature course with a racially mixed group of students, I was especially interested in learning more about multicultural literature and teaching. Since the topic of youth violence was frequently addressed in news, music, and film, I also hoped to integrate the study of mass media and popular culture into the class. Thus, as I approached teaching and learning about the youth violence crisis, I wanted to bring together traditional literature and new texts and approaches.

As the course began, I found that one of the classic novels of the African American literary tradition was an effective work for exploring the causes of youth violence. A hard-hitting and graphic text, Richard Wright's

Native Son allowed us to examine ways in which racism and economic inequality are tied to violence, crime, and mounting racial hostility. In the first section of the novel, Bigger Thomas, a teenager in Chicago's Black ghetto, attempts to establish his authority among his circle of friends by planning the robbery of a White store owner. This scene became pivotal in our discussion when Chet, a first-year African American student from Detroit, argued that while the robbery was clearly wrong, it nonetheless served as a positive psychological step for Bigger in that it allowed him, for the first time in his life, to reject the submissive and docile role that Wright's White society would prefer to cast him in. Andraya, also African American, was able to appreciate this line of thinking. She later wrote, "I think for Bigger to rob Blum, a White man, was the ultimate sin yet the ultimate high at the same time. To go through with the plan would show that Bigger wasn't letting the White man control him totally, which, in essence, would be Bigger's only way of showing his hatred of the White man."

As we progressed with Wright's work these insights became still more disturbing. Students compared the first section of the novel, where Bigger's frustration and anger are tied to his limited options as a Black person, to the second section, where murder leads him to feel free and powerful for the first time in his life:

> And, yet, out of it all, over and above all that had happened, impalpable but real, there remained to him a queer sense of power. *He* had done this. *He* had brought all this about. In all of his life these two murders were the most meaningful things that had ever happened to him. He was living, truly and deeply, no matter what others might think, looking at him with their blind eyes. Never had he had the chance to live out the consequences of his own actions; never had his will been so free as in this night and day of fear and murder and flight. (Wright 225)

Why should murder lead Bigger to feel free and powerful? The students groped toward understanding the racism and oppression that produces Bigger's anger and alienation. Wright shows how violent criminal behavior lets Bigger step outside of the powerless position that the dominant society expects of him. His job as chauffeur to the Dalton family becomes a role that he can play, while his inner life and thoughts become, for the first time, independent and self-directed. Ironically, it is only when Bigger enters into a life of crime that he is able to realize that he might exercise control over his own destiny.

In their reading of *Native Son* my students thus struggled to understand the causes of alienation and violence even more evident in the United States today than in the 1939 of Wright's novel. Scott, a White pre-education student from a small town, proposed that Bigger might have suffered from "Attention Deficit Disorder." (Sound familiar?) Other students took issue with Scott's interpretation, pointing out that this view simply located the problem entirely in an individual person and "took society off the hook" for Bigger's frustration and anger. Jamail, a first-year African American male student from Detroit, wrote in our electronic conference:

> I have lived as an observer of the system everyday in my neighborhood. It seems to me once you got in there was no way out. All the friends I have who were in the system are either still in, back to old crimes hoping not to get caught, or a few even dead. As a young black male, I feel the system is just another way of contributing to making the black male extinct. I have yet to see the system rehabilitate anyone I know.

Through open discussion in a mixed-race classroom, Scott's viewpoint evolved. He later wrote:

> Consider the high school freshman with a second grade reading level, who is told he cannot go to college. He hates school—he has no future goals—he knows he can't get a good paying job if he can't go to college. But, a-ha, he has an older brother who told him he can make 400 dollars a day if he sells crack after school. His brother has cool clothes, he has a cool car, he has a car phone, and he's only 19! I think I would choose to sell drugs too! But, you say, why doesn't he overcome these temptations, overcome this oppression, and focus his energies to finish school and go to college! This is the "right" decision. Yes, maybe this is the right decision, but it takes a very strong-willed person, especially if that person is a 16-year-old kid, to pass up those material goods and the money. Especially when they can have it RIGHT NOW! If our government and other political organizations are doing nothing to help change the environment in which these "offenders" live and are more concerned with beefing up police forces, building more prisons, and locking more people up, then could these people be considered political prisoners?

As the course progressed, student interest was high, and discussions and writing were as energized as any I have seen. What really made the difference in this class was the opportunity for students, via a response-based cultural studies approach, to enter into dialogue with each other about the contemporary crisis, consider its effect on their own lives, and begin to think about how they could address our culture of violence.

We moved from an examination of violence in *Native Son* to a consideration of the creative and transformative power of nonviolence in the civil rights struggle. Our reading included a chapter on the civil rights era from Howard Zinn's *A People's History of the United States* as well as Martin Luther King Jr.'s frequently anthologized "Letter from a Birmingham Jail." Many of my college students, particularly the White students, had never studied this era of American history. For them, viewing videos from the Eyes on the Prize series came as a surprise and revelation. The powerful footage in *Eyes on the Prize* of fire hoses and dogs turned on nonviolent protesters marks only what 1960s television was able to capture; as we discussed these images, students came to realize that anyone who seeks to understand issues of violence in the African American community needs to understand the history of that violence, a history that includes slavery, lynchings, and ongoing police brutality. Among many things my students learned from the *Eyes on the Prize* series was the way in which movement participants themselves bore the violence of Southern police and jails and, nonetheless, created a powerful nonviolent solidarity as they sat, marched, and rode together, as they were arrested together, sang in their cells, and refused to cooperate with guards and jail authorities.

My students came to see that King's nonviolent strategy was based on a strategic plan to overwhelm the state's power to imprison and force authorities to the bargaining table. For King, as for his model Mahatma Gandhi, nonviolence was not only a spiritual philosophy but also an activist commitment to social justice. As students focused on the relationship of crime and race, they found themselves moving past stereotyping and negative images and toward a more dynamic understanding that included themselves as active participants in social change.

After learning about Martin Luther King Jr., my class turned its attention to Malcolm X, whose experience as a street hoodlum, incarcerated felon, member of the Nation of Islam, and African American leader offered a paradigm for rethinking America's violence problem. While my African American students had an immediate identification with Malcolm X, after reading his story they began to recognize the commitment and determination entailed in a desire to follow in his footsteps.

As we carefully worked through Malcolm X's challenging autobiography, White students were frustrated; many began to undergo intense self-examination. Some reported feeling a sense of guilt. Since I don't believe in collective or racial responsibility, such guilt was at first hard for me to understand. Yet I think that we should recognize that for those of our students who live in relative safety and prosperity, learning about the experience of others in different circumstances may lead them to take personally the unfairness and inequalities of our world. When this happens, teaching about violence and the conditions that produce it is likely to prick students' consciousness and lead them to ask, Why didn't I know about this? What can I do about it? In my view these are questions that ought to direct our teaching rather than arise as its outcome.

The mixture of students in my classroom allowed for a vital cross-racial dialogue to take place, a dialogue that has been all too infrequent in my own teaching. Small-group discussion and the ready moving of desks and students helped keep the atmosphere open. As a White teacher I made an effort to get to know my African American students and help them feel welcome in the classroom. There were times when the mood of the class became tense, and there were moments when one group of students or another felt that they were misunderstood or disrespected. Yet differences of opinion did not usually develop strictly along racial lines, as individuals in each racial group expressed a variety of viewpoints and were willing to challenge each other's thinking. As we focused on the texts and issues at hand, students brought their own experiences into the discussion.

The Rodney King incident, the Los Angeles uprising, the O. J. Simpson trial, and the continuing barrage of highly charged racial incidents, depictions, and debates in the mass media demonstrated the high level of racial tension in our society. Young people are very conscious of and concerned about racial matters. This is true at all high schools and colleges, but especially in institutions where students of different racial groups regularly come into contact. A few days before I sat down to write these pages, I took an informal poll in a racially mixed classroom of high school juniors and seniors. On a scale of one to five, students were asked to respond to the question, "How much racial tension is there in your school?" Two students responded with a three ("moderate"), and twenty-seven with a five ("very high"). Yet in this school teachers are uncomfortable directly discussing issues of race in the classroom. The English curriculum, like that at most high schools, is almost exclusively monoethnic and Euro-American (Applebee, "Stability"). The lack of opportunities to discuss racial and cultural differences doesn't help these students come to know and respect each other.

While opinions are mixed, no public school or college English teacher today could deny the increasing interest and enthusiasm in the profession for the inclusion of multicultural approaches—something we see in new textbooks, anthologies, syllabi, and professional conferences. The impetus for teaching multicultural literature has come from the civil rights movements, school integration, and the changing demographics of "minority" ethnic students in schools and universities, as well as from an outpouring of marvelous writing by American minority authors. As scholars have explored minority literatures, a wide variety of rich and important works have been recovered, and richly interconnected traditions have come to be recognized.

Multicultural Studies

Multicultural studies brings new and broader conceptions of literature to teaching. Reworking traditional philological approaches, scholars recover oral and popular traditions and stress the importance of understanding literature in cultural and historical contexts. There are important differences in the issues, approaches, and emphases in the scholarship on various American minority groups. Oppression and resistance, assimilation and cultural continuation, diversity within each so-called "ethnic group"—all of these may be common themes, yet the differences are important as well, and what each minority tradition means to the dominant tradition—and what they mean to one another—are rich and interesting questions open to classroom exploration.

Multicultural studies, like women's studies, has recovered lost literary voices, helped connect literature to cultural and social movements, and helped establish a theoretical base for understanding minority—and majority—cultural traditions. Conventional forms of literary criticism have been necessary but are also insufficient to address the particular qualities of multicultural literatures, the outpouring of high-quality minority writing, and the remarkable force and potential for multicultural literature in the classroom.

For example, scholars of African American studies such as Henry Louis Gates Jr., Houston Baker, Barbara Christian, Cornel West, and Toni Morrison have forged new paradigms for reading and teaching literature that are beginning to reach secondary and college classrooms. Their work has helped emphasize American literary traditions not as a series of universal stages, such as Puritanism, Transcendentalism, or Realism, but as an ongoing and energetic dialogue of viewpoints and experiences that fracture any one "period" into multiple perspectives. They recognize African American literature as a coherent and self-reflective—"signifying" to use Gates's word—tradition that is both informed by the dominant culture and that serves as an alternative narrative from which the dominant tradition can be reinterpreted.

Textbook makers have made significant efforts to address the implications of ethnic studies scholarship and the demands of teachers and school districts for more relevant textbooks. For example, Harcourt, Brace has produced full-length Mexican American and African American literature textbooks for high school. *The Norton Anthology of African American Literature* is a rich resource that comes with its own CD-ROM including African American music. Other texts attempt to bring together multiple ethnic groups—for example, *Braided Lives,* published by the Minnesota Humanities Commission. Perhaps the anthology that goes farthest in this direction is the *Heath Anthology of American Literature*, designed for college yet rich in

▶

materials for all levels. Wonderful new trade collections and anthologies of multicultural literature are appearing all the time; many could serve as classroom texts.

A primary issue for all of the multicultural textbooks is that their incorporation of multicultural literature often becomes an assimilation of new texts to old literary approaches. "New Critical" textbooks that isolate the literary work from its author and culture, as well as reader response approaches that fail to assist students to bridge social, cultural, and historical distances in works outside their own cultural experience, are inadequate or misleading when used exclusively as an approach to multicultural materials. Using a book like *Native Son* solely to examine the literary features of the novel—while it can be done—would seem to miss the point of the work. Students also need to consider the vital questions that the novel raises about racism, urban poverty, crime, youth violence, and criminal justice, and they may also need to look at the way that such a book tends to be read differently by majority and minority Americans. Multicultural literature makes more sense and works more effectively in the classroom when it is read within a cultural studies curriculum.

Teachers working in areas outside their own background or training need to move with care. Regarding Native American literature, Joseph Bruchac, an Abenaki poet, storyteller, and teacher, stresses the importance of non-Native American teachers listening to Native people. He advises:

> Much of Native America's traditional culture is living in the strongest sense of that word. Revealing that culture to the uninitiated is sacrilegious. A good teacher of Native American literature needs to know enough to be able to know which works need to be shown special respect. I cannot emphasize that word respect strongly enough. In some cases it may even mean NOT discussing something. This is a hard direction for people with the western mindset to follow, that western mindset which says, "Tell it all, show it all, explain it all." I feel that those with that mindset would be better off avoiding the teaching of Native American literature. (149)

Yet sensitivity must not silence discussion. The need to address issues of race and ethnicity as part of the curriculum is more pressing today than ever before. Given the fact that in America nearly 50 percent of high school students do not go on to college (25 percent start a two-year or technical program, and 25 percent start a four-year program), these sensitive and important discussions must not be "saved" only for college where they are supposedly "safer." While our population is increasingly, even dramatically, more multiethnic, our country is also increasingly racially divided. In the 1990s, schools in many states were more racially separated than in the 1950s before the famous *Brown v. Board of Education* decision. Failing to teach multiculturally is part of what has divided us. Mary Louise Pratt writes:

> Multiculturalism seeks to multiply the number of socially defined groups that have access to the society's dialogues about itself and to place those groups in dialogue with each other. Inevitably, the dialogue is initially anchored in the groups' differences from each other—but this does not constitute Balkanization; in fact, it constitutes the opposite, for the groups are in the same room and are talking and listening to each other. The real Balkanization is what we had before— the legal and de facto segregations around which this country's institutions were built. Nothing could be more Balkanized than American higher education in the 1920s or the 1950s. The momentum of multiculturalism is meant to counter fragmentation produced by social disenfranchisement and segregation. (12)

Years ago, Rodney King asked a simple question: "Can't we all just get along?" I submit that the answer to this question depends significantly on high school and college English teachers and our willingness and courage to draw on the wisdom of minority writers and scholars and address racial issues in our classrooms openly and maturely.

Multicultural studies was certainly vital to my class's examination of race and violence in contemporary America. One important contribution was the rap music that several of my African American students suggested we look at. While rap's reputation for glorifying violence and objectifying women must be considered, I learned through my students that it would be a mistake to lump all rap together and fail to recognize the relevant social critique made by many rap artists. One song my students brought to class, called "Trapped" by the late rap artist Tupac Shakur, tells a story about a young man who dreams of escaping the ghetto but finds himself unable to evade the path that leads to violence.

> All we know is violence, do the job in silence.
> Walk the city streets like a rat pack of tyrants.
> Too many brothers daily headed for the big pen,
> Niggas coming out worse off than when they went in.
> Trapped in a corner, dark, and I couldn't see the light
> Thoughts in my mind, was the 9, and a better life. [9: 9mm gun]
> What do I do, live my life in a prison cell?
> I'd rather die, than be trapped in a living hell.

Powerful beat, vivid rhyme and images, and an "on the street" perspective make rap, based on my experience with this class, one of the most energized forms of poetry for English classes to examine. Teachers need to take care in its use, as language may be strong and inappropriate for some classrooms. Contemporary films about inner-city life offer another powerful medium in which students can explore the violence crisis (see the list headed "Works for Teaching about Youth Violence" at the end of this chapter for suggestions). While the works I have been discussing emphasize the experience of the inner city, it is also important to recognize that violence is by no means confined to ghettos and that youth gangs are formed by all racial groups in many different parts of the country.

Regardless of the age level of the students we work with, exploring literature that addresses issues of violence may hit close to home. Victimization by robbery, assault, rape, and sexual harassment of teenagers and college students, as well as abusive home environments, cut across all racial and social lines. Indeed, bullying and harassment are all too common even in many of the institutions in which we teach—situations of which students are often more aware than are teachers. While some students will be reluctant to bring their feelings privately to the teacher or professor, others may not. When my classes address such issues, I am surprised by how often students will share with me—via their journals, in person, or even with the whole class—that they have been the victims of one or another form of violence. I am also disturbed by how rarely they have been able to seek help and counseling. Even though my class is a "literature" class, I have felt it essential to address these concerns as they arise. Thus I have invited speakers from the women's shelter and the local YWCA sexual assault program to visit my classes, to speak with all my students about developing respectful relationships, about safety issues, and about the survivor process, and to provide them with information about resources in our community.

Made famous by a song about a sweet and innocent hometown gal, the city of Kalamazoo, Michigan, where I now live may appear at first glance to be a comfortable town of tree-lined streets, churches, and universities; yet our community is increasingly showing the "big city" problems of crime, drugs, and gangs that have led our county to have the highest juvenile arrest rate in the state. The scene Cindy describes in the quotation that heads this chapter took place only a few blocks from my home. (Less than two weeks after I finished this chapter, a student who had dropped out of the high school I describe below was shot and killed. About ten days later, two college students were brutally murdered in the robbery of a video store three blocks from the school.) Many White families have fled to the suburbs or placed their children in private schools, and as a result our two large high schools are about 50 percent African American and a majority of the students are from low-income families.

In working with a racially mixed group of lower-track sophomores at one of the downtown high schools, two of my former students, Amy Kruzich and Christine Bundy, have developed a unit for exploring the causes of violence and the perspectives of inner-city youth. The centerpiece is the powerful book *Monster: The Autobiography of an L.A. Gang Member* by Sanyika Shakur, a.k.a. Kody Scott. Scott, who entered gang life at the age of eleven, portrays the brutal battle for territory, the idiosyncrasies of the criminal justice response, and the breakdown of community that drew him away from middle school and senior high. He writes from jail where he is currently serving a sentence for armed robbery. For teachers and students who wish to understand gang life, this text is a must-read.

While views about gangs differed widely, these at-risk students found Scott's story compelling. Some of the most "difficult" students had considerable street knowledge about gang life and, perhaps for the first time in their educational career, they became the class "experts," able to inform classmates and their teachers on a number of the issues raised in the text. Working in small groups, writing, and later meeting as a whole class, the students spent several weeks examining and arguing about the influences on Kody's life and the choices that he makes.

After being repeatedly beat up for his lunch money, Kody determines never again to be a victim. Students understood the intensity of Kody's decision, his sense of honor and the conflicting allegiances his decision creates. Attempting to explain Kody's violent "down for anything" actions, one student described the requirements of gang patriotism in this way: "Kody got to do whatever he have to do to respect his flag." To the students it was clear that the adults didn't know, understand, or appreciate Kody's world. In discussion one student pointed out, "Kody has respect for his mother, but still he goin' to stand up for what he believe in." Melinda wrote,

> He felt he had to join a gang to survive and to fit in with others. Kody found the closeness of the gang appealing and decided to be part of it. His mom was always working and the gang became his family.

The emphasis these students placed on Kody's sense of honor and his need for respect fits closely with the analysis of academic experts like urban anthropologist Elijah Anderson:

> At the heart of the street code is the issue of respect—loosely defined
> as being treated "right," or granted the deference one deserves. . . .
> Many of the forms that dissing (disrespecting) can take might seem
> petty to middle-class people (maintaining eye contact for too long, for
> example), but to those invested in the street code, these actions
> become serious indications of the other person's intentions. (82)

James Garbarino, perhaps the leading scholar on the effect of violence on young people, maintains that children raised in an unsafe environment develop a form of "hyper vigilance" where ambiguous stimuli are treated as threatening.

The students in this class would understand Garbarino's analysis; they could sympathize with Kody's sense of a constant insecurity, his turning to the gang for safety. These students knew how important it was that the gang offered Kody respect and a family that could partly substitute for an absent father. Some felt that an eleven-year-old Kody could not be held responsible for his decision to join the gang. Others insisted that Kody always had a choice. I observed one class discussion where it was obvious that the passionate debate over Kody's freedom to choose versus the pressures of his environment was tied to the difficult decisions that the students found themselves making on a daily basis. Using *Monster* and addressing gangs and violence in these English classrooms was a way of providing these students with a forum for thinking about their own lives. While they didn't condone Kody's violence, the students began to explore ways to address this violence and to avoid it themselves.

In working with these teachers I was intrigued by the way that *Monster* was integrated into their existing literature curriculum. After *Monster* they turned to the familiar play *Twelve Angry Men*. Coming to the play after examining contemporary issues of gangs and violence helped both teachers and students see the relevance of the more traditional work. The teachers tied the study of the play to the trial of Rodney King and the challenges facing largely White juries attempting to understand the point of view and experience of minorities. If *Twelve Angry Men* is a powerful statement of the possibility of fairness and justice in the American legal system, then connecting the play to the real world helped students explore how precarious such justice can be, how prejudices can cloud judgment, and how inadequate the justice system is to remedy fundamental issues of poverty, racism, and inequality.

While the portrayals students are presented with on television or in theaters may desensitize them to violence, it has been my experience that reading and exploring certain texts with violent passages can have the opposite effect, resensitizing students to the pain of others. Based on what I have observed in these classrooms, *Monster* is in that category. Firsthand testimonials of people struggling for peace, justice, and equality—works like *Narrative of the Life of Frederick Douglass, Night,* or *I, Rigoberta Menchú,* which include violent scenes but position the reader to experience them from the point of view of the victim—can be used in the same way to examine alternatives to violence. Works such as these ought to be a regular part of language arts teaching (see Chapter 7 for further discussion of this point).

We can also consider teaching about violence with many of our traditional works. For years, teachers have segued from *Romeo and Juliet* to *West Side Story,* connecting these stories to the current crisis of gangs and violence would seem only natural. The popular 1996 Baz Luhrmann version of *Romeo and Juliet* staring Leonardo DiCaprio certainly makes this connection. In the past I tried to interest students in *Macbeth* by emphasizing the violence of the early scenes. A more effective and humane reading of the play might seek to reflect critically on issues of violence by examining Macduff's agonizing over the loss of his family, Macbeth's own dehumanization as he wades further into killing, and, as I mentioned in the last chapter, the problematic code that seems to equate manhood with violence throughout the work as well as in society today.

Examining the mass media has also been a tradition in language arts teaching; perhaps doing so today is more important than ever. As many other teachers have done, I have had students keep "video logs" where they could record incidents of violence they have seen on television. This simple form of documentation has made them more aware of what they are exposed to and led to important discussions about how the media affects us.

Media Studies

In the 1960s, Marshall McLuhan claimed that the "medium is the message," that we live in an electronic "global village," and that new forms of emerging media technology profoundly influence us.

> The medium, or process, of our time—electric technology—is reshaping and restructuring patterns of social interdependence and every aspect of our personal life. It is forcing us to reconsider and reevaluate practically every thought, every action, and every institution formerly taken for granted. Everything is changing—you, your family, your neighborhood, your education, your job, your government, your relation to "the others." And they're changing dramatically. (*The Medium Is the Massage* 8)

As newspapers, magazines, film, television—and now the Internet—have evolved, so have scholarship and teaching in English, journalism, and communication studies. Scholars such as Albert Bendura have undertaken empirical studies of the effects of media, including examining the effects of media violence. The mass media has become a topic for writers exploring wide-ranging topics such as the representation of minorities and women, the influence of media on children, advertising, and the domination of the media by large corporations. Jerry Mander's *Four Arguments for the Elimination of Television* (1978) presents a convincing case. Neil Postman's *Amusing Ourselves to Death* (1985) examines the way that television reduces public discussion to show business and raises profound questions about democracy in the media age. The well-known 1978 film *Killing Us Softly* has for decades introduced students to issues in the portrayal of women in advertising.

Four years of teaching high school mass media classes served as my introduction to the relevance of media education. Close-reading the media often meant careful analysis of brief clips and images. But such close reading could not take place without an awareness of questions to ask and social issues to explore, as well as a sensitivity to the power of media and advertising in our society. Thus my classes included reading that would take students out of familiar contexts and allow them to examine the media from an "outside" perspective. I found science fiction novels effective, and books such as *1984* by George Orwell, *Fahrenheit 451* by Ray Bradbury, *Brave New World* by Aldous Huxley, *The Giver* by Malcolm Lowry, and even Ayn Rand's *Anthem* helped students develop perspectives on the media as a societal force.

Students discovered ways to respond to and speak back through the mass media, to develop their own media voices, so to speak. They enjoyed making advertisements, designing radio and television programs, and creating storyboards and film scripts. Today, I would also encourage developing their own Web sites. Creating their own media "texts" sharpened their literacy, their understanding of language, texts, and images, and their ability to read and "deconstruct" the world that surrounds them. In addition to experimenting with various media genres, students engaged in projects where they imagined taking over a television or radio station and restructuring the programming, or they developed grassroots campaigns to influence the media through letter writing, petitioning, and other direct actions.

Many teachers have generated enthusiasm and critical thinking by teaching about popular culture and mass media. Comic books, television programs, romance novels, popular music, music videos, alternative newspapers, fashion magazines, advertisements, movies, and films are all properly a part of English language arts teaching. Yet, rather than mounting separate courses of the kind I was given to teach, perhaps the most effective way to address media studies is to integrate media study into literature and cultural study. Understanding film, popular culture, or the mass media is serious intellectual work; combining media and literary studies allows a wide range of creative and critical possibilities.

Directly addressing issues of violence and gangs in students' lives is an approach supported by Linda Christensen in her article "Building Community from Chaos" in the hopeful book *Rethinking Our Classrooms: Teaching for Equity and Justice* (edited by Bigelow et al.). Writing out of her classroom, Christensen examines ways for English teachers to address the increasing anger of students who are frustrated by wasting time on meaningless assignments in low-track classes, as well as their hostility toward school and toward each other. Rather than outlawing the subject, she let her students talk about it and discovered literature that could powerfully address their lives and experiences. These connections did not always have to be as immediate and direct as those made in *Monster*. For instance, she found one of the most effective texts to be *Thousand Pieces of Gold* by Ruthann Lum McCunn. Christensen writes:

> In an attempt to get them involved in the novel, I read aloud an evocative passage about the unemployed peasants sweeping through the Chinese countryside pillaging, raping, and grabbing what was denied them through legal employment. Suddenly students saw their own lives reflected back at them through Chen, whose anger at losing his job and ultimately his family led him to become an outlaw. Chen created a new family with this group of bandits. Students could relate: Chen was a gang member. I had stumbled on a way to interest my class. The violence created a contact point between the literature and the students' lives. (Bigelow et al. 51)

Building on this connection, Christensen seeks to have her students develop empathy, think critically about violence and its causes, and find ways to become active in working against it.

Community is also the focus of one of my former students, Eva Kendrick, teaching English in an alternative school and working with some of the most endangered adolescents in our community. Eva begins the year by developing a contract with her students to establish her classroom as a neutral, violence-free zone. Since her students have failed to fit into traditional classrooms, she has them engage in extensive dialogue, writing, and discussion about what roles they believe teachers should take to make the class successful as a learning community. Eva invites her students' participation in decision making as she goes about creating a more democratic classroom environment. Her emphasis is also on the word *respect* and that seems to resonate with the students. By identifying vandalism as *disrespectful* to all members of the community she has been able to greatly reduce this behavior in her classroom. As trust is developed with her students, discussion and personal writing begin to reveal the issues of violence that pervade their lives.

After meeting her students, reading their writing, and recognizing the power their voices were developing in Eva's class, I invited Eva and her students to join me at a conference sponsored by the Michigan Council of Teachers of English to speak to teachers on the subject of the problem of violence in students' lives. Eight of her students, all of them either presently or formerly gang members, served as a panel addressing an overflow crowd of 130 English teachers. The students were nervous, a couple huddling inside winter jackets they didn't want to remove. At the outset I was uncertain, fearful that the students might not be able to speak, unsure what was going to happen next. Yet gathering strength from each other, one by one they began to tell about their own experiences and to analyze them. Individually and collectively, they shared how they had been expelled from traditional high schools, how they had become involved with the juvenile court system, and the role that violence played in their daily lives. They spoke of the decisions they had made to join gangs and the safety and security they hoped to find there. One student explained that what she got from the gang and nowhere else was "People watching my back. People that will be there for me no matter what. People that I can count on." Tyesha told us about three older students who continually harassed her in the halls when she was a first-year student and how reporting them to the vice principal only made matters worse. She explained:

> I got hemmed in corners of deserted hallways during and after school by groups of girls. It got to the point where I just couldn't take it anymore. So I'd fight, figuring they would leave me alone. But I was wrong. . . . It got to the point where I was afraid to come to school. So I went and used my lunch money to skip school which caused my grades to drop and me to get kicked off the swim team because I didn't come to practice. . . . I came to the conclusion that if I was in a gang maybe the girls would leave me alone. . . . They helped me by solving most of the fighting problems by talking to some of the girls. I stopped skipping school and tried to bring my grades back up. My new friends were there for me when my mother and family wasn't and when no one would help me.

> I am sorry that I joined a gang. Not because of the trouble I got into, but because I hurt a lot of people. I did what I had to do to help myself. I am a gang member because I chose to be one and no one can change that.

These students told the audience about the prevalence of weapons and fighting in the schools they had attended—information that surprised a couple of the teachers who worked in the very schools these students were describing. As gang members they were able to analyze why gangs existed as articulately as any social scientist I have heard on the subject, and they offered specific suggestions for what schools needed to do to address them. Overall, they spoke from their hearts about their desire for respect and belonging.

The audience of English teachers was spellbound; several told me later that they had been on the verge of tears. Here were the educational throwaways of our community—poor Black, Hispanic, and White kids, school "troublemakers" who skipped and flunked out of classes, who, when they were given the microphone, were wonderfully articulate, clearly intelligent thinkers with much to tell us about what our schools were really like. Listening to them I realized how desperately important it is that the voices of "marginal" students like these be heard and, indeed, be placed at the center of attention. Such students can be found in every educational institution, and if we are willing to listen to them then there is much we can learn about how schools and colleges need to change to become safer and more productive places. In the weeks after their presentation, Eva was convinced that although the lives of these students remained troubled and chaotic, the opportunity they had had to be heard at the conference was important to them, even transformative. Eva struggles to keep them together as a group and find other forums in which her students can speak. We have taken these and similar students to NCTE conferences in Minneapolis and Chicago, where they have joined with local students, told their stories, shared their wisdom, and had similar reactions from English teachers.

But the need for these young people's voices to be heard should not be limited to the occasional teachers' conference. The best place to start is our own classrooms. Having students write about the violence in their lives can be therapeutic, even lifesaving. While not all of our students have had direct encounters with violence, they can all benefit from the humanizing experience of examining the lives and testimonies of other young people whose experience differs from their own.

Such teaching involves taking risks. Allowing students to journal in their own voices and tell their own stories may mean that we sometimes receive writing that makes us uncomfortable. As teachers, we also have an important responsibility to protect our students' privacy. Incorporating literature that addresses the current crisis of violence or gangs means we may need to rethink the canon and even the purposes of literature study. Listening to marginalized students may mean hearing things that we might rather not hear, not only about students' families or their experiences with poverty, drugs, and violence, but also about our own classrooms, our teaching, our schools and institutions. It may be difficult for some schools to openly recognize problems of violence and listen to students without being defensive, yet we must take into consideration the high correlation between youth violence and school failure. Administrators and teachers may worry that if "distorted" information about the presence of harassment, violence, or weapons on campuses "gets out," school reputations, even budget levies, may be in jeopardy. At the university level, colleagues, department chairs, or administrators may view such topics as not sufficiently "academic."

When we do respond, it is often to the symptom, not the cause. As a society, we turn to increasing the numbers of police, building prisons, and trying juveniles as adults; in schools we develop more rules, use more aggressive disciplinary measures, increase detention and suspension, create special at-risk classes, create special at-risk alternative schools, and, in general, attempt to get the kids out of the building and out of mind. But the issue should be seen not as one of exclusion, but as one of inclusion, of finding ways for all of us to listen to each other. Open discussions about gangs are far less likely to lead to gang recruitment than refusing to address the issue. Examining issues of date rape or racial harassment can and should take place in classrooms as well in college dorms.

It is time to stop blaming and demonizing young people for the violence in their lives. Indeed, it is not so much that we have a youth violence problem in this country, but that throughout our society we have endemic problems of family and community breakdown, of increasing inequality, of readily available weapons, of a harsh get-ahead-at-any-cost ethic, even of glorifying violent behavior itself. As families, children, and schools continue to be underfunded, levels of desperation rise. In such a world, violence in the lives of our children and young people must come to us as no surprise. Yet, developing sensitivity to what we read and see, heightening our awareness of the feelings and experience of other people, is at the heart of both antiviolence training and good English teaching.

In this chapter I have explored ways in which cultural studies teaching might address a pressing contemporary issue. Cultural studies also provides powerful and exciting ways to view the past, to reconsider literary traditions, and to attempt to better understand and connect to the "classics." Thus in the next chapter I focus on Shakespeare and the possibilities of teaching his plays within an engaging multicultural approach to British and world literature.

Works for Teaching about Youth Violence

- Luis Rodriguez's autobiography *Always Running: La Vida Loca, Gang Days in L.A.* (1993) addresses the rise of Hispanic gangs in California from an insider's viewpoint. Rodriguez addresses the book to his son in an effort to keep him out of gangs.

- *The Autobiography of Malcolm X* also addresses youth violence in the context of America's racial dilemmas.

- *Deadly Consequences: How Violence Is Destroying Our Teenage Population and a Plan to Begin Solving the Problem,* by Deborah Prothrow-Stith with Michaele Weissman, is an introduction to the youth violence crisis, including chapters on the perspective of adolescents, on gangs, and on helping schools prevent violence.

- The issue of *English Journal* for September 1995 (volume 84, number 5) focuses on violence in schools. The *English Journal* issue for May 2000 (89.5) focuses on developing peace-centered curriculums.

- To understand violence in the United States, one should probably start with the treatment of native peoples. James Welch's *Fools Crow* is a compelling novel set in nineteenth-century Montana.

- The classic young adult novels by S.E. Hinton (*The Outsiders; That Was Then, This Is Now; Rumble Fish*) demonstrate to students that gangs are by no means confined to minority youth.

- Narrated from the point of view of a nineteen-year-old girl, James Baldwin's *If Beale Street Could Talk* offers a readable and compelling look at the inequities of the criminal justice system and the effect on the families of young people who are caught up in it.

- Herbert Kohl's essays in *I Won't Learn from You: And Other Thoughts on Creative Maladjustment* invites teachers to enter into the perspective of resistant students and to transform their teaching to more authentically meet student needs.

- A powerful picture book that would work well with a variety of age groups, *Life in the Ghetto* is written and illustrated by a twelve-year-old girl, Anika Thomas, and tells about the violence of her daily life in a poor neighborhood.

- Nathan McCall's *Makes Me Wanna Holler: A Young Black Man in America* describes a life of violence and gangs in Virginia. By reading *Native Son* and *The Autobiography of Malcolm X* while in prison, McCall turned his life around and became a journalist for the *Washington Post.*

- Starting with his middle school years when he joins The Crips, Kody Scott's *Monster: Autobiography of an L.A. Gang Member* chronicles the violence and human cost of America's failure to address the needs of inner-city youth.

- As described above, I think Richard Wright's *Native Son* is an effective text for examining the role of racism in the contemporary youth violence crisis.

- *Scorpions* by Walter Dean Myers is a Newbery Award–winning young adult novel addressing the youth violence crisis.

- Another picture book, *Stop the Violence Please* by Michele Durkson Clise, will stimulate discussion with any age group and includes an appendix of information on the youth violence crisis and strategies for youth involvement to address it.

- A number of compelling inner-city African American "gangsta" movies address violence among minority youth. Although they may not be appropriate for classroom viewing, my first choice would be *Strapped*. Others include *Boyz N the Hood, Juice, South Central,* and *Menace II Society.*

- *Voices from the Future: Our Children Tell Us about Violence in America,* edited by Susan Goodwillie, is a disturbing collection of interviews with children across America who have experienced violence in their lives. Created by a group of dedicated teenagers, the book is a monument to what young people can do to learn about and address our violence crisis.

Readings in Multicultural Studies

General

- *Redefining American Literary History* edited by A. LaVonne Brown Ruoff and Jerry Ward and published by the Modern Language Association in 1991 is a resource for teachers of American literature. It includes not only a number of useful essays (especially "The Literatures of America: A Comparative Discipline" by Paul Lauter) but also a bibliography of literature and secondary reading in African American, American Indian, Asian American, Chicano, and Puerto Rican literatures.

- Howard Zinn's *A People's History of the United States* retells American history from the point of view of minorities, women, immigrants, and working-class people and is an indispensable companion for teachers seeking to broaden and deepen an historical approach. Many chapters will work well in the classroom in tandem with literature.

African American

- *African American Literary Criticism 1773 to 2000* edited by Hazel Arnett Ervin is a compendious, important, and useful collection of essays by leading thinkers about African American writing. The table of contents is organized chronologically and by critical approach. Among the more than sixty essays included are Langston Hughes's "The Negro Artist and the Racial Mountain" (1926) and pieces by W.E.B. Dubois, Alain Locke, James Baldwin, Ralph Ellison, Toni Morrison, and bell hooks.

- Barbara Christian's *Black Feminist Criticism: Perspectives on Black Women Writers* is a pathbreaking collection of essays addressing autobiography, slave narrative, and contemporary fiction.

- *The Black Image in the White Mind: The Debate on Afro-American Character and Destiny, 1817–1914* by George Fredrickson is a rich and accessible historical study of the development of "scientific" racial thought in the nineteenth century. Addresses pro- and antislavery thinking, including *Uncle Tom's Cabin*, social Darwinism, and progressivism.

- *Conjuring: Black Women, Fiction, and Literary Tradition,* edited by Marjorie Pryse and Hortense Spillers, is another collection of essays addressing autobiography, slave narrative, and contemporary fiction by African American women.

- Houston Baker's *The Journey Back: Issues in Black Literature and Criticism* is a sound overview of African American writing from slave narratives to nationalism and the Black aesthetic. More approachable than Gates's *The Signifying Monkey.*

- Toni Morrison's *Playing in the Dark: Whiteness and the Literary Imagination* attempts to rethink major figures of American literature from an African American perspective.

- Ralph Ellison's *Shadow and Act* is a classic that traces Ellison's own development as a writer and includes essays from 1946 to 1964 on *Huckleberry Finn,* Hemingway, Faulkner, Stephen Crane, Richard Wright, and Black writing in general.

- Henry Louis Gates Jr. is the W.E.B. Dubois Professor of African American Studies at Harvard University; his major book *The Signifying Monkey: A Theory of African American Criticism* rewards the diligent reader.

- Eric Sundquist's *To Wake the Nations: Race in the Making of American Literature* is a rich and accessible study of the role of race in the work of African American and Euro-American male writers of the nineteenth century. The focus is on Frederick Douglass, Herman Melville, Mark Twain, Charles Chesnutt, and W.E.B. Dubois.

Native American

- *American Indian Literatures: An Introduction, Bibliographic Review, and Selected Bibliography* by A. LaVonne Brown Ruoff is an essential and concise introduction that addresses both traditional oral and contemporary written literatures and includes useful bibliographies.

- *Coming to Light: Contemporary Translations of the Native Literatures of North America,* edited by Brian Swann, is a large collection of recently translated, regionally organized poetry and stories, each piece introduced by useful commentary.

- Susan Berry Brill de Ramírez's *Contemporary American Indian Literatures and the Oral Tradition* uses storytelling and the "conversive" tradition to examine contemporary writers like Momaday, Silko, Alexie, and Welch.

- Andrew Wiget is editor of the *Handbook of Native American Literature*, a rich collection of over seventy essays by leading scholars addressing oral literatures and the emergence of Native American writing and the Native American Renaissance (post-1967). There are many pieces on well-known individual authors. Wiget is also the author of *Native American Literature*, a sound, quick overview of oral literature, fiction, and poetry.

- Dell Hymes's *"In Vain I Tried to Tell You": Essays in Native American Ethnopoetics* explores the complexity of understanding traditional Native American oral narrative.

- Peter Nabokov's *Native American Testimony: An Anthology of Indian and White Relations; First Encounter to Dispossession* offers an enormous variety of short pieces that could work well in the classroom, particularly to give historical and cultural context.

- *Roots and Branches: A Resource of Native American Literature—Themes, Lessons, and Bibliographies* by Dorothea Susag is NCTE's first effort to bring Native American literature to teachers.

- *The Sacred Hoop: Recovering the Feminine in American Indian Traditions* by Paula Gunn Allen (Laguna/Sioux) addresses the role and perspective of women in Native American literature.

- Native American literature and scholarship represent an enormous and often compromised body of work—mistranslation, inauthentic renderings, and appropriation by the dominant culture are common. A short essay by Joseph Bruchac (an Abenaki), "Thoughts on Teaching Native American Literature," offers an important cautionary note for non-Native teachers approaching Native American literature.

Mexican American

- *Aztlán: Essays on the Chicano Homeland,* edited by Rudolfo Anaya and Francisco Lomelí, explores the myth of Aztlán, the Aztec and Chicano homeland in the American Southwest, by leading Chicano scholars.

- Gloria Anzaldúa's *Borderlands = La Frontera* is an influential and moving combination of essay and poetry about identity, Aztlán, the Chicano movement, language, writing, and borders by a leading feminist.

- Ramón Saldívar's *Chicano Narrative: The Dialectics of Difference* is a careful and theoretically informed examination of Chicano writing as a resistance literature. Saldívar addresses the *corrido* song tradition, as well as individual writers, including Paredes, Rivera, Anaya, Hinojosa, Cisneros, Rodriquez, Galazara, and others.

- *The Identification and Analysis of Chicano Literature* edited by Francisco Jiménez is an older but still informative collection of essays and talks by well-known Chicano authors.

- Teresa McKenna's *Migrant Song: Politics and Process in Contemporary Chicano Literature* is a similar and high-quality work. It includes a chapter on Hispanic literature and pedagogy.

- Rodolfo Acuña's *Occupied America: The Chicano's Struggle Toward Liberation* is an influential historical study examining the Chicano experience in America from a colonial perspective.

- *"With His Pistol in His Hand": A Border Ballad and Its Hero* by Américo Paredes is a rich and approachable study of early Mexican American culture focusing on the *corrido* (ballad) and the real-life story of Gregorio Cortez, an outlaw hero of the nineteenth century.

Asian American

- Frank Chin and a group of Asian American writers put together *Aiiieeeee! An Anthology of Asian-American Writers* in 1974 that was reissued as *The Big Aiiieeeee!* in 1983. This volume is an important early collection emerging from the social protest of the 1960s and has been criticized by a few prominent contemporary Asian American women writers.

- Elaine Kim's *Asian American Literature: An Introduction to the Writings and Their Social Context* is an early and still valuable book-length study of Asian American literature, including chapters on images of Asians in Anglo-American literature and comments on frequently taught Asian American texts such as *Farewell to Manzanar* and *Woman Warrior.*

- David Leiwei Li's *Imagining the Nation: Asian American Literature and Cultural Consent* is a valuable and theoretically informed survey of issues and texts of Asian American literature.

- *An Interethnic Companion to Asian American Literature* edited by King-Kok Cheung is a fine introduction for the general reader and a rich resource for teachers. Separate chapters by leading authorities introduce the reader to Chinese American, Filipino American, Japanese American, Korean American, South Asian American, and Vietnamese American literatures. A general introduction and five chapters survey key issues in Asian American literature. Addresses Asian American writing from the early *Aiiieeeee!* anthology to contemporary feminist and exile/diaspora challenges.

Materials on Popular Culture and Media Studies

- *Amusing Ourselves To Death* by Neil Postman is an accessible and important critique of the danger of a media-as-entertainment approach to American politics.

- The January 1998 *English Journal* (volume 87, number 1) is focused on media literacy and includes a wide variety of articles written by teachers about their examination of media in the classroom.

- *Four Arguments for the Elimination of Television* by Jerry Mander argues that television prepares people for autocratic control, is dominated by narrow interests, adversely affects the human body and mind, and does not have potential to be a democratic medium.

- *Killing Us Softly,* directed by Margaret Lazarus and Renner Wunderlich in 1979, is a popular and powerful film about women in advertising. The film was followed in 1987 by *Still Killing Us Softly* and in 2000 by *Beyond Killing Us Softly: The Strength to Resist*, and the most recent version may be the best one. On the same theme, see the books *The Beauty Myth* by Naomi Wolf and *Where the Girls Are: Growing Up Female with the Mass Media* by Susan Douglas.

- A useful text for students seeking to understand the complexity of the media and violence issue is *Media Violence: Opposing Viewpoints,* edited by William Dudley, in the Opposing Viewpoints Series from Greenhaven Press.

- *Screening Images: Ideas for Media Education* by the Canadian Chris Worsnop is a good introduction to media education for teachers.

- Written in England, *Teaching about Television* by Len Masterman is one of the richer books for media teachers.

- *Understanding Media* made Marshall McLuhan a household name in the 1960s and brought attention to media studies. Terrence Gordon's *McLuhan for Beginners* is a visually appealing synthesis of McLuhan's thought that would appeal to high school and college students.

- The representation of minorities in the media is explored in many works including *Representing "Race": Ideology, Identity, and the Media* by Robert Ferguson and *Split Image: African Americans in the Mass Media* by Jannette Dates and William Barlow.

- Historical studies of the media that I have found interesting are *A History of Mass Communication: Six Information Revolutions* by Irving Fang and *Images of American Life: A History of Ideological Management in Schools, Movies, Radio, and Television* by Joel Spring.

- Writing from a revolutionary Chile to an overwhelming American political and cultural power, Ariel Dorfman and Armand Mattelart create a critique of Walt Disney in their short book *How to Read Donald Duck : Imperialist Ideology in the Disney Comic*, a work that can still resonate with students today. Later, in exile in America, Dorfman wrote *The Empire's Old Clothes: What the Lone Ranger, Babar, and Other Innocent Heroes Do to Our Minds,* examining politics and nationalism in comic books and popular publications such as *Reader's Digest.*

- *Understanding Mass Media* (fifth edition) by William Jawitz is a textbook for high school classes focused on the mass media. The approach is better suited to helping students consider careers in mass communications than to helping them think critically about the media. *Mass Media and Popular Culture* by Barry Duncan is the most popular media studies text in Canada, where mass media study is more fully incorporated into K–12 teaching.

Web Sites for Media Literacy Teaching

- The Assembly of Media Arts is a section of NCTE, and its Web site is located at: http://www.ncte.org/assemblies/#AMA.

- The Center for Media Literacy has a wide variety of materials for teachers: http://www.medialit.org/.

- The Media and Communications Studies site is located at: http://www.aber.ac.uk/media/Functions/mcs.html.

- The Media Awareness Network offers practical support for media education: http://www.media-awareness.ca/eng/.

- The Media Literacy Organizations page offers links to national and international organizations and sites dedicated to media literacy: http://www.eggplant.org/ideas/media/media1.html.

- The Media Literacy On-Line Project at the University of Oregon can be found at: http://interact.uoregon.edu/MediaLit/HomePage.

- The National Telemedia Council focuses on media literacy among K–12 students: http://danenet.wicip.org/ntc/.

5 Shakespeare and the New Multicultural British and World Literatures

When I was a high school student I had a wonderful English class devoted to the plays of William Shakespeare. We viewed an Encyclopedia Britannica film featuring the countryside of Stratford-upon-Avon, boys studying in the grammar school, the commercial bustle of London, even a hint of scandal about how old Shakespeare was when he married Anne Hathaway. I remember our enthusiastic teacher, Mrs. Perko, showing us a built-to-scale wooden model of the Globe Theatre. How small it was! How clearly everyone was in their place, crude groundlings on their feet in the open enclosure, rising classes and aristocrats in the roofed balconies. We learned about the "great chain of being," the religious and philosophical framework that, we were told, ordered the Elizabethan conception of the universe. Students from previous classes had done projects on heraldry, and brightly colored shields decorated the walls of the classroom.

It was a surprise, then, to learn in graduate school that this colorful, bucolic, and orderly picture of Renaissance England was, at best, a limited way to think about Shakespeare's time. During Shakespeare's day, as during our own, there were many contentious, violent, and disorderly things going on, and far from there being one "Elizabethan point of view," Shakespeare's day was a time of social upheaval, political and economic oppression, and serious religious, sexual, and philosophical disagreement. During Elizabeth's reign, rural and urban poverty was on the rise, and the fear of peasant revolt and rebellion led to strict laws against "masterless men." Dozens of men were charged with attempted regicide and drawn and quartered, their heads stuck on spikes along the Thames bridges where they were left to rot (and stink), not far from the Globe Theatre. Open and intense dispute about the place of women, of "half-humankind," was carried on in a war of street pamphlets, in sermons, and on the stage. Religious and philosophical controversies raged, and the very identity of English nationhood was conflictive and emerging. Shakespeare lived during the period of the colonization of the Americas and, with the Spanish Armada in 1588, England began to replace Spain as the great world power.

During Shakespeare's day, Native Americans were undergoing a massive genocide—some were captured and brought back to England where they were on regular display in the London streets. By 1611, the year in which Shakespeare wrote his last play, there were more than a million African slaves in the so-called "New World."

The way we think about Shakespeare's day has great implications for the way we think about Shakespeare's plays. It certainly affects our ideas of how we should teach them. Controversy, social issues, political questions—the very stuff that generates debate, engages students, and makes literature relevant to us—is washed out by traditional approaches. The influence of New Criticism and its emphasis on literary artistry and "the text itself" has, ironically, led many academics to fail to make good close readings of Shakespeare's language because they failed to concern themselves with the many social, historical, and political issues foregrounded in the plays. In the classroom, New Critical approaches have also, all too often, reduced Shakespeare's vitality. On the other hand, putting Shakespeare in context, examining the relevance of his work to the controversies of his day, and developing conceptions of history that connect Shakespeare's time and our own, offer to rescue Shakespeare from an abstract "greatness" and make his works meaningful to students and their lives in today's world. This is precisely what a cultural studies approach to teaching Shakespeare proposes to do.

In this chapter I want to share with you some of the experiments that I and a former student have attempted in order to bring cultural studies approaches to the teaching of Shakespeare and British and world literature. Shakespeare is obviously central to our teaching of English at the high school and college levels, and there are many different cultural studies concerns that can emerge from his plays. In the last chapter, I mentioned connecting *Romeo and Juliet* to the theme of gangs and youth violence. Shakespeare's plays provide wonderful forums for addressing the roles and relationships of men and women, and many interesting female characters are found in his comedies. In chapter three we looked at addressing issues of gender both in Shakespeare's day and in our own through the teaching of *Macbeth*. In the first chapter, in regard to addressing anti-Semitism and literature, I suggested *The Merchant of Venice*. In relation to the theme of homelessness, I mentioned *King Lear* and *Henry IV* as potentially interesting. In this chapter I will focus on *The Tempest,* a play that, as I will explain, literary and cultural studies scholarship has made not only more interesting to teach but also increasingly relevant to British, world, and even American literature.

My interest in *The Tempest* comes significantly from my experience in teaching the play. Until a few years ago, I thought of it as one of Shakespeare's stuffiest works, a sophisticated commentary on his own art perhaps, but a deliberate piece, weak in characterization, and unsuited to the tastes of young people. Yet in teaching it from a cultural studies perspective, I found that, far from being stuffy or slow, *The Tempest* is engaging and highly relevant. It is a play in which students can discover Shakespeare's magic, spectacle, and magnificent language through accessible themes of romance, the relations of parents and children, and political intrigue. Now understood as one of the earliest works of English literature set in the Americas, the play addresses the relationship of European and non-European people that has shaped much world history since Columbus. The historical context of the play connects it to issues such as colonialism, slavery, racism, indentured servitude, the domination of women, native resistance, social rebellion, and the founding of political utopias. And while *The Tempest* can accommodate historically grounded multicultural teaching, it is a difficult work to force into a "politically correct" interpretation. Students found that the questions raised by the play cannot be addressed with simple or clichéd answers.

Recent new historicist scholarship has developed our understanding of the connection between *The Tempest* and contemporary English settlement in America. The joint-stock Virginia Company that founded the early Virginia Colonies was one of the world's first multinational corporations; two of its wealthy owners were also Shakespeare's patrons. A letter written in 1609 by the colonist William Strachey about the second Virginia expedition is now considered the primary source for *The Tempest*. Strachey records a hurricane, the landing of the Virginia's governor's ship on Bermuda, the wintering over of the passengers on the island, and a settlers' rebellion. It is clear that Shakespeare either read Strachey's letter or was familiar with its contents, and this letter is frequently included with annotated versions of the play (see, for instance, the Oxford or Arden editions).

In addition to fashioning the primary action of *The Tempest* from the adventures recounted in the colonial letter, Shakespeare loaded the play with references to the New World. Ariel describes "the still-vexed Bermudas," and the mood of the play certainly belongs to the turbulent and mysterious "Bermuda Triangle." Caliban worships the god "Setebos," a name found in Magellan's journals. Called a "Man of Ind," Caliban is himself repeatedly compared by other characters in the play to American Indians kidnapped for display in London (during the voyages of Frobisher and Raleigh). A speech about an island utopia given in the play by the character Gonsalo borrows directly from the 1603 English translation of Michel de Montaigne's interesting (and teachable) essay on the New World, "Of Cannibals." In Gonsalo's speech—and for the only time in Shakespeare—the word "plantation" appears. According to the *Oxford English Dictionary*, in Shakespeare's day "plantation" meant "the planting of a colony, colonization."

The New World setting of the play is stressed as Shakespeare derives "Caliban" from the now familiar "cannibal," another word with a relevant etymology. On his first voyage in 1492 Christopher Columbus was, of course, looking for trade routes to "Cathay" and the Indies and expecting to find not only "Indians" but also the fabled Great Khan (*El gran can* in Spanish). Looking for the "*gran can*" Columbus coined the term "*canibale*" ("cannibal" in English) when he recorded what he thought was the name used by the people he met (the Arawaks) to describe another people farther north who were reported to eat their enemies (the Caribs). Since "cannibal" did not take on a separate meaning in English from "Caribbean islander" until 1796, Shakespeare's derivation of "Caliban" from "Cannibal" connects his character to the Carib tribe, and, perhaps inadvertently, to Columbus's first voyage.

New Historicism

New historicism is an approach to the study of literature and history that attempts to incorporate insights from many of the emerging schools of thought that we have been examining, such as multicultural studies, gender studies, political criticism, media studies, popular culture, cultural studies, and so on. When new historicists or "cultural materialists" look at the past, they distrust expressions like "in the eyes of the later Middle Ages" or monolithic cultural explanations such as the "great chain of being." They tend to see historical periods not as consistent or coherent, but instead as made up of differing social groups in contest with one another. Thus, for new historicists, literature should not be thought of as always transcending the time in which it was written, but as deeply involved in its time and thus reflecting and refracting the tensions and diversity of any historical moment. Stephen Greenblatt says that new historicists have "been less concerned to establish the organic unity of literary works and more open to such works as fields of force, places of dissension and shifting interests, occasions for the jostling of orthodox and subversive impulses " (*Power* 6). New historicists also try to be conscious of how our positions in the present shape our views of the past and of ways in which understandings of literature and history change over time.

In secondary school and college literature classes, writers and works from the past are too often presented in narrow and one-dimensional ways. A new historicist approach creates the possibility of making the study of traditional literature more contentious, controversial, and considerably more interesting. Teaching informed by new historicism might try to bring together different kinds of texts, literary and nonliterary, that bring out controversy and contentious viewpoints. The way this chapter explores teaching *The Tempest* in light of colonial letters, historical and contemporary essays, Columbus's voyage, and new perspectives on colonialism, slavery, and Native Americans is only one example of the way that new historicism can be put to use in the classroom.

As I have suggested, comparing a range of historical texts and materials with Shakespeare's plays opens up cultural studies possibilities. While considering gender issues, the teacher might ask students to compare Shakespeare's portrayal of women with street pamphlets from his day arguing vociferously about women's rights; or, the teacher might have students explore the Elizabethan treatment of peasant revolts and public forms of torture of disloyal subjects against Shakespeare's presentation of treason and regicide; or, have students analyze contemporary sermons about Jews along with Shakespeare's presentation of Shylock in *The Merchant of Venice* (and/or the treatment of Jewishness in Chaucer's "The Prioress's Tale"). All of the historical materials I am mentioning here are readable, relatively brief, and available (see the list at the end of this chapter titled "Resources for Cultural Studies Teaching of Shakespeare"). Yet the textbooks and literature anthologies currently available to us isolate Shakespeare from the tensions and controversies of his age and those of our own time, making it harder for students to see what is really interesting about Shakespeare's time (or that of any writer's) and why it might be relevant to them. The list titled "Reading in New Historicism and Cultural Materialism" at the end of this chapter includes new historicist scholarship for all periods of British and American literature.

While the language of *The Tempest* constantly invokes New World settlement, Shakespeare's depiction of characters and events offers students an opportunity to reflect on the relationship of American Indians and Europeans in the founding period of American history. Caliban describes himself as initially receptive to Prospero's arrival.

> The island's mine, by Sycorax my mother,
> Which thou tak'st from me. When thou cam'st first,
> Thou strok'st me and made much of me, would'st give me

Water with berries in 't, and teach me how
To name the bigger light, and how the less,
That burn by day and night; and then I loved thee,
And show'd thee all the qualities o' th' isle,
The fresh springs, brine-pits, barren place and fertile. (I.ii.331–39)

With Caliban Shakespeare creates an indigenous New World character who initially welcomes the Europeans and later finds himself cheated of his birthright. Caliban is vociferous about this mistreatment. He explains that now "you" (Prospero) "sty me / In this hard rock, whiles you do keep from me / The rest o' th' island" (I.ii.342–44). He asserts, "I am subject to a tyrant, a sorcerer that by his cunning hath cheated me of the isle" (III.ii.40–41).

Prospero and Caliban are important figures not just because they can be connected to English settlement in Virginia, but also because their relationship serves as a metaphor for historical relationships between Europeans and non-Europeans more generally. When Shakespeare wrote *The Tempest* in 1611, Spain, Portugal, England, Holland, and France were well under way in their invasion of Central, South, and North America, and they were actively initiating colonies in Asia, Africa, and the South Pacific. Millions of New World peoples had perished under Spanish rule; in the years soon afterward, millions more would suffer under the English, and, later, the Americans. Similar tragic histories were repeated elsewhere around the globe.

Rather than have the teacher lecture students about this connection, it is more engaging for them to begin to uncover the significance of the play's colonial relationships on their own. To help put their reading into a historical and cultural studies frame, I had students read the first chapter of Howard Zinn's *A People's History of the United States* before encountering the play. Zinn tells the story of the first Spanish and British colonies in the New World from the perspective of Native Americans, and his compelling narrative raises questions about the ways in which we traditionally think of history. (Zinn's book is indispensable to teachers of American literature.) After reading Zinn, my students turned to Shakespeare and were able to start making their own connections between *The Tempest* and colonial history. Possibilities for additional research, class presentations, papers, and additional reading rapidly emerged.

New historicist approaches, like any other, are not without problems and risks. For example, my students were too quick to see Caliban as a spokesman for the colonized. Despite Caliban's objections to Prospero's rule over him, I asked students to think about whether or not Caliban speaks with an "authentic" Native American voice. The students were then able to point out that, of course, Shakespeare had never visited America, nor did he know a New World language, nor likely had he spoken with Native Americans.

Students did argue, based on the language of *The Tempest*, that it was at least likely that Shakespeare saw "freak show" displays of Native Americans—or at least of people dressed up as half-humans, half-savages. Following up on the discussion, I learned that monster displays in England had a long history; the Bartholomew fair, for instance, which included exhibits of "freaks," lasted from the twelfth to the nineteenth century. In an essay entitled "Monsters in the Marketplace: The Exhibition of Human Oddities in Early Modern England," Paul Semonin writes that,

> from Elizabethan times, when the first inhabitants and specimens of animal life from the new world began to arrive in England, there appeared among the exhibits a startlingly diverse array of monstrous creatures, many of whom were already familiar to their audiences through popular fables, the bestiaries, pictorial prints and biblical lore. (70)

In *The Tempest* Caliban is presented as one of these "monstrous creatures," a singular figure, removed from family, tribe, and community. Clearly, the details of his portrayal have little to do with the real world of indigenous peoples.

In my class it was more effective to examine Caliban not as a "true depiction" of a Native American but as a freakish representation of the European imagination. Set on his island utopia, the character Caliban could even be considered a sort of European literary or philosophical experiment on the nature of other races, New World "savages," and European "wild men." Historically, the depiction of welcoming natives was part of the promotion of colonial settlement and, ironically, the shattering of their "noble savage" image by eventual resistance was considered by Europeans to justify violence, even genocide. As an example of the European stereotype of a childlike "savage" or nonhuman, Caliban could still be "educated" and become "civilized"—that is to say, more like the Europeans. If this education fails to take hold, the Europeans can justify putting Caliban, and others like him, to different uses. One student put it better than I could.

> Prospero tries to "save" Caliban by teaching him civilized languages, fails to reform him, and can [then] rationalize Caliban's enslavement and treatment because he has proved to be "savage."

In short, the Caliban figure allowed my students to examine the ways in which the portrayal on the Elizabethan stage of a Native American supports—or challenges—the ideological system which was used to justify European colonialism and rule over native people for centuries.

The Caliban character constitutes not only one of the earliest portraits of Native Americans in English literature, but also, perhaps, the first treatment of African Americans. Caliban's mother is from Africa, and Caliban himself is born on the island. He is specifically referred to by Prospero and Miranda as their "slave" on five occasions. Shakespeare could not have known, of course, that the first slave ship would arrive in Jamestown a mere eight years after the staging of *The Tempest,* or that by the time of the French and Native American wars, fully as much as 40 percent of the population of Virginia would be Black slaves. Yet Shakespeare was obviously aware of the slave trade and the presence of slaves—both Africans and Native Americans—in the Caribbean plantations. By 1611 the African slave trade was 170 years old, and a million Africans had already been brought to the New World by the Spanish, Portuguese, Dutch, and English slave traders.

That there should be confusion as to whether or not Caliban is an American Indian or an African American slave is not surprising, given that Elizabethans tended to lump together Africans and North American "Indians." From the English perspective, there were reasons to do so. As Native Americans were killed or died off or escaped, Africans were brought in to replace them in the established slave system. Escaped Africans frequently joined Native American bands in the Caribbean, forming rebel "maroons." Relationships between Europeans and Native Americans resembled those between Europeans and African slaves. As is the case with Caliban as a "Native American," Caliban as a "slave" must recognize Prospero's authority. In both relationships, from the English perspective it was necessary to subdue and discipline Caliban and to educate him in "the ways of civilization."

Thus my students were correct in using the Prospero/Caliban dichotomy as a sort of paradigm for colonial relationships. They were not the first to do so. Octave Mannoni titled his 1956 study of the dependence of colonized people, *Prospero and Caliban: The Psychology of Colonialism.* "Third World" writers objected to Mannoni's conclusions but continued to borrow the paradigm. The Jamaican novelist George Lamming examines the play as a metaphor for the relationships of colonialism in his autobiographical work *The Pleasures of Exile* (1961). Aimé Césaire (a Martinican poet and founder of the African/Caribbean Negritude movement) rewrote *The Tempest* in 1969. In his version Ariel becomes a sort of Martin Luther King Jr. and Caliban a version of Malcolm X. Responding to a famous essay by the Uruguayan José Enrique Rodó on Latin American identity entitled *Ariel* (1900), the Cuban writer Roberto Fernández Retamar, in an equally well-known essay titled "Caliban" (1989), claimed that

Prospero invaded the islands, killed our ancestors, enslaved Caliban, and taught his language to make himself understood. . . . I know of no other metaphor more expressive of our cultural situation, of our reality. (14)

Given the specific role of the play in contemporary thought, as well as its broader metaphorical possibilities, reading and discussing *The Tempest* from a historical and multicultural perspective was a way of preparing my students to understand world history and literature from a colonial perspective, a perspective scholars in postcolonial studies have been exploring for some time. No wonder, then, that *The Tempest* is increasingly taught in British and world literature courses.

Even as I try in my teaching to develop cultural studies curriculums that maintain a focus on a particular theme (or several themes), I also find that student response to the literature may take us on side trips or useful tangents. For the teacher, there are always complicated choices when we explore such issues. In teaching *The Tempest,* for example, in addition to an examination of colonialism and the New World, my students were also engaged by other historical and social issues. The play is filled with Renaissance political intrigue. Prospero is deposed by Antonio, Sebastian schemes against Alonso, the common people (in the person of the butler, the clown, and Caliban) attempt to overthrow Prospero's rule. Gonzalo's discourse on political utopia is scoffed at by his self-interested auditors. Also, rather like *Romeo and Juliet, The Tempest* addresses young love and the tensions of parent/child relationships. Ever submissive to her father's will, Miranda develops a relationship that crosses socially acceptable lines (as long as Prospero is out of favor) and culminates in Prospero's presentation of a Renaissance wedding masque. Unlike *Romeo and Juliet*, my students pointed out, tension arises not only between families but also, even primarily, between social classes—the masque is startlingly interrupted by Caliban's insurrection.

As with any of Shakespeare's plays, approaches such as reading the text in class, listening to recordings, viewing taped performances (of which there are many), and enacting scenes are necessary in order to help students of all levels appreciate Shakespeare's language and stagecraft. Yet the special opportunities to explore the complexities of Shakespeare's era and its relationship to our own are best brought out by a new historicist approach that pairs the play with thematically similar works.

Comparing different works with *The Tempest* is a strategy for developing a cultural studies curriculum that fosters intellectual liveliness, critical thinking, and meaningful reading and writing. Students can use role playing and persona writing to attempt to understand the cultural and historical perspectives involved in *The Tempest* and the texts that correspond to it. Exercises in which students imagine characters or authors from contrasting works speaking to each other are also effective. Issues raised by *The Tempest* are timely, and the play can usually be connected to current events. In the 1990s my students discussed the Rodney King beating and the Los Angeles riots vis-à-vis their relationship to characters and themes in *The Tempest*. In this type of discussion, relevant newspaper and magazine articles can be brought into the classroom.

By using *The Tempest* and choosing from a variety of other works, it is possible to develop survey courses in English and/or world literature with interrelated themes and intertextual relationships. It is also possible to begin to create historically and literarily sound British literature curriculums that are increasingly multicultural and relevant to today's world.

A wonderful way to start such a course is with Sir Thomas More's *Utopia*. Written in 1516, it is one of the first and most interesting European works to respond to the discovery of the New World. Based on reports from a member of the Vespucci expeditions, the book paints an imaginative and evocative picture of Native Americans living in an egalitarian state without private property. Coining the term "utopia" (literally "no-where"), More creates a society that invites students to explore comparisons with his contemporary Europe, with the actual lived reality of the New World before colonialism, and with our own society today. The fascinating legacy of utopian and dystopian literature is a testimony to the power of More's ideas, and his book should also inspire a variety of creative student projects and papers. As we move toward a more multicultural British literature, we will want to start placing British depictions of non-British natives into comparison with the self-representations of colonized and formerly colonized peoples. Teaching *Utopia*, for example, provides an opportunity for student investigation of any number of Native American histories and literary texts. (While you may want to use a few pages from *Utopia*'s Part I to set up the frame of the story, it is Part II of the complete text that is the famous and most interesting part of the work.)

One of the texts that works especially well alongside *The Tempest* is Daniel Defoe's fascinating novel *Robinson Crusoe* (1719). A famous tale of adventure, *Robinson Crusoe* is also a classic of English literature deeply rooted in the history of colonialism in the New World. Beginning his voyage on a slave-trading mission to North Africa, Crusoe travels to Brazil to found a tobacco plantation before he is shipwrecked in the Caribbean off the northern coast of South America. On his island he brings European science, technology, and order to an untamed natural environment. As with Prospero and Caliban, the relationship between Crusoe and the

Native American Friday becomes a metaphor that students can explore in order to consider the European vision of colonial "civilization." Crusoe settles on the island, kills and frightens cannibals in order to save Friday, and returns to the island with shiploads of colonists to make a fortune by running an island corporation. In the ensuing centuries of the British Empire, *Robinson Crusoe* was enormously popular and likely read by every boy who entered the British colonial service.

Another work that makes a fascinating addition to this curriculum is Aphra Behn's 1688 novel *Oroonoko, or, The Royal Slave*. Considered the first novel written in the English language, *Oroonoko* was written by a woman living in the same century as Shakespeare. *Oroonoko* is a fast-paced, well-written story about an interesting subject and, for a seventeenth-century text, is a relatively easy read. Despite all of these good reasons to include *Oroonoko* in survey courses for college and high school students, it remains a relatively unknown work. That is a shame. *Oroonoko* is told from the point of view of a female English colonist in Surinam in the British West Indies who visits isolated Native American tribes and, in the colony, comes to know and sympathize with an African slave named Oroonoko. (Aphra Behn herself visited Surinam in the 1650s.) Oroonoko tells the narrator his story, that of an African prince who allows himself to be sold into slavery to protect the woman he loves. Like Caliban, Oroonoko rebels against his colonial masters and, with his beloved, attempts an escape to freedom. Though I won't give away the novel's conclusion, suffice it to say that it has been compared to *Othello*.

An eighteenth-century text that would fit nicely into this curriculum is the slave narrative of Olaudah Equiano, titled *The Life of Olaudah Equiano, or, Gustavus Vassa, the African*. Though occasionally included in American literature courses, this narrative was written and published in London and can more properly be considered a work of English literature. Moreover, it is an important text to include in our British literature curriculums to help us understand the increasingly multicultural dimensions of English literature and culture. Equiano surely lived one of the most astounding lives of his age. Born in a village in Africa in 1745, captured by slave traders, and shipped to the Caribbean, Equiano worked on plantations and later as a crewman on trading ships before eventually attaining his freedom and settling in England, where his accounts were published in 1789. One of the most traveled men of his century, Equiano's experiences also include living with Central American Indians, visiting Philadelphia before the American revolution, traveling in Turkey, joining one of the first expeditions to the North Pole, and returning to Africa as a Christian missionary. As much as Equiano assimilates to Christianity and English culture, his inside descriptions of slavery and life in the English New World colonies make for interesting comparisons with *The Tempest, Robinson Crusoe,* and *Oroonoko,* as well as with other slave narratives. His text allows us to examine the British anti-slavery movement, an important force in the British empire both before and after the British abolition of slavery in 1837.

Many well-known nineteenth-century British novels feature the colonies and the British Empire as their backdrop. Mr. Micawber in *David Copperfield* lives in Australia—the same place to which Magwitch of *Great Expectations* goes to earn his fortune. Pip himself ends up as an employee in the colonial administration. The Bertram Estate described in Jane Austen's *Mansfield Park* is funded by its slaveholding sugar plantations in Antigua. Found in the port city of Liverpool, Heathcliff of *Wuthering Heights* is a figure of racial difference. One of the most interesting colonial connections is with Charlotte Brontë's *Jane Eyre.* Mr. Rochester and his family make their fortunes from Caribbean plantations, and Bertha Mason, the insane wife he locks in the attic, is a Caribbean Creole. One of England's twentieth-century novelists, Jean Rhys, recreated the story of Bertha Mason in her interesting novel *Wide Sargasso Sea* (since turned into a sensuous movie). Another contemporary work to compare with these two would be *Abeng* by the Jamaican novelist, Michelle Cliff.

Other nineteenth-century works foreground European colonialism. Of course Kipling wrote a great deal about the British service in India. His novel *Kim* addresses cultural and racial mixing within the framework of the colonial adventure novel, and works like "The Man Who Would Be King" continue the myth of Europeans ruling natives and becoming rich (also a film, starring Sean Connery). Kipling's short story "Wee Willie Winkee" and much of his poetry provides a disturbing metaphor for colonial relationships. E. M. Forster's *A Passage to India* (1924) explores the difficulty of relationships across colonialism's racial barriers. These works of English literature open into a rich range of possibilities for reading postcolonial and commonwealth literature from India, the Caribbean, Australia, and around the globe.

The colonial adventure novel finds its most important practitioner and critic in Joseph Conrad, whose novella *Heart of Darkness* is an ideal text to include in a course focused on colonial themes. *Heart of Darkness* is one of the most frequently taught books in U.S. colleges and one of the most frequently used in AP English classes, yet many students and teachers find it difficult. The first time I taught the novel was in a high school AP English class before I knew much about Belgian exploitation of the Congo and the novel's colonial themes. At that time, I tried to explore the rich language and symbolic or allegorical possibilities of the work, but students found the text obscure, depending more on my interpretations than on their own. Eight years later, as I had begun to learn more about colonialism, I taught the work in a world literature survey course for first-year college students, with completely different results.

Reading the book as a critique of colonialism gave the novel more impact. Conrad visited Africa at the height of European colonialism, during a period when more than six million Africans were killed in the forced labor system used by the Belgians to operate rubber plantations and to extract raw materials, such as the ivory that is the focus of the novel. With this historical context in mind (the new Norton Critical Edition of the novel includes many good source materials for teaching), the novel simply makes more sense and becomes more meaningful. Scenes of forced labor on the railroads and in the ivory trade, images of exhausted and starving workers dying under the trees, of raided and deserted villages, of tribesmen in chain gangs, of Europeans firing guns at Africans or into the jungle, of insanely greedy European traders and "explorers," of hypocritical reports by the "Society for the Suppression of Savage Customs" that end in scrawled passages such as "Kill all the brutes"—all of these scenes become compelling as students start to understand "the horror, the horror" of Belgian colonialism that Conrad is talking about.

When I taught the novel the second time, I drew on approaches from postcolonial studies, foregrounding the colonial context and pairing *Heart of Darkness* with a number of other works that helped my students make connections both forward and backward in time. Considered a critical work in the transition to twentieth-century narrative techniques, *Heart of Darkness* has also been enormously influential for twentieth-century writers around the world, especially in areas of European colonialism. Many African novels can be read as direct responses to *Heart of Darkness*. Bringing together Conrad's novel and other colonial European works with corresponding literature from Africa, India, the Caribbean, and South America creates a fabulous literary and cultural dialogue and opens up for students many of the primary issues and themes of world literature today.

In reading postcolonial and "Third World" literatures, and in examining their significance to their own lives and traditions, students discover that despite differences of nationality, language, culture, and income, our shared colonial histories and the living global economy we are all part of link us closely together. Much of our food and clothing, as well as many of the objects, images, and cultural artifacts that surround us every day, are products of an economy that links North and South, East and West. Under what conditions were these everyday items produced? How did they get here? How has the international economy shaped conditions of life around the world? How has it affected life in our own communities? How has it influenced employment, salaries, and future job opportunities for our students? How has it affected the development of literature and culture worldwide?

Just as the "Third World" comes to "modernize" and look more and more like the first, so does the "First World" come to resemble the "Third." Stark contradictions between rich and poor, jarring cultural contrasts, families and communities pulled apart by economic forces, religious revivalism and tenacious holds on fundamentalist truths in the face of rapid social change—all of these recognized realities of the "Third World" are more and more the reality of the "First World" as well. The internationalization of culture and economy affects all of us every day and is something that our students need to understand, given the increasingly global society of the future. Postcolonial studies aspires to address these questions.

Postcolonial Studies

By 1914, the European powers had conquered 85 percent of the earth's surface and created the districts of colonial administration that were eventually to become, through anticolonial resistance, nation-states. Forging the modern world system through military conquest, slavery, and economic exploitation, as well as political, cultural, and linguistic domination, European colonialism created the dramatic inequalities we know today as the distinction between "First World" and "Third World." Postcolonial studies looks with a critical eye not only at European economic and military authority but also at the cultural traditions and Eurocentric legacy that identified colonized peoples as "savage," "uncivilized," "backward," or "underdeveloped."

Like ethnic studies, postcolonial and "Third World" studies have a great deal to say to literary scholars and literature teachers. They direct our attention to rich and rapidly growing literary traditions, ask us to rethink the literary canon, and raise issues for classroom consideration such as the existence of "Third Worlds" within the "First World" and vice versa. There are literatures written in European languages and emerging from former European colonies in Latin America, Africa, Asia, and the Caribbean, and much of this writing is suited to American university and secondary school teaching. Textbook makers and teachers are taking notice of a few of the superstar Nobel prize winners, but there are hundreds of possibilities (for some initial possibilities, see the list headed "Sampling of Postcolonial Works for the Classroom" at the end of this chapter).

"Third World" nations often had their borders drawn and their peoples grouped together by European colonizers who cared little for indigenous ethnic differences. "Third World" writers in Africa, India, Latin America, and the Caribbean have been and continue to be educated in the European-oriented schools put in place during the colonial period. Thus English, French, and Spanish often serve as national languages in many countries with a great variety of indigenous tongues. While these contradictions may differ from the experiences of many of our students, finding one's voice in a foreign medium, struggling with contradictions between home and school life, addressing discrimination and inequality, attempting to understand and come to terms with national cultures and identities are issues relevant to "First World" as well as "Third World" students. The connections that our students are able to make between their own lives and people in the "Third World" are, given the separations between us, especially precious.

One analysis of postcolonial writing is *The Empire Writes Back* by Ashcroft, Griffiths, and Tiffin, and there is indeed an important sense in which postcolonial writers and postcolonial scholarship and theory respond to and rethink European culture and literary canons. The defining of "Western Civilization" has always by implication suggested the "East," the "Orient," the "Non-Western," the "noncivilized," which is considered to be the West's "Other" in a series of binary oppositions including rational versus mysterious, organized versus chaotic, individualistic versus collective, materialistic versus spiritual, energetic versus lethargic, masculine versus feminine, and so on. Postcolonial scholars argue that these simplistic oppositions have little descriptive value, and that rather than being the result of objective science, they provided racist justifications for the military takeover and economic exploitation of most of the globe in the name of "civilization." Postcolonial writers and scholars reexamine many of the classic British authors and reveal disturbing colonial dimensions in their work. Issues of this kind have been raised in respect to Shakespeare, Defoe, Dickens, Eliot, Kipling, Hardy, Forster, Brontë, Thackeray, Austen, and Conrad, and exploring these questions in the classroom adds significantly to the interest and complexity of student learning.

After *Heart of Darkness* my students read Chinua Achebe's novel *Things Fall Apart*, about the life of the Ibo people of Nigeria, before and during the first contacts with the British colonists. Achebe modifies and adapts the English language and the form of the novel in order to express Ibo and African experiences and perspectives. He shows us that Africa's "primitive tribes" were, in fact, sophisticated cultures with rich verbal expression, involved social relationships, complex individuals, and a moral and religious system with its own strengths and contradictions. He also shows us the process of colonial "pacification" from the other side.

While *Things Fall Apart* "writes back" to *Heart of Darkness*, Achebe also wrote a compelling and much-discussed essay in which he directly analyzes *Heart of Darkness* from an African point of view and criticizes Conrad as "a thoroughgoing racist" ("Image" 257). Achebe's essay split my class down the middle and generated an intense debate. It seemed as if some students were almost personally offended that a revered European author should be charged with "racism," and they defended Conrad with vigor. Others found Achebe convincing and, rather than apologize for Conrad, these students began talking about European misunderstanding of indigenous peoples in Africa and beyond. Throughout the conversation we turned again and again to passages and events in Conrad's novel, trying to determine their meaning and significance both from European and African perspectives.

Recently, I visited Melinda Dobson's twelfth-grade English class in the small town of Otsego, Michigan. Her students were discussing the same essay after reading *Heart of Darkness* and before reading *Things Fall Apart*. This group of small-town, Euro-American students was very interested in the charges that Achebe brought against Conrad; I would say that the debate they had was at least as sophisticated as if not more so than the one that took place in my college classroom. Listening to them, I began to think about the way the Conrad/Achebe dialogue was helping these students investigate complicated literary issues relevant to many texts in addition to *Heart of Darkness*. Here are some of the comments these high school students made (from my notes on the discussion):

> "Marlow can by no means be seen as identical with the author, and Achebe failed to adequately separate the two in his essay."

> "The novel is fiction and the author has a right to portray as he wants. In an adventure story there is always going to be cannibals, savages, bad guys, or whatever. Conrad wrote what he knew about."

> "Why should we accept it if adventure stories use racism as a form of personal entertainment."

> "Achebe destructs the book through his modern eyes; but racism was not truly the same issue when Conrad was writing. If the book is racist today it is something we are making of it."

> "We have to look at how the author uses the color 'black' in this book."

> "Racism, what is it? It doesn't just deal with color but also with culture."

"Conrad used the African woman only as a counter-point to show the European woman as more refined. The African woman was used as just a part of the story."

"*Heart of Darkness* is just a novel; we have to look at the context in which it was written if we want to pass judgment on it."

In my own class the rich intertextual dialogue between Conrad and Achebe was something that continued to shape our reading. As Conrad's novel describes the experience of Kurtz, a sophisticated European venturing into the "heart of darkness" of Africa, many African novels portray just the opposite experience—African peoples journeying to and living in European capitals. In my class we next read Cheikh Hamidou Kane's novel *Ambiguous Adventure*, about a Senegalese man who leaves the study of Islam to earn a Ph.D. in philosophy at the Sorbonne in Paris. We also read Buchi Emecheta's novel *Second-Class Citizen,* about a Nigerian woman living in London, and we concluded with the African American writer Paule Marshall's *Praisesong for the Widow,* about a middle-class African American woman who takes a very different journey to a "heart of darkness" in the Caribbean. Recently, in another course, I taught a wonderful new postmodern novel by the writer Michelle Cliff, *No Telephone to Heaven,* about a Jamaican woman who travels to London before returning to participate in the violent and ongoing social struggle in her own country. Students were fascinated by the novel's incorporation of popular culture, cinematic technique, and kaleidoscopic cultural interplay (and there are many other possibilities—again, see the Sampling of Postcolonial Works). Reading these works together allowed students to explore the burgeoning of contemporary world literature in our increasingly interconnected world, with cultural as well as economic and political systems emerging from a history of European colonialism. (For additional discussion of this class, see Carey-Webb, "Tarzan".)

Beyond exploring the Achebe/Conrad exchange, Melinda Dobson has been increasingly focusing her high school British literature course on colonial themes. Drawing on the traditional textbook, Melinda has been able to develop a curriculum that focuses on the perceptions of colonizer and colonized. She begins her course with discussion of the successive waves of colonization of the British Isles by Romans, Danes, Anglo-Saxons, and the French, as well as the effects of colonial history on the early development of the English language and English literature. Her students read the excerpts of *Beowulf* found in their textbook and explore both the Anglo-Saxon code of honor and adventurousness, as well the perspective of Grendel, particularly as they read John Gardner's imaginative recreation of the epic from Grendel's point of view (*Grendel*). Examining the characteristics of both the Anglo-Saxons and the "indigenous" monster Grendel sets up a counterpoint that proves useful when Melinda's class reads other works with colonial themes. For instance, her students have examined similarities and differences between Grendel and Caliban. Melinda tells me that her high school students responded well to *Oroonoko*. She is curious not only about how traditional literary works portray "the natives," but also about the complexity of English traits and traditions that both support *and challenge* British expansionism. Drawing on her anthology's collection of Romantic poets, for example, Melinda and her students examine the Romantic critique of industrialism as well as Romantic utopian aspirations for communication with nature.

As Melinda moves to the second half of her course, she includes a great variety of short stories from twentieth-century postcolonial writers; several of the stories have now been included in the standard textbook she uses. Indeed, the colonial theme curriculum I am describing opens up possibilities for the inclusion of twentieth- as well as nineteenth-century and earlier British literature. Almost all of Conrad's writing has colonial themes. Works by George Orwell—such as "Shooting an Elephant," an essay about his experience of British colonialism in Burma—could enrich the discussion. William Golding's *Lord of the Flies* can be connected in interesting ways to works such as *Utopia, The Tempest, Robinson Crusoe,* and *Heart of Darkness*. And, as we think about twentieth-century English literature, we come to recognize that English has become a world language, that many works of world literature belong in English literature courses and vice versa.

South African literature is a good example—a rich area of writing that can broaden the perspectives of British literature students. I have taught short stories by Nadine Gordimer to both high school and college students; these stories would fit perfectly into such a course and would in this context be more comprehensible to students. I mentioned *Cry, the Beloved Country* in the first two chapters as a novel I found successful with both high school and college students. Apartheid and its aftermath are easier to understand in the context of a course with colonial themes. My students have contrasted Alan Paton's *Cry, the Beloved Country* with South African writing from a black perspective, such as the autobiography *Kaffir Boy* by Mark Mathabane or poetry by Denise Brutus.

Advances in publishing and scholarship make a multicultural British literature course of this kind increasingly possible. Dover Thrift Editions, costing between $1 and $2 each, are now available for many of the works I have discussed, including *Utopia, The Tempest, Robinson Crusoe,*

Olaudah Equiano, Heart of Darkness, and Kipling's "The Man Who Would Be King" and other stories from *Plain Tales from the Hills.* At the same time, richly edited versions of many of these texts, including many documents and essays addressing colonial history, are also now available and could serve as ideal teacher editions (see, for instance, the Norton Critical Editions of *Utopia, The Tempest, Oroonoko, Robinson Crusoe,* and *Heart of Darkness*). These classic texts of English literature are also available for free on the Internet, as are postcolonial criticism, critical responses, e-mail discussion lists, and a great variety of historical materials. (I hope to develop a textbook for British and world literature courses focused on postcolonial and multicultural themes that should be an additional resource.)

This multicultural British literature curriculum also facilitates the introduction of literature written by people from the former colonies who now reside in Europe. For millions of immigrants from Asia, Africa, Latin America, and the Caribbean, Europe itself has become the "New World," and the migration of "Third World" peoples to the "First World" has not always been easy. Harkening back to colonial history, these new settlers have proclaimed, "we are here because you were there." Many works explore this important aspect of globalization: *Second-Class Citizen* and *In the Ditch* by Buchi Emecheta (a Nigerian immigrant to England), *Bye-bye Blackbird* by Anita Desai, the difficult and controversial *Satanic Verses* by Salman Rushdie (portraying immigrants from India), *Season of Migration to the North* by Tayeb Salih (Sudan), and *Ambiguous Adventure* by Cheikh Hamidou Kane (Senegal) all detail the experience of colonized and formerly colonized people in the European metropole. These works can be considered to form an increasingly important part of contemporary multicultural European experience and European literature. In a sense these writers narrate the reverse of the story of colonial works such as *Heart of Darkness*; many "Third World" "been to" novels make for interesting comparison with Conrad's writing or other European works.

Though this chapter is primarily focused on British and world literature, I cannot resist pointing out that, as one of the earliest literary depictions of America in English, *The Tempest* is also a fascinating work to pair with works of American literature. Comparing Caliban to more authentic depictions of Native Americans or Africans creates a fascinating dialogue of stereotypes and representations. My students became aware of Caliban's singularity and isolation when we read *Morning Girl*, a contemporary young adult novel by the Native American writer Michael Dorris. In this novel, Dorris uses the point of view of a pre-teenage girl to imaginatively recreate the life of a family of Carib Indians five hundred years in the past. On the last page of the novel the Carib girl sees Christopher Columbus's ship arriving and swims out to greet it. Thus the work pairs very nicely with *The Tempest* and the Zinn chapter about Columbus. I described teaching *Native Son* in the chapter addressing youth violence, but it is also an interesting work to compare with *The Tempest*. Students can consider the ways in which the fatherless Bigger works for Mr. Dalton and is charged with the rape of his daughter, just as is Caliban with Prospero and Miranda. Like Caliban, Bigger creates his own ineffective rebellion against the system, and, in the end, is hunted down. Many other African American writers draw on *The Tempest* for inspiration; consider John Edgar Wideman's novel *Philadelphia Fire* or Toni Morrison's *Tar Baby*.

The approach Melinda Dobson and I have taken with *The Tempest* and other English classics demonstrates that well-known texts of the "canon" can be reexamined and can serve as entry points to sound cultural studies teaching. Cultural studies approaches, such as new historicism and postcolonial studies, can help us link literary works together and weave richer and more meaningful curriculums. Through this process it becomes clear that rather than conveying eternal truths about a supposedly "universal" human nature, Shakespeare or any literary artist exists within a particular cultural, historical, political, and social context, a context that our students can and should explore. If your students are like mine, then when they read *The Tempest,* for example, they will begin to wonder about the way in which Shakespeare portrays Caliban or Miranda, about the role of his work in questioning stereotypes or its complicity in continuing them. While this brings students back to the text, it can also lead them to critical thinking about other "great works," as we saw with *Heart of Darkness.* As students become better critical thinkers, they may begin to wonder about why we study literature and whose perspectives are featured in established literary canons. A next step might be to have them learn about some of the different schools of literary theory and to examine their own literary education. Such an approach is likely to make them far stronger readers, a point my friend Lisa Schade makes in her forthcoming book about teaching literary theory to high school students.

It is through his book learning that Prospero gains the magical power he needs to dominate the island and the people on it—people he must discipline and instruct in English in order to maintain his authority. If students come to doubt Prospero, to question his authority, will they begin to wonder about the system in which they are learning as well? Will Spanish-language students confronted by an "English only" curriculum— or inner-city African American students facing dismal future prospects—

raise questions about the schools and classrooms in which they find themselves? Might they say, like Caliban, "You taught me language, and my profit on't / Is I know how to curse. The red plague rid you / For learning me your language!" (I.ii.362–64)

Bringing a cultural studies approach to teaching literature from earlier historical periods involves exploring and thinking critically about the past. Putting together reader response and cultural studies approaches may mean reevaluating curriculum, textbooks, and traditional pedagogical relationships. In this chapter we have seen one way in which new historicism and postcolonial studies might lead us to rethink our teaching of British and world literatures. In the next chapter, we will see how cultural studies perspectives are also leading us to rethink pedagogical relationships and a key canonical literary work in the American tradition, *Adventures of Huckleberry Finn.*

Resources for Cultural Studies Teaching of Shakespeare

- *Half Humankind: Contexts and Texts of the Controversy about Women in England, 1540–1640* by Katherine U. Henderson and Barbara F. McManus is a collection of street pamphlets circulated during Shakespeare's day that intensely debate the roles and capacities of women. Placed next to any one of Shakespeare's plays, these works would bring new life to the classroom.

- Stephen Greenblatt's *Learning to Curse: Essays in Early Modern Culture* has wonderful chapters on *The Tempest, The Merchant of Venice*, and *King Lear.* His *Shakespearean Negotiations: The Circulation of Social Energy in Renaissance England* is somewhat more difficult but offers innovative ways of thinking about the history plays.

- *Masterless Men: The Vagrancy Problem in England 1560–1640* by A. L. Beier is a fascinating look at the lives of vagrants, public attitudes toward the poor, and social policies during the time of Shakespeare. Chapters or sections read along with *Lear* or the Henry IV plays would lead to interesting discussion and fresh insights.

- *Masters and Servants in English Renaissance Drama and Culture: Authority and Obedience* by Mark Burnett is a clear and careful study of Renaissance servitude that opens up new issues and perspectives for examining the relationships of masters and servants in many of Shakespeare's plays.

- *The Moor in English Renaissance Drama* by Jack D'Amico draws on the historical relations of England, Morocco, and the Islamic world, and provides a reference point for exploring *The Tempest* and *The Merchant of Venice,* as well as *Othello* and ongoing attitudes toward Islamic peoples.

- Dollimore and Sinfield's *Political Shakespeare: New Essays in Cultural Materialism* is an important collection of new historicist essays on Shakespeare. It includes Greenblatt's famous (and difficult) essay "Invisible Bullets," which connects Shakespeare's history plays with colonialism in the New World, along with fine essays on Irish colonialism and *The Tempest*, spying in *Measure for Measure*, feminist criticism, homoeroticism, and prostitution.

- *Shakespeare and the Jews* by James Shapiro and *Anti-Semitic Stereotypes without Jews: Images of the Jew in England, 1290–1700* by Bernard Glassman are both useful books for exploring anti-Semitism in Shakespeare's day as well as rich resources for reading *The Merchant of Venice*. (Glassman's book also addresses Chaucer's "The Prioress's Tale.")

- *Shakespeare and the Nature of Women* by Juliet Dusinberre explores the Protestant attitude toward women and Puritan feminist sympathies in the plays.

- *Surveillance, Militarism, and Drama in the Elizabethan Era* by Curtis Breight is somewhat difficult but strips away the myth of a benign Shakespearean England and opens up possibilities for rethinking Shakespeare's treatment of kinship and power.

Works for a Postcolonial Approach to British and World Literature

These works are presented in chronological order.

- *Utopia* (1516) by Thomas More is based on accounts of the New World from the Vespucci expeditions. A fascinating imaginative work to compare with both European and Native American societies, it inspires debate and interesting creative projects. (Students need not read most of Part I; Part II is the most interesting and relevant).

- *The Tempest* (1611) by William Shakespeare is at the center of a rich discussion about colonialism and cultural encounter. Drawn in part on the basis of early accounts of the Virginia colonies, Prospero and Caliban have come to be regarded as emblematic figures of European and native relations.

- *Oroonoko* (1688) is the first novel written in English—and it was written by a woman. Drawing on her voyage to the Caribbean, Aphra Behn tells the story of an African prince taken into slavery who rebels against his masters.

- *Robinson Crusoe* (1719) by Daniel Defoe is one of the most popular classics—read, it is said, by every young man who ever went into service in the British empire. Interesting study of an Englishman bringing "order" and "civilization" to the "savages" and the "untamed" New World. Compare with J. M. Coetzee's *Foe* (1986), an experimental fiction by the South African author of *Waiting for the Barbarians.*

■ "A Modest Proposal" (1729) by Jonathan Swift is set in England's oldest colony, Ireland, and is a critique of English absentee landlords.

■ *The Life of Olaudah Equiano, or, Gustavus Vassa, the African* (1789), an amazing slave narrative, is a work of English literature (published in English, in England, by an English citizen). It would make for a rich comparison with works such as *The Tempest, Oroonoko,* and *Robinson Crusoe.*

■ *Jane Eyre* (1847) by Charlotte Brontë has a fascinating colonial connection through Rochester's Caribbean plantations and his Caribbean wife, Bertha Mason. Many other nineteenth-century novels have similar colonial connections (consider Magwitch in *Great Expectations,* Mr. Micawber in *David Copperfield,* Heathcliff in *Wuthering Heights,* or even the Bertram estate funded by Antigua plantations in *Mansfield Park*). Compare *Jane Eyre* with *Wide Sargasso Sea* by Jean Rhys, which constructs the story of Bertha Mason, and compare both of these with *Abeng* by Michelle Cliff.

■ *Heart of Darkness* (1899) by Joseph Conrad is most meaningful when read in the context of European colonialism. Many other works by Conrad explore colonial themes. Connect with the essay by Achebe, "Racism in Heart of Darkness," Achebe's novel *Things Fall Apart,* and many other postcolonial texts.

■ *Kim* (1901) by Rudyard Kipling addresses the "Great Game" of British and Russian struggle for control over India. Many other works by Kipling would fit perfectly into such a course, including *Plain Tales of the Hills, Gunga Din and Other Poems,* and "The Man Who Would Be King."

■ *A Passage to India* (1924) by E. M. Forster treats the arrogance of British colonialism in India. Students may find the film more approachable than the novel.

■ George Orwell's "Shooting an Elephant" (1936), set in the British colony of Burma, is an excellent essay on the role of the English as colonial administrators.

■ *Lord of the Flies* (1954) by William Golding can be seen as a work in the colonial tradition and makes an interesting comparison with *Robinson Crusoe* and *Heart of Darkness.* It can also be compared with the R. M. Ballantyne's *The Coral Island,* a British adventure story mentioned in and critiqued by *Lord of the Flies,* as well as with Marianne Wiggins's *John Dollar,* a truly disturbing novel about girls on a deserted island, or even H. G. Wells's *The Island of Dr. Moreau,* a colonial story which could be read along with several of the classic British works. The connections between colonial history and many works of science fiction are also interesting to explore.

Sampling of Postcolonial Works for the Classroom

- Chinua Achebe's novels *Things Fall Apart, No Longer at Ease, A Man of the People, Arrow of God*, and *Anthills of the Savannah* trace the history of Nigeria. All are approachable classics.

- Ayi Kwei Armah's *The Beautyful Ones Are Not Yet Born* is a challenging radical novel from Ghana.

- Dennis Brutus's *A Simple Lust* is a collection of political poetry from the apartheid period in South Africa.

- Michelle Cliff's dazzling novels *Abeng* and *No Telephone to Heaven* address the brutal violence and poverty of Jamaica.

- Tsitsi Dambarembga's *Nervous Conditions* is an engaging and disturbing coming-of-age novel from Zimbabwe.

- Anita Desai's *Bye-bye Blackbird* treats the experience of Indians living in England.

- Buchi Emecheta's *Joys of Motherhood* is an ironic novel about moving from the village to the city in colonial Nigeria—a great work for exploring the role of women in modern Africa, tribal versus modern customs, and the "Third World" urban crisis. *Second-Class Citizen* and *In the Ditch* address the challenges that face Nigerians living in London.

- Nadine Gordimer won the Nobel prize for her brilliant writing on the theme of apartheid in South Africa. Her short stories are classroom favorites; try the collection *Something Out There*.

- Wilson Harris's *Palace of the Peacock* is a colonial fantasy set in British Guyana (South America) that could be read along with *Heart of Darkness*.

- Cheikh Hamidou Kane's *Ambiguous Adventure* is justly one of the most famous works in the Francophone African tradition. It works well in the classroom as it examines European civilization from the point of view of an African from Senegal.

- Camara Laye's *Dark Child*, another Francophone classic, describes the distance that a young boy travels from his tribe when he enters a colonial school.

- René Maran's *Batouala* is one of the early Francophone texts written by a Black Martinican administrator in French West Africa in 1921; the novella portrays the vitality of African culture.

- Kamala Markandaya's *Nectar in a Sieve* narrates the struggle of an Indian farming family to survive drought and their migration to the city.

- Mark Mathabane's *Kaffir Boy* reveals the nature of South African apartheid from the point of view of a teenage African boy who falls in love with the sport of tennis. In the next volume of this autobiography, Mathabane tells the story of his immigration to the United States. His story was made into a film.

■ R. K. Narayan was called by Graham Greene "the greatest living writer in English." Sample his charming novels from India and perhaps you will agree. You and your students might begin with *The Guide, The Painter of Signs,* or *The Man-Eater of Malgudi.*

■ Ngugi Wa Thiong'o is one of the best-known East African writers. His novels are challenging and politically engaged. One might begin with *Weep Not, Child.*

■ Flora Nwapa's novel *Efuru* describes, from the point of view of female characters, the life of an Ibo tribe (in what is now Nigeria) before its first contact with Europeans. Nwapa is considered one of the most important African women writers, and her work makes for productive comparison with Achebe's *Things Fall Apart.*

■ Michael Ondaatje is a Canadian writer of Ceylonese origins. His autobiographical novel *Running in the Family* is a nostalgic visit to the life of his family in Ceylon in the 1920s and 1930s.

■ Alan Paton's *Cry, the Beloved Country* is the old chestnut of South African literature. Written in 1949 at the start of apartheid, it chronicles the separations of race and economics that still mark not only South Africa, but also the world.

■ Due to the infamous "Rushdie affair" over *The Satanic Verses,* Salman Rushdie may be the best-known postcolonial writer. His novels are long and involved, and thus challenging in the classroom. Some may opt for his light children's novel, *Haroun and the Sea of Stories,* but I recommend a fascinating short story that touches themes of colonial espionage, "Chekov and Zulu."

■ Tayeb Salih's *Season of Migration to the North* is a compelling Sudanese novel about the lasting and disturbing effects of receiving a European education.

■ Ousmane Sembène, a Francophone writer from Senegal, is regarded as one of the founding fathers of African literature. His radical novel *God's Bits of Wood* works well in the classroom. *Xala* is a short but powerful novella that becomes an allegory of contemporary Africa. There are fine short stories in *Tribal Scars and Other Stories.*

Readings in New Historicism and Cultural Materialism

■ Stephen Greenblatt is credited with coining the term "new historicism." His books *Marvelous Possessions* (see the list headed "Reading in Postcolonial Studies," below), *Learning to Curse,* and *Shakespearean Negotiations* (see Resources for Cultural Studies Teaching of Shakespeare, above), are good starting points for new historicism in British literature.

- Marjorie Levinson's book *Wordsworth's Great Period Poems: Four Essays* is a study of the social, biographical, and political contexts of Wordsworth's most "literary" poems, including "Tintern Abbey" and the "Intimations Ode."

- *The American Renaissance Reconsidered,* edited by Walter Benn Michaels and Donald Pease, is a collection of fine and approachable essays by leading American literature scholars rethinking the "American Renaissance" in ways that include race, class, and gender issues and that offer historical and international perspectives on the high canon of nineteenth-century American writers.

- *The New Historicism Reader,* edited by Aram Veeser in 1994, is an attempt to marshal the best new historicist essays. The introduction provides a useful overview of the fundamental assumptions of scholars who use this approach.

- *The New Historicism,* also edited by Aram Veeser, is an earlier collection (1989) of essays attempting to define, explain, demonstrate, and critique new historicism. It includes chapters by Greenblatt, Montrose, Arac, Graff, Spivak, and others.

- *New Historicism and Renaissance Drama*, edited by Wilson and Dutton, is a collection of new historicist essays, many on Shakespeare's plays; it includes well-known pieces such as Greenblatt on *Henry IV* and *Henry V*, Montrose on *A Midsummer Night's Dream,* Barker on *Hamlet,* and Sinfield on *Macbeth.* The book's introduction explains the new historical approach.

Readings in Postcolonial Studies

- One of the best ways to get started with postcolonial studies is to learn about colonial history from the point of view of those who have been colonized. Several important and approachable titles are: *The Black Jacobins,* by C. L. R. James (Haitian revolution); *American Holocaust: Columbus and the Conquest of the New World* by David Stannard or *Bury My Heart at Wounded Knee: An Indian History of the American West* by Dee Brown (Native Americans); *Capitalism and Slavery* by Eric Williams (slavery within the colonial system); *How Europe Underdeveloped Africa* by Walter Rodney (colonialism in Africa); *The Open Veins of Latin America: Five Centuries of the Pillage of a Continent* by Eduardo Galeano (neocolonialism in Latin America); or, Gandhi's autobiography, *The Story of My Experiments with Truth,* or Nehru's autobiography (independence struggle in India).

- *The Empire Writes Back: Theory and Practice in Post-Colonial Literatures* by three Australian scholars, Bill Ashcroft, Gareth Griffiths, and Helen Tiffin, offers a comprehensive summary of scholarship on postcolonial literature in English.

- *Rethinking Columbus: The Next 500 Years,* edited by Bill Bigelow and Bob Peterson, is a wonderful compendium of resources for postcolonial teaching about the impact of the arrival of Columbus in the Americas.

- *The Wretched of the Earth* by Frantz Fanon was written during the Algerian Revolution and offers a powerful interpretation of colonial experience that has greatly influenced subsequent postcolonial studies.

- Stephen Greenblatt's *Marvelous Possessions: The Wonder of the New World* examines the Renaissance British travel writer Mandeville, as well as Columbus and Bartólome de Las Casas, to explore the ways in which the New World was imagined and possessed by the early European colonists.

- Peter Hulme's *Colonial Encounters: Europe and the Native Caribbean, 1492–1797* examines Columbus's letters, Shakespeare's *The Tempest, Robinson Crusoe,* and other European works in light of colonialism. It is well-written and includes illustrations.

- *Decolonising the Mind: The Politics of Language in African Literature* by the Kenyan writer Ngugi Wa Thiong'o is a good introduction to the issues facing postcolonial writers.

- Edward Said, a Palestinian émigré and professor at Columbia University, is a leading intellectual and literary scholar in the field of postcolonial studies. *Culture and Imperialism* explores European and especially British and French literature as they are involved in the colonial enterprise. His discussion may change the way you think and teach familiar British writers; it also introduces postcolonial authors. His earlier work, *Orientalism,* about how Europeans' views of the Middle East have been clouded by colonial politics, has been highly influential.

- *Regeneration Through Violence: The Mythology of the American Frontier, 1600–1860* by Richard Slotkin is not usually considered a postcolonial study but does offer an interpretation of American literature that foregrounds colonial expansion.

- *The Post-Colonial Critic: Interviews, Strategies, Dialogues* by Gayatri Spivak is a collection of short pieces by one of the leading feminist critics in postcolonial studies.

- *The Conquest of America: The Question of the Other* by Tzvetan Todorov looks closely at documents from the Spanish colonization of the New World in order to understand the logic of cultural difference.

6 *Huckleberry Finn* and the Issue of Race in Today's Classroom

A masterpiece.

T.S. Eliot

One of the world's great books and one of the central documents of American culture.

Lionel Trilling

All modern American literature comes from one book by Mark Twain called Huckleberry Finn. . . . *There was nothing before. There has been nothing as good since.*

Ernest Hemingway

For the past forty years, black families have trekked to schools in numerous districts throughout the country to say, "This book is not good for our children," only to be turned away by insensitive and often unwittingly racist teachers and administrators who respond, "This book is a classic."

John H. Wallace

Huckleberry Finn may be the most exalted single work of American literature. Praised by our best-known critics and writers, the novel is enshrined at the center of the American literature curriculum. According to Arthur Applebee ("Stability"), the work is second only to Shakespeare in the frequency with which it appears in the classroom, and it is required in 70 percent of public high schools and 76 percent of parochial high schools. The most-taught novel, the most-taught long work, and the most-taught piece of American literature, *Huckleberry Finn* is a staple from junior high (where eleven chapters are included in the Junior Great Books program) to graduate school.

Written in a now-vanished dialect, told from the point of view of a runaway fourteen-year-old, the novel conglomerates melodramatic boyhood adventure, farcical low comedy, and pointed social satire. Yet at its center is a relationship between a White boy and an escaped slave—an association freighted with the tragedy and the possibility of American history. Despite a social order set against interracial communication and respect, Huck develops a comradeship with Jim for which, at least at one point, he is willing—against all he has been taught—to risk his soul.

Despite the novel's sanctified place in the canon and its ostensibly antiracist message, since school desegregation in the 1950s a number of Black Americans have raised objections to *Huckleberry Finn* and its effect on their children. Linking these complaints with the efforts of other groups to influence the curriculum, we English teachers have often seen the issue as one of censorship and thus have responded by defending the novel and our right to teach it. In so doing, we have been properly concerned: the freedom of English teachers to design and implement curriculum must be protected, as censorship undermines the creation and maintenance of an informed citizenry able to make critical judgments between competing ideas.

Yet, considering the objections to *Huckleberry Finn* only in terms of freedom and censorship does not resolve potentially divisive situations that can arise in either high school or college settings. To do this, we need to listen to objections raised against the novel and reconsider the process of teaching it. Entering into a dialogue with those who raise objections to *Huckleberry Finn* can help us think about the dynamics of race in literature courses and about the ways in which literature depicts, interrogates, and affirms our national culture and history. This chapter, then, will help us formulate a response-based cultural studies approach to one of the most vexing pedagogical issues in American literature courses.

A "communication shutdown" is the way I would describe what happened in November 1991 in a largely White suburb just next door to where I train English teachers. Concerns expressed by African American students and parents during the teaching of *Huckleberry Finn* led to a decision to immediately remove the text from the classroom in the district's two high schools. Required to read a brief statement to their students stating that the book had been withdrawn, teachers were prohibited from further discussion of *Huckleberry Finn* or of the reasons for its removal until "more sensitive" approaches were found.

Local television and newspaper reporters learned of the story, and English teachers, students, parents, and administrators suddenly and unexpectedly found themselves at the center of a difficult and very public controversy. An impassioned meeting at the high school made the nightly news. A subsequent meeting with the school board was broadcast on the cable access channel. Expressing sentiments that might be echoed by many across the country, these teachers felt that they had been teaching appropriately all along. One teacher told the local paper, "We have shown a concerted effort to express what we call sensitivity," and "we feel a very strong kinship to this book because of what we believe it stands for" (*Kalamazoo Gazette*). Upset that their freedom in the classroom was impinged upon, these teachers were also confused and pained that parents should find the text and their methods insensitive.

On the other side, Black students who raised concerns with teachers about the book felt they had not been listened to, and Black parents concluded that a tight-knit group of narrow-minded White English teachers had shut out and demeaned their legitimate concerns. Some White students were angry that the complaints of the Black students meant they couldn't finish reading the book. Some Black students felt that long friendships with White students were in jeopardy. In sum, parents were angry with teachers, teachers felt threatened and misunderstood, administrators went in various directions but failed to follow policies already in place, and students were alienated from the school and from one another. In the following year, the novel was reinstated, but to this day teachers remain understandably nervous about using it, unclear as to why African American parents object to it, and uncertain just how it should best be taught. As with many similar incidents that have occurred again and again around the country, this controversy over *Huckleberry Finn* only exacerbated problems of interracial communication and respect.

We can and must do better. Doing better begins with English teachers at all levels taking a careful look at the complex racial issues raised by the novel and actively listening to views expressed by African Americans and by teachers, scholars, writers, parents, and students of all races. That *Huckleberry Finn* draws the attention of Black families should not be a surprise. Since no text by a Black writer—or any other minority group member, for that matter—has yet made it to the list of most frequently taught works (according to Applebee's research), *Huckleberry Finn* has a peculiar visibility. The novel remains the only one of the most-taught works in high school to treat slavery, to attempt representing a Black dialect, and to have a significant role for an African American character. The length of the novel, the demands it places on instructional time, and its centrality in the curriculum augment its prominence. Add to this the presence in the novel of the most powerful racial epithet in English—the word appears 213 times—and it is evident why *Huckleberry Finn* legitimately concerns African American parents sending their children into racially mixed classrooms.

Censorship and Teacher Freedom

Since cultural studies teaching seeks to explore controversies in open, constructive, and pedagogically sound ways, cultural studies teachers, especially, need freedom to shape their curriculums, and they need the support of their departments, administrations, and communities if they are to teach meaningfully and effectively. Depending on the contexts in which we work and the particular individuals who hold authority over us, such freedom and support may be easier or more difficult to come by. Yet, regardless of context or individuals, there are ways to address the various forms of censorship that limit our ability to create sound curriculums.

The censorship we probably fear the most is that which comes from direct challenges against curricular materials, assigned reading, or library holdings—challenges made by students, parents, administrators, community members, or religious or political groups. Such objections are more likely to be an issue for middle school or high school teachers; yet university teachers also occasionally find their syllabi under question. Many institutions have specific censorship policies and procedures for curricular complaints. Schools that don't have such policies should develop them, as the existence of a policy and a form to fill out can do a great deal to protect teachers and defuse potentially adversarial situations (see the list at the end of this chapter titled "Further Reading about Censorship"). In the case I describe in this chapter, policies and forms were in place, but administrators forgot to use them, and the crisis rapidly escalated.

Clear communication reduces the vulnerability of teachers and facilitates more adventurous curriculums. Cultural studies teachers need to remind students, probably on the syllabus and on the first day of class, that controversial issues are part of the learning process, and they need to inform students that diverse points of view will be welcomed and explored. Discussions are more open and students become more authentically involved when a true diversity of perspectives is available in the reading. Many secondary school teachers have written letters explaining their course and approach to parents. As a high school teacher, I found it useful to invite administrators, colleagues, and parents to my classroom to participate in the discussions my students and I were engaged in. These invitations helped create trust and freedom. Alternative assignments for students for whom parents believe particular reading is not appropriate can also defuse concerns.

Other forms of censorship are more subtle. Sometimes schools or departments have particular policies—or budget restrictions—that limit the selection of books or reading. Yet, curricular policies often involve folklore. I once had a series of conversations with three English teachers who had worked in the same high school for many years. Teacher X told me, "Our

▶

curriculum in this district is set. We have a list of books and we have to teach every book on the list. Nothing can be added or taken away." Teacher Y told me, "The district has a long list of approved books and we have a wide variety of choice about which books we choose from the list." Teacher Z, working just down the hall, told me, "I teach what I want to teach; in this district we have complete freedom." Perhaps the example is extreme, but I am intrigued by the way that certain teachers seem to find creative ways to interpret policies, obtain materials, and create leeway, while their colleagues in the same institution consider themselves constrained or limited.

The most pervasive form of censorship is self-censorship. It takes place when teachers choose to stay away from texts, issues, or discussions that might be best for their students because they fear that materials or ideas might be challenged or disapproved of by someone else. In the case of self-censorship, we "play it safe" rather than engage students in important issues. Ironically, self-censorship is probably more damaging to students than open censorship because it specifically avoids public discussion of the constitutional freedoms on which democracy is based. Fear of risk taking, reluctance to stand up for what one believes in, or even a lack of interest in new and challenging ideas is destructive to the teaching process and to the teacher as a person and a professional. While there are many resources and organizations ready to help teachers create intellectual freedom in the classroom, the courage teachers most need must come from within.

Huckleberry Finn has consistently attracted the attention of prominent Black scholars and writers who, since the 1950s, have thought carefully about the work, its cultural contexts, and its role in the curriculum. We are fortunate to have much of their analysis readily available in a paperback volume, edited by James S. Leonard, Thomas A. Tenney, and Thadious M. Davis, and titled *Satire or Evasion? Black Perspectives on Huckleberry*. Every contributor is concerned with the role of *Huckleberry Finn* in the classroom; most are professors and teachers at leading universities, and some have high school experience. The diverse and divergent cultural studies essays in *Satire or Evasion?* demonstrate the complexity of Twain's novel and the racial issues it raises. In addition to the articles, *Satire or Evasion?* contains an annotated bibliography on issues of race, the novel, and the classroom.

The collection begins with an essay by John H. Wallace, the Black school administrator at Mark Twain Intermediate School in Fairfax, Virginia, who played a prominent role in the debates over the novel in the early 1980s. Wallace's essay is followed by others that take significantly different and more subtle positions, but most contributors agree on several key points. First, they make a persuasive case that Twain's depiction of Jim owes much to the popular nineteenth-century blackface minstrel show where White actors darkened their skin to the color of coal to render supposedly comic burlesques of African American speech and manners. This insight is not entirely new: more than fifty years ago, Ralph Ellison wrote that "Twain fitted Jim into the outlines of the minstrel tradition, and it is from behind this stereotype mask that we see Jim's dignity and human capacity—and Twain's complexity—emerge" (65). While Ellison noted Twain's talent, he remarked on a fundamental ambivalence in Jim's portrayal that justified the discomfort of the "Negro" reader. He found Jim "a white man's inadequate portrait of a slave" (72). (Ellison's essay "Change the Joke and Slip the Yoke," frequently referred to in *Satire or Evasion?*, is found in its entirety in Ellison's *Shadow and Act*.)

Satire or Evasion? considerably elaborates Ellison's remarks. The contributors offer significant evidence that Twain himself was an avid fan of blackface minstrelsy. Bernard Bell, a professor of English at the University of Massachusetts, quotes from one of Twain's letters: "The minstrel used a very broad Negro dialect; he used it competently and with easy facility and it was funny—delightfully and satisfyingly funny" (128). Bell also notes that when the shows appeared to be dying out in the early twentieth century, Twain lamented the loss of "the real nigger show—the genuine nigger show, the extravagant nigger show—the show which to me has no peer and whose peer has not arrived" (127). As his affection for the minstrel show indicates, and as the contributors point out, Twain's personal attitudes toward Blacks were contradictory. His father and uncle owned slaves, yet his wife was the daughter of a prominent abolitionist. He fought briefly with the Confederate army, yet later in life paid a Black student's way through Yale Law School. Though he protested against lynching and discrimination, he loved minstrel shows and "nigger jokes." In their essay, Frederick Woodward and Donnarae MacCann, a professor and (at the time) a graduate student, respectively, at the University of Iowa, argue that Twain's affection for the minstrel show is fundamental to the portrayal of Jim: "The swaggering buffoonery of the minstrel clown is represented early in the novel when Jim awakes and finds his hat in a tree (one of Tom's tricks), and then concocts a tale about witches and the devil" (145). They argue that

> the "stage Negro's" typical banter about wife troubles, profit making, spooks, and formal education is echoed in episodes in *Huckleberry Finn*, and their inclusion can be traced to a period when Twain was in the midst of planning a new tour of stage readings. Jim gives his

impression of "King Sollermun" and his harem in a minstrel-like repartee (chap. 14) and his confusion about stock market profits is seen in a farcical account of how Jim's stock—his cow—failed to increase his fourteen dollar fortune when he "tuck to specalat'n'" (chap. 8). Throughout the novel Jim is stupefied by information that Huck shares with him, as when they discuss Louis XVI's "little boy the dolphin." (145)

Several scholars in *Satire or Evasion?* point out that in the sequels that Twain wrote to *Huckleberry Finn* (*Tom Sawyer Abroad* and the unfinished *Tom Sawyer's Conspiracy*), Jim also appears as "the patient simpleton," and "Huck and Tom amuse themselves while risking Jim's dignity and even his life" (152). In this view, even the affection that Huck and the reader feel for Jim fits with the minstrel tradition where the comic Black characters are congenial and nonthreatening to White audience members who may, knowingly or unknowingly, hold racist attitudes.

While a couple of the contributors to *Satire or Evasion?* develop complex explanations of how the end of the novel serves as "Twain's satire on the extremes to which the defeated Confederacy went to keep the Black population enslaved" (213), for the most part these African American scholars and teachers are profoundly disappointed with *Huck Finn*'s final chapters. Although Jim runs away early on in the book, his independence is downplayed because he never makes his own way to freedom; it is Miss Watson's benevolence rather than Jim's intelligence or courage that gain him his liberty. Further, the believability of the *deus ex machina* freeing of Jim depends on an unsustainably innocent view of racial relations. Speaking of the public knowledge that Jim is suspected of killing Huck, writer and English professor Julius Lester comments, "Yet we are now to believe that an old white lady would free a black slave suspected of murdering a white child. White people may want to believe such fairy tales about themselves, but blacks know better" (203).

In examining the conclusion of the novel, these scholars are troubled by the way that the developing relationship between Jim and Huck abruptly seems to lose its meaning as Huck accedes to Tom Sawyer's cruel and senseless manipulations. Rhett Jones, an English professor at Rutgers, writes: "The high adventures of the middle chapters, Huck's admiration of Jim, Jim's own strong self-confidence, and the slave's willingness to protect and guide Huck are all, in some sense, rendered meaningless by the closing chapters, in which Twain turns Jim over to two white boys on a lark" (186). Jones views Huck's failure to speak up—his only protest being to compare stealing "a nigger" to stealing "a watermelon, or a Sunday school book"—as Huck's finally rejecting Jim's humanity. He points out that Huck

> in the closing paragraph is careful to tell the reader all about Tom and himself, including Aunt Sally's plans to adopt him. But the reader who is interested in learning what Jim intends to do, how he intends to rejoin his family, and what plans he has for freeing them is left in the dark when Huck flatly concludes, "There ain't nothing more to write about." Huck is not interested in the fate of Jim—much less that of his family—nor is Tom; nor, evidently, was Twain. (190)

Bernard Bell puts it simply: "Twain—nostalgically and metaphorically—sells Jim down river for laughs at the end" (138).

Seen from the points of view of some of these scholars, even the most cherished aspects of the book begin to appear ambiguous, compromised. Focusing on the portrayal of Jim in the latter part of the book, particularly the testimony of the doctor who recaptures Jim after Jim has risked freedom to stand by the injured Tom, Julius Lester comments:

> It is a picture of the only kind of black that whites have ever truly liked—faithful, tending sick whites, not speaking, not causing trouble, and totally passive. He is the archetypal "good nigger," who lacks self-respect, dignity, and a sense of self separate from the one whites want him to have. A century of white readers have accepted this characterization because it permits their own "humanity" to shine through with more luster. (203)

Some of the scholars are even critical of Huck's reasoning when he decides to "go to hell" for Jim. Jones points out that while Huck considers "Jim's love for him, Jim's humanity, and, most important, the ways in which Jim has served Huck," Huck "concludes that Jim has done a great deal for him but in none of his reflections does he consider Jim's own needs, much less those of his wife and children" (188).

Shelley Fisher Fishkin puts forward a well-publicized argument in *Was Huck Black?: Mark Twain and African-American Voices* that Twain patterned Huck's speech on that of African Americans, thus suggesting a close interrelationship between racial identities in the novel. Her position is anticipated in *Satire or Evasion?* by Arnold Rampersad, professor of English at Princeton, who makes the case that *Huck Finn*, with its stress on folk culture, on dialect, and on American humor, can be seen as "near the fountainhead" for African American writers such as Hughes, Hurston, Ellison, and Walker. Rampersad explores issues of alienation in the novel, comparing Twain to Wright, Baldwin, and Morrison, yet he argues that the major compromise of the novel is not the ending, but the fact that Jim never gains the intellectual complexity of Huck, that Jim never becomes a figure of disruptive alienation, nor does he even seem capable of learning this from Huck: "Assuredly Twain knew that Huck's attitude could be contagious, and that blacks had more reason than whites to be alienated and angry" (226). Consequently, despite the close relationship Huck and Jim develop on the raft—and the possibility that Huck's own language may owe something to Black dialect—their roles and human possibilities are kept irresolutely separate and unequal.

In her study of American fiction *Playing in the Dark: Whiteness and the Literary Imagination,* Toni Morrison—winner of the Pulitzer Prize for her own novel about slavery, *Beloved*—goes further in criticizing *Huckleberry Finn* than the contributors to *Satire or Evasion?* Morrison believes that in the novel there is a close "interdependence of slavery and freedom, of Huck's growth and Jim's serviceability within it, and even of Mark Twain's inability to continue to explore the journey into free territory" (55). She is struck by two things in the novel: "the apparently limitless store of love and compassion the black man has for his white friend and white masters; and his assumption that the whites are indeed what they say they are, superior and adult" (56). According to Morrison,

> Jim permits his persecutors to torment him, humiliate him, and responds to the torment and humiliation with boundless love. The humiliation comes *after* we have experienced Jim as an adult, a caring father and a sensitive man. If Jim had been a white ex-convict befriended by Huck, the ending could not have been imagined or written. (56)

What is most disturbing about the novel, Morrison argues, is not its portrayal of Jim, "but what Mark Twain, Huck, and especially Tom need from him" (57). Rather than merely offering a White man's limited portrait of a slave, the novel demonstrates the inadequacy of Euro-American utopian aspirations; Morrison says *Huck Finn* "simulates and describes the parasitic nature of white freedom" (57). In her reading, then, the American dream of freedom may well be embodied in Huck and Jim's time on the river, but, if so, then that very dream itself is fundamentally flawed, resting on a shedding of social responsibility and a failure to examine relations of subservience.

The racial problematics of *Huckleberry Finn* are partly "corrected" in the 1994 Hollywood film version. The film shuns the complexities of irony and satire that make understanding the novel difficult. All points of view are simply and directly argued, and offending passages are cut away. All 213 repetitions of the racial epithet are simply eliminated. The Widow Douglas espouses an explicitly abolitionist position. Above all, Jim is a far stronger character. His superstitiousness becomes a self-conscious put-on, and rather than being frightened of Huck and thinking him a ghost when they meet on Jackson Island, it is Jim that surprises and frightens Huck. Running away with a plan and a map, Jim exercises planning and foresight.

Still ridiculed by being dressed up as an "African" by the Duke and King, Jim is for the most part more articulate: he directly argues for the elimination of slavery.

Also enhancing the depiction of Jim is the film's elimination of Tom Sawyer. Without Tom, the scene in the second chapter where Jim is mocked by Tom's theft of his hat disappears. The problematic final eleven chapters of the novel—where Jim is a helpless and gullible figure for Tom's scheming—are simply done away with. By making Huck (instead of Tom, as in the novel) the injured boy that Jim must save, the climax of the film becomes a reciprocating act of friendship, rather than a *deus ex machina* revelation that Jim has all along been free. Although far from examining slavery from an African American perspective or telling its full horror, the film does add scenes of a plantation with a cruel overseer whipping slaves, Jim among them. Huck views this brutality, consciously examines his own complicity in the system of racial inequality, explicitly and determinedly rejects slavery as an institution, and makes a personal apology for his own complicity with slavery to Jim. None of this is in Twain's novel. Rather than serving as a contemporary testament to Twain's greatness, the radically revised film simply points to significant problems with the text. After watching the film with my school-age son, I had a troubling and, for an English teacher, iconoclastic thought: might this Hollywood production be more effective with students than the novel itself?

My own experience with students in the classroom would seem to verify the observation that one's cultural background influences one's reaction to the novel. Recently I taught *Huckleberry Finn* in two classes with racially different student populations and saw clearly divergent results. The first class occurred in the fall, a college-level Black American literature class with a cultural studies approach to the theme of slavery. The class included a wide range of primary and secondary material from the seventeenth century to the present. We studied depictions of slavery by Black authors such as Olaudah Equiano, Frederick Douglass, Linda Brent (Harriet Jacobs), Nat Turner, Langston Hughes, Ishmael Reed, and Toni Morrison, and White authors Aphra Behn, Harriet Beecher Stowe, Caroline Lee Hentz, Herman Melville, and Mark Twain. We viewed segments of *Roots* and read historical essays (including chapters from Howard Zinn's *A People's History*) and contemporary studies about slavery (see the "Works for Teaching about Slavery" list at the end of this chapter). The course enrollment was half African Americans and half White students, from Detroit and medium-sized towns throughout Michigan.

Given the historical and thematic integration of the course, each new text we read was examined in light of what we already knew, and, simultaneously, the new texts led us to fundamentally rethink our previous readings. For example, it wasn't until after reading Frederick Douglass, Linda Brent, and Nat Turner that my students, both White and Black, were able to fully recognize the stereotyping in *Uncle Tom's Cabin*. Stowe's Black characters appeared as stock figures in a White abolitionist imagination only after coming to know the intellectually questing Douglass, the trapped and emotionally conflicted Brent, and the violent and unrepentant Turner. Focusing on a historical theme and putting the texts next to each other created a cultural studies experience that encouraged students to make sophisticated judgments, write complex papers, and engage in increasingly meaningful discussions.

After reading and discussing *Huckleberry Finn* in the context of this class, my African American college students from first to senior year—many of them planning to become teachers themselves—were concerned about the use of *Huckleberry Finn* in the high school, an institution they themselves had only recently left. Some of these students talked about their own experience as the only or nearly the only African American student in an otherwise White classroom. In this situation, they resented being turned to as experts by their White teachers, and they were uncomfortable being stared at by their fellow students. One of the brightest and most outspoken students—a popular college junior and an actor who had done stage appearances as Malcolm X—spoke of how, as a high school sophomore, he had read *Huckleberry Finn*, felt demeaned and angry in the process, and yet considered himself so isolated by his situation as the only Black person in the classroom that he was unable to share his reaction even privately with his teacher. What does it tell us about the challenge we teachers face in attempting to teach the novel that such a student, in this case the son of two college professors, lacked confidence to raise the issue?

I read several passages of the book aloud to the class to set up a discussion. One of the passages was the paragraph where Tom and Huck trick Jim in the second chapter. In this paragraph the epithet occurs seven times. Although I read the passage gently and as "sensitively" as I could, it was clear that hearing the word come out of my mouth made my African American college students bristle. One African American student (who was, in fact, of a mixed racial background and thus particularly acute on the question) was quite direct with me in the discussion afterwards. He pointed out that while this word may be used by Blacks with other Blacks, it simply must not be used by Whites. In his opinion, while a Black teacher might be able to read *Huckleberry Finn* aloud, a White teacher, no matter how "sympathetic," simply could not read the work aloud without offending Black students.

Still trying to understand the issue of *Huckleberry Finn* in the classroom, I taught the novel again during the following semester, this time in a literature teaching methods class for fifth-year English majors who themselves would soon be student teachers in high school and middle school language arts classrooms. In addition to reading *Huckleberry Finn,* we read Frederick Douglass, Nat Turner, Linda Brent, and several of the essays from *Satire or Evasion?* In contrast with the African American literature class, nearly all the students in this methods class were of Euro-American background (as are 98 percent of all the education students at our university). This particular term there was one African American student. She told me after the course was over that the only day that she really felt completely comfortable in the room was the day that we had a Black professor—and eight Black students from my course in the fall—come to join us for a discussion of the novel. Simply having more people of color in the class and listening to their point of view had a powerful impact on all the students. Up until that day all of the White students were confident that they would be able to teach *Huckleberry Finn* in appropriate and sensitive ways; after that day, although most of them decided that they would teach the novel, their final projects indicated that they realized it would be a complex task indeed.

Those who still want to teach *Huckleberry Finn* after reading this chapter and exploring the perspectives offered by *Satire or Evasion?* can marshal impressive arguments for their cause, not the least of which is the importance of having students examine the issue for themselves. In literature courses, we are sometimes so busy trying to "cover all the material" or "expose" our students to "great literature" that we fail to take the time to focus in, develop connections between works and contexts, and explore the relevance of what we read to the present. It is crystal clear to me that *Huckleberry Finn* should not be taught in a curriculum that simply showcases literary works without developing student skills at challenging the classics and thinking critically about literature, history, politics, and language. In other words, *Huckleberry Finn* should not be taught simply within a New Critical perspective.

To teach this novel ethically involves entering into a response-based cultural studies approach that, at a minimum, requires:

1. teaching *Huckleberry Finn* in a way that is sensitive to the racial makeup and dynamics of the classroom;

2. openly addressing the presence of the racial epithet in the text and developing a strategy for use or avoidance of the term in the classroom;

3. examining objections to Twain's portrayal of African Americans

and reading texts about slavery written by Black authors (see the "Works for Teaching about Slavery" list at the end of this chapter);

4. informing the parents of high school–age students that the text will be used, and offering intellectually meaningful alternative assignments when students or parents are uncomfortable with the novel.

Several of these points need clarification. For example, the dynamics of teaching *Huckleberry Finn* differ considerably from classroom to classroom, based on the race of the teacher and the proportion of minority students in the classroom, as well as on local social, cultural, and political factors. Talking across racial lines about questions of race always carries emotional impact in high school or college. The issues require a sensitivity and intellectual maturity from students that is not ordinarily found below the eleventh grade. Teachers and students who undertake to read *Huckleberry Finn* must be committed to respecting and learning from minority views, yet I do not recommend that a classroom vote or even a consensus process be used to decide whether or not *Huckleberry Finn* should be read. This difficult decision should be made by the teacher; letting students decide may put unfair pressure on those students who might object to reading the work, alienating them from their classmates. The racial makeup of the classroom is a complex factor in teaching *Huckleberry Finn* that requires further consideration.

While we might wish that fifty years after *Brown v. Board of Education,* classrooms without Black students would be increasingly rare, a *de facto* racial segregation is still the norm in many of America's suburbs, rural areas, and private schools. Even in racially mixed urban schools, tracking often leads to racially segregated classrooms. And universities are often just as segregated as secondary schools, if not more so. In a classroom without African Americans or other students of color, teachers often mistakenly believe that they are "off the hook" and need not deal with racial issues. However, as the country and the world become increasingly interrelated and as the White majority in this country becomes a minority in the not-so-distant future, it will be all the more imperative for White students to learn a multicultural literature and history and to participate in cultural studies curriculums.

Indeed, a classroom without African Americans (students or teacher) presents particular difficulties for the teacher and students reading *Huckleberry Finn.* Lacking Black voices, it will be difficult for "sympathy" or "understanding" to be more than superficial. Issues of race may be treated at a safe though somewhat uncomfortable intellectual distance: "I think that they would think . . . ," or, "If I were Black I would feel . . ." In a classroom without Blacks some students may seek to relieve the tension that a discussion of race brings by making supposedly funny, but actually inappropriate, racial remarks. A White teacher in this situation needs to make it clear from the outset that such remarks are not acceptable whether or not Blacks are present to hear them. Students and parents in such contexts may resent *any* time spent on racial questions or on Black history and culture as "too much" time, yet for these students *more* time is necessary to understand the literature and prepare for democratic citizenship. Inviting Black speakers to the class, whatever their viewpoint, is especially important. It is relatively easy for White teachers to argue for the importance of multicultural perspectives and racial understanding, while teachers of color, whether Black or otherwise, who attempt the same pedagogy may be perceived as "hypersensitive" or "activist," or may be accused of "reverse racism."

When issues of race come up in classes where students of color constitute a small minority, these students will sense, often accurately, that they are being singled out, that the other students are looking at them, waiting for a reaction. In a letter to the *New York Times* Allan Ballard describes his experience in a predominantly White junior high school in Philadelphia in the 1950s:

> I can still recall the anger I felt as my white classmates read aloud the word "nigger." In fact, as I write this letter I am getting angry all over again. I wanted to sink into my seat. Some of the whites snickered, others giggled. I can recall nothing of the literary merits of this work that you term "the greatest of all American novels." I only recall the sense of relief I felt when I would flip ahead a few pages and see that the word "nigger" would not be read that hour. (qtd. in Henry 29)

Non-Black teachers need to understand that it may be difficult for Black students, even the most able, to express their reservations or concerns about matters of race to their teacher. Silent refusal to read the novel, distracting comments or behavior, an excess of humor in the classroom by students asked to read *Huckleberry Finn* should be seen by teachers not as student insubordination or narrow-mindedness but as inchoate expressions of resistance to a possibly inappropriate curriculum or pedagogy. Since a special burden falls on them, African American students have a right to expect that they will be consulted in advance of reading and discussing the novel. Particularly if the teacher is Euro-American, it is important that minority students know that their teacher is aware of their position. Minority students can be told that when they write or participate in discussion that they can either speak "just as a person" or, if *they* choose to, identify their viewpoint with that of other African Americans.

In a classroom where half or more of the students are Black, African American students are less likely to feel isolated. Yet in these classrooms teachers still need to find ways to affirm student voices and facilitate communication between racial groups. Small group discussion plays a particularly important role in this classroom. Such groups will probably be more racially mixed if students are assigned by "counting off," though group self-selection may be important in helping to build comfort level and confidence. Unless their purposes are made explicit, teachers should avoid overtly separating groups by race. As a White teacher with about half African American students, I observe an evolution in class discussion. In the first weeks the majority of large group discussion volunteers are often White. As we work with small groups, as I show an interest in listening to minority perspectives, as Black teachers and colleagues visit my classroom, and as I invite nonvolunteers to participate, a more balanced class discussion evolves.

African American—or any other minority—voices are not automatically affirmed just because African American students are present in the classroom. Since African American or minority culture is not the focus of academic attention in most schools or universities—even institutions with a majority of "minority" students—it is not fair for teachers to assume that these students know "their" history or literature. Thus it may be just as important for students in a class with a larger percentage of Black students, for example, to acquaint themselves with complementary materials from African American perspectives.

In addition to carefully considering the racial dynamics of the classroom, it is important in reading *Huckleberry Finn* to recognize the power of language, and in particular the power of racial epithets. Teachers make a mistake when they excuse Twain's use of the term on the grounds that it was accepted in his time. All of the scholars I have read on the subject agree with professor David L. Smith that, "Even when Twain was writing his book, 'nigger' was universally recognized as an insulting, demeaning word" (107).

Peaches Henry, formerly a high school teacher, describes the history and politics of the word:

> To dismiss the word's recurrence in the work as an accurate rendition of nineteenth-century American linguistic conventions denies what every black person knows: far more than a synonym for slave, "nigger" signifies a concept. It conjures centuries of specifically black degradation and humiliation during which the family was disintegrated, education was denied, manhood was trapped within a forced perpetual puerilism, and womanhood was destroyed by concubi-

nage. If one grants that Twain substituted "nigger" for "slave," the implications of the word do not improve; "nigger" denotes the black man as a commodity, as chattel. . . . "Nigger" encapsulates the decades of oppression that followed emancipation. It means not only racist terror and lynch mobs but that victims "deserve it." Outside Central High in Little Rock in 1954 it was emblazoned across placards; and across the South throughout the 1950s and into the 1960s it was screamed by angry mobs. . . . So to impute blacks' abhorrence of "nigger" to hypersensitivity compounds injustice with callousness and signals a refusal to acknowledge that the connotations of "that word" generate a cultural discomfort that blacks share with no other racial group. (31)

Henry believes that in teaching texts such as *Huckleberry Finn* or *To Kill a Mockingbird,* the word should be "forced . . . into active class discourse" in a controlled classroom setting because, in her experience, "students (black or white) could only face sensitive issues of race after they had achieved a certain emotional distance from the rhetoric of race" (41). She describes her experience with ninth graders:

Unable to utter the taboo word "nigger," students would be paralyzed, the whites by their social awareness of the moral injunction against it and the black by their heightened sensitivity to it. Slowly, torturously, the wall of silence would begin to crumble before students' timid attempts to approach the topic with euphemism. Finally, after tense moments, one courageous adolescent would utter the word. As the class released an almost audible sigh of relief, the students and I would embark upon a lively and risk-taking exchange about race and its attendant complexities. (41–42)

An open classroom discussion of racial epithets in a mixed classroom of ninth graders with a sensitive and able Black teacher clearly offers important opportunities for learning. With a different student population and a different teacher, the results might have been less positive. Some teachers forbid the use of the word in the classroom and simply skip over it when the work is read aloud. Others speak the word only when they are quoting from a secondary source, such as the novel itself. Others use the expression "n-word" or "the racial epithet." No approach is guaranteed, but whatever approach is taken it should be done explicitly and be discussed by the students, in college or in high school. Discomfort with the word on the part of teachers or students may not be overcome by even the most sensitive approach, and the problem of the racial epithet in the novel constitutes reason enough for some teachers to choose not to teach the work. No teacher should be required to teach this novel. (The ethics of requiring teachers to teach *Huckleberry Finn* are explored by Wayne Booth in *The Company We Keep: An Ethics of Fiction.*)

There was a time when I thought it was silly not to teach *Huckleberry Finn* on the grounds that it was a racist novel. After reading and listening to African American scholars, teachers, parents, and students, I have changed my mind.

Gerald Graff has urged English teachers to "teach the conflicts," and at teachers' conferences in Oregon and Michigan I have advocated using the novel along with other works in a cultural studies framework to develop critical thinking about literature, racism, and the literary canon. Given the prominence of *Huckleberry Finn* in the curriculum, the attempt to teach it in a truly antiracist way marks a starting point, a much needed improvement over business as usual. I realize that sometimes it is necessary for English classrooms to be uncomfortable, and that if we fail to challenge established ways of knowing, to contrast viewpoints, and to broaden perspectives, then we fail to do our job.

Yet we must be careful that such discomfort is experienced equally rather than focused on an oppressed group that is desperately struggling for school success. It is timely for us English teachers to look beyond *Huckleberry Finn*, to find other works that might be more appropriate for all of our students and more effective in creating multicultural communities of learning in our classrooms. Educating White students about prejudice with a text that is alienating to Blacks perpetuates racist priorities, does it not? There is no excuse for the fact that not even one of the most-taught works in American high schools is written from a minority perspective—or that many college courses still include very little African American literature. Why aren't the great African American novels of Richard Wright, Zora Neale Hurston, Ralph Ellison, or Alice Walker more central to our teaching?

Moreover, race is not the only disturbing issue when we consider the role of *Huckleberry Finn* in the classroom; we also need to ask other questions—about the novel's treatment of women, for instance, about its effect on women students, and about the overwhelming male orientation of our curriculum. Julius Lester states:

> [In *Huckleberry Finn*] civilization is equated with education, regularity, decency, and being cramped up, and the representations of civilization are women. . . . The fact that the novel is regarded as a classic tells us much about the psyche of the white American male, because the novel is a powerful evocation of *puer*, the eternal boy for whom growth, maturity, and responsibility are enemies. (205)

Clearly, attempting to create appropriate response-based cultural studies approaches to teaching *Huckleberry Finn* brings us squarely into contact with issues of what the "canon" of American literature is and should be.

We now use the expression "literary canon" to mean the collection of "great works" that have been established through tradition, the evaluation of critics, and frequency of appearance in classrooms, anthologies, and textbooks. But despite the sense in which "the canon" is an established and venerable assortment of works, it is important to understand that "literary canons" are actually relatively recent inventions and have, all along, been the subject of political struggles.

Canons

What makes one literary work better than another? This question hinges on the fact that competing schools of literary scholarship value different types of texts and promote different works of literature. Mythology, folk literature, and epics were important to philologists (among the earliest literary critics) who sought to show that modern European literatures were the equal of classical literatures in Greek and Latin. If the Romantics depreciated Metaphysical poets and largely succeeded in removing them from the canon, the New Critics valued Metaphysical poetry and, years later, were able to restore this poetry to attention and classroom teaching. In line with competitive nineteenth-century racial and national theories, literary scholars "discovered" ancient ethnic oral traditions, and works such as *Beowulf*—which had been virtually unknown for centuries—were elevated to canonical status. In the United States, scholars rejecting the dominance of British literature developed an American canon to demonstrate American "exceptionalism." Given this history we are right to find something suspect in literature classes that emphasize the "special quality" of American or British literature, language, or culture.

The inclusion of minority and women writers in an expanding conception of "the canon" offers possibilities for rethinking the canon itself. Autobiography, slave narrative, testimonial, and the autobiographical novel— forms typically marginalized as being of "lesser merit" in traditional literary studies—emerge as centrally important. As we have seen throughout *Literature and Lives*, including minority perspectives means that familiar works such as Dickens's *Oliver Twist* (discussed in Chapter 2), *Romeo and Juliet* (Chapter 3), *The Tempest* (Chapter 4), and *Huckleberry Finn* may be seen from new and rich perspectives. As I have suggested, marginally canonical works such as *Uncle Tom's Cabin, Robinson Crusoe,* and *The Jungle* may become newly interesting and important, depending on the themes and issues under investigation. Rather than simply surveying the "great works," a cultural studies approach asks us to move away from an isolated examination of "high" literary texts and toward a more encompassing study of cul-

▶

ture, where popular forms, oral narratives, and musical and visual "texts" expand how we define the "literary."

Expanding the canon is a hard—and exciting—concept because it never means a simple adding on or fitting in, but fundamental change in the ideas and institutions that are already in place, a rethinking and renegotiation of purposes and methods. The recent outpouring of new scholarship and new and recovered literary texts underscores the need for teachers to continue their learning, to reflect on and, at times, reevaluate their own literary educations.

Expanding the canon takes us to the concept of "cultural literacy"— what it is that our students most need to know. Rather than a narrow list of sacred "great works" or an impossibly long list of everything under the sun, "cultural literacy" as conceived from a cultural studies perspective is not a list at all, but an activity of investigation and analysis. Rather than being handed a set of works and told, "These are great," students should be engaged in making comparative judgments, exploring criteria of evaluation, and considering the issues involved in text selection and canon formation. In this sense, rather than "covering" all the great works, "cultural literacy" entails thinking critically about a wide range of texts—and their various cultural, social, and historical contexts—both inside and outside the canon.

The teaching of *Huckleberry Finn* presents a complex problem that I continue to think about. Contrasting Twain's work with other texts addressing slavery locates *Huckleberry Finn* within a larger cultural studies undertaking, exploring the topic of slavery. The contrasts between many texts on the topic helped me appreciate Paul Lauter's notion of American literature as a comparative discipline within itself. This process of comparison, of bringing together works from the mainstream with texts from minority traditions—such as women's literature and African American, Latino, and Native American literatures—is most effective when there are common themes, a variety of textual materials, and closely overlapping historical situations.

Helping students situate themselves within this historical and social fabric, and yet also develop their particular voices and perspectives, is the challenge that I explore in the next chapter.

Works for Teaching about Slavery

Slave Narratives

- Frederick Douglass wrote three autobiographies; *Narrative of the Life of Frederick Douglass* is the first, shortest, and best known. A master of language, Douglass contrasts the cruelty of slavery with the desire of slaves for knowledge and freedom. No Jim, Douglass learns to read, explicitly adopts and develops abolitionist arguments, teaches other slaves, fights back—at one point punching his master—and plans a careful escape. (The collection *The Classic Slave Narratives,* edited by Gates, is not only inexpensive, but also includes three other important slave narratives, those of Olaudah Equiano, Mary Prince, and Linda Brent [a.k.a. Harriet Jacobs].)

- *The Life of Olaudah Equiano* begins with his birth in Africa in 1745. Equiano was one of the best-traveled men of his age; his adventures take place in Africa, the Caribbean, South America, London, Philadelphia, Spain, Turkey, and the Arctic Circle. His account is one of the earliest views of African society by an insider and is an interesting indictment of slavery by a man who significantly assimilated to European culture and religion.

- *Incidents in the Life of a Slave Girl* tells the story of a teenager, Harriet Jacobs (a.k.a. Linda Brent), who had to withstand the cruelty and sexually harassing advances of her master. As a young woman, she hid for years in order to be out of slavery but near her children. Students will find in this story of resistance to slavery a very different perspective from that of *Huckleberry Finn.* Brent was a sophisticated thinker and writer.

- *Confessions of Nat Turner* should not be confused with the novel of the same name by William Styron. Turner's original confessions as recorded by a journalist named T. R. Gray may be the most riveting fifteen pages you or your students will ever read. Throwing caution to the winds, Turner and his group of rebelling slaves would arrive at one plantation after another, slaughter the White families, and be joined by many of the slaves before moving on. Though the rebels, including Turner, were eventually caught and hung, their revolt reveals that anger and violent resistance were very much a part of slavery. (Students who read Gray's account carefully may uncover ways in which this White journalist may have embellished or distorted Turner's words.)

Fiction and Drama

- *Clotel: or, The President's Daughter* by William Wells Brown is an early African American novel that explores the life of Thomas Jefferson's illegitimate slave daughter. Given the new research about Jefferson's offspring, students will find it fascinating.

- Charles Chesnutt's *The Marrow of Tradition,* a turn-of-the-century novel by a somewhat lesser known but excellent Black novelist, is perfect for high school and college students. Set in the period just after the end of slavery, the novel uses a detective fiction format to explore the experience of Blacks in the South after the Civil War.

- Though some of us may have seen Alex Haley's *Roots* as a television movie or read the book, many of our students have not encountered it. The video series is a good way to complement other reading about slavery and presents one of the few depictions I know of slave capture and transportation to America.

- Langston Hughes's play *Mulatto* offers a compelling look at personal and social relations in the "big house" between slave masters, their slave mistresses, and mulatto children. There is a certain mystery about the period in which the action takes place that makes possible a reading of the play either as a historical recreation from the days of slavery or as a drama suggestive of more recent experience.

- "Tribal Scars" by Ousmane Sembène is a short story by the renowned Senegalese author (found in a collection with the same name). This work examines the effect of the slave trade on African culture.

- *Jubilee* by Margaret Walker is more approachable for most students than other contemporary Black fiction on slavery such as Toni Morrison's *Beloved*, Ishmael Reed's *Flight to Canada*, or Charles Johnson's *Middle Passage*. *Jubilee* is a powerful and compelling novel of one woman's journey through slavery and its aftermath.

- *Our Nig, or, Sketches from the Life of a Free Black* by Harriet Wilson is the first novel by an African American woman. It focuses on the oppression of Black servants in the North rather than on slavery per se. Alice Walker says of Harriet Wilson, "It is as if we'd just discovered Phyllis Wheatley—or Langston Hughes. . . . She represents a similar vastness of heretofore unexamined experience, a whole layer of time and existence in American life and literature."

Historical Accounts

- *The Slave Community* by John W. Blassingame is a classic study of the life and culture of American slave communities. A valuable classroom resource that is readable and contains numerous illustrations; students at all levels will find it helpful.

- Elizabeth Fox-Genovese has done important work on slave culture, particularly on the experience of women. Advanced students might want to examine her book *Within the Plantation Household: Black and White Women of the Old South.*

- *Roll, Jordan, Roll: The World the Slaves Made* by Eugene Genovese (Elizabeth Fox-Genovese's husband) is a massive and masterful study of slave culture written by a leading African American historian. The work is surprisingly approachable, though encyclopedic. *A People's History of the United States* by Howard Zinn offers a version of U. S. history from "the people's" point of view. For use with *Huckleberry Finn* or as part of a unit on slavery, the chapters "Drawing the Color Line" and "Slavery without Submission, Emancipation without Freedom" would be essential.

Web Sites Addressing *Huckleberry Finn* and Racism

- This site, mounted by the Electronic Text Center at the University of Virginia and titled simply "Adventures of Huckleberry Finn," includes historical essays, promotional materials, and illustrations from the novel that facilitate students' exploration of the issue of racial representation: http://etext.virginia.edu/railton/huckfinn/huchompg.html.

- In 2000, the Culture Shock series on PBS aired an interesting program on teaching *Huckleberry Finn* entitled "Born to Trouble." Along with the program, the producers created a Web site called "*Huck Finn* in Context: A Teaching Guide," with high-quality curriculum materials and lesson plans for teachers: http://www.pbs.org/wgbh/cultureshock/teachers/huck/index.html.

- "Teacher CyberGuide: Censorship and *The Adventures of Huckleberry Finn*" is a site mounted by the San Diego County Office of Education to help teachers bring the censorship debate into the classroom, providing texts, lesson plans, and links for teachers and students. It can be found at http://www.sdcoe.k12.ca.us/score/huckcen/huckcentg.html.

- My own Web site contains a page titled "Teaching *Huck Finn*: The Controversy and the Challenge," with materials by Peaches Henry that coordinated with a visit she made to our campus. See http://vms.cc.wmich.edu/~careywebb/huck.html.

Further Reading about Censorship

- *Academic Freedom to Teach and Learn: Every Teacher's Issue,* edited by Anna Ochoa and published by the National Education Association, is an essential resource. It provides clear and compelling arguments for academic freedom, explains the origins of censorship challenges, clarifies the laws protecting academic freedom, explores lessons learned from censorship challenges, and provides standard policies and forms for reconsideration of school curriculum.

- Each year, the American Library Association creates a kit to help librarians and teachers celebrate "Banned Book Week." The kit includes lists of banned books, posters, bookmarks, and resources for addressing censorship.

- *Banned in the U.S.A.: A Reference Guide to Book Censorship in Schools and Public Libraries* by Herbert Foerstel includes a sur-

vey of major book banning incidents; a careful examination of
the laws and legal history that address book banning, including
the 1988 Hazelwood decision on student newspapers; interviews
with banned young adult authors; and descriptions of the charges
made against books in the 1990s.

- *Battle of the Books: Literary Censorship in the Public Schools, 1950–1985* is written by Lee Burress, former chair of the NCTE Standing Committee Against Censorship. The book offers lucid and historically interesting examples of censorship, information on "secular humanism," and an extensive survey of titles that were objected to.

- *Book Burning* by the conservative commentator Cal Thomas is an attack on the media establishment, the women's movement, the ACLU, the "anti-censorship movement," and atheistic secular humanism, and it is dedicated to Jerry Falwell. Thomas advocates that parents be vigilant about curriculum, but that rather than banning books, they should urge libraries and schools to purchase conservative Christian materials.

- *Caught Off Guard: Teachers Rethinking Censorship and Controversy* by Ellen Brinkley helps teachers better understand and prepare for curriculum challenges.

- *The Day They Came to Arrest the Book* by First Amendment activist Nat Hentoff is a young adult novel that fictionalizes the story of a school seeking to censor *Huckleberry Finn*. A good introduction to censorship issues for secondary students.

- *The Future of Academic Freedom* edited by Louis Menand is a rich collection of essays by a variety of leading university professors on the centrality of academic freedom to university life.

- *Rationales for Challenged Books* is a CD-ROM produced by NCTE and featuring a wide variety of arguments for teaching frequently challenged literary works. The CD-ROM format makes it easy for teachers to cut and paste arguments suitable to their needs.

- *Reading Stephen King: Issues of Censorship, Student Choice, and Popular Literature,* edited by Power, Wilhelm, and Chandler, is an offbeat collection of essays from a conference on Stephen King addressing censorship and popular literature.

- *The Student's Right to Know* by Lee Burress and Edward Jenkinson is a forceful fifty-page pamphlet published by the NCTE Standing Committee Against Censorship; it articulates the case for academic freedom, distinguishes between selection and censorship, and offers a sample complaint form for people who seek to object to curricular materials. All teachers, librarians, and administrators should have a copy. (See also "Students' Right to Read: Dealing Responsibly with Challenges to Literary Works" on the NCTE censorship Web site, listed below.)

Web Sites to Challenge Censorship and Support Teacher Freedom

- The American Library Association offers materials on intellectual freedom and banned books, materials for coping with censorship challenges, and extensive Web links: http://www.ala.org/alaorg/oif/censors.html.

- NCTE's censorship site offers a variety of resources, including the full text of "The Student's Right to Read: Dealing Responsibly with Challenges to Literary Works," "Guidelines for Selection of Materials in English Language Arts Programs," and a list of contents and samples from the *Rationales for Challenged Books* CD-ROM. See http://www.ncte.org/censorship/.

- The People for the American Way maintains a site focused on freedom of expression, with links related to censorship in public schools and libraries: http://www.pfaw.org/issues/expression/index2.shtml.

- A site created and maintained by Dr. Mary Ellen Van Camp in the English Department at Ball State University has links to banned books available online: http://nova.bsuvc.bsu.edu/~00mevancamp/enged.html.

Further Reading about Literary Canons

- *American Literature and the Culture Wars* by Gregory Jay provides a history of canon formation in American literature and examines the relationships between multicultural literature, nationalism, the literary discipline, and the syllabus.

- *Beyond PC: Toward a Politics of Understanding,* edited by Patricia Aufderheide, is a good collection of essays on both sides of the political correctness debate.

- *Canons,* edited by Robert Von Hallberg, is a collection of closely argued essays addressing issues of canonization of literary works. Published in 1983 and for the most part ignoring multicultural issues (with the significant exception of Arnold Krupat's fine essay on Native American literature), the best essays here are the most general (see those by Altieri, Guillory, Ohmann, and Krupat).

- *Canons and Contexts* by Paul Lauter is a collection of essays about American literature and includes revised versions of his important pieces "The Literature of America—A Comparative Discipline" and "Reconstructing American Literature—Curricular Issues."

- *The Closing of the American Mind: How Higher Education Has Failed Democracy and Impoverished the Souls of Today's Students* by Allan Bloom was a bestseller when it came out in 1987.

Arguing that due to cultural relativism the university no longer provides students with the great tradition of philosophy and literature, Bloom maintains that high schools have failed (they are filled with teachers from the 1960s), feminism is the enemy of the vitality of the classics, and democratization of the university has destroyed real learning. The media frenzy that followed Bloom's book can be explored in *Essays on the Closing of the American Mind* by Robert Stone, a volume which collects sixty-two essays on both sides of the issue.

- *Cultural Literacy: What Every American Needs to Know* propounds E. D. Hirsch's theory that America needs a common cultural vocabulary—and his extended appendix offers a list of terms that "every American should know." The book spawned a mini-industry of cultural literacy books, lists, teaching, and testing programs.

- *Decolonizing Tradition: New Views of Twentieth-Century "British" Literary Canons,* edited by Karen Lawrence, is a collection of essays on the politics of canons, genre, cultural legitimation, and postcolonial perspectives.

- *Illiberal Education: The Politics of Race and Sex on Campus* by Dinesh D'Souza uses a variety of anecdotes to argue that American college campuses are dominated by politically correct multicultural curriculum and ideas. Another bestseller.

- Arthur Applebee's *Literature in the Secondary School: Studies of Curriculum and Instruction in the United States,* the most complete research study of the contents of the secondary school literary canon, finds that, in 1988, secondary literature curriculums continued to focus on established Euro-American authors, and that minority and women writers have yet to significantly enter secondary classrooms.

- *Loose Canons: Notes on the Culture Wars* by Henry Louis Gates Jr. is a collection of essays—some first appearing in the *New York Times Book Review,* other in journals of literary scholarship, such as *SAQ* and *PMLA*—that offer an accessible, even playful approach to issues of the role of African American writing in the literary canon.

- *The Opening of the American Mind: Canons, Culture, and History* by Lawrence Levine is a defense of the university against Bloom, D'Souza, Hirsch, and others. The books offers a lucid, brief, and balanced history of the American university's movement toward openness; an exploration of metaphors of American identity, from the melting pot to pluralism; and a defense of multicultural education.

7 Testimonial, Autoethnography, and the Future of English

My name is Rigoberta Menchú. I am twenty three years old. This is my testimony. I didn't learn it in a book and I didn't learn it alone. I'd like to stress that it's not only my life, it's also the testimony of my people. . . . The important thing is that what has happened to me has happened to many other people too: My story is the story of all poor Guatemalans. My personal experience is the reality of a whole people.

So begins *I, Rigoberta Menchú,* an urgent firsthand account of a poor, rural Guatemalan Indian community in the 1970s and early 1980s. Speaking to us from within another culture that she is determined to protect, a twenty-three-year-old Quiché Indian woman describes the cultural flexibility and community solidarity that have allowed the Quiché to survive horrific violence and economic oppression. Recorded and transcribed by a South American anthropologist, Rigoberta Menchú's account describes her people and their struggle in her own words. In recognition of her ongoing work in civil rights, this former servant girl was awarded the Nobel Peace Prize in 1992, a year which marked five hundred years of European colonialism of the New World. Her story has been included in college and high school courses and has generated complex and interesting discussions (see Beverley; D'Souza; Gugelberger; Carey-Webb and Benz; Stoll; Arias; and this book's Appendix B, "The Truth of Rigoberta Menchú's Testimonial: A Note to Teachers"). Without doubt this work is the most powerful book I have read or taught.

When I was a college student, I wrote a research paper on Guatemala, so I had heard of the terrible inequalities in that country, its long history of repression of indigenous peoples, and the dark pages of American interventionism. After college, I traveled in Mexico and other countries, where I saw Third World poverty, the kind of poverty in which, according to statistics, the majority of the world's people live. I knew this much before I started to read Menchú's story. Nonetheless her descriptions of the daily life of her community as they worked on coffee plantations, recognized births and marriages, were assaulted by the army, tried to bury their dead and maintain their identity—these detailed experiences, directly and simply narrated, left me profoundly shaken. How, at the end of the twentieth century, can such poverty, exploitation, and violence exist? How did the Quiché survive and go on living? Why wasn't the media informing us about these issues? After reading *I, Rigoberta Menchú,* I knew I needed to share it with students and fellow teachers. It was another work that would deepen and complicate the study of literature and culture.

When I teach *I, Rigoberta Menchú,* as I have now done several times, I realize that it presents a kind of experience to which my students have precious little access. Trying to sort out the moral and political dimensions of inequality, injustice, poverty, violence, and oppression in the world presents a challenge. Some students are immediately sympathetic to Menchú's story and anxious to know more, to involve themselves. Others are disappointed that the Quiché are so attached to their culture that they appear to teach their children to accept their situation rather than give up their identity. As with the reading of Holocaust narratives, some students are overwhelmed by the losses that Rigoberta Menchú suffers. Others are engaged by the role of Christianity as a tool of liberation in her community. Often we discuss what type of work this book is, whether or not it is literature, and how we might compare it with literary works we have read. Many students want to know more about what they can do about the kind of poverty in which Menchú's people live.

After teaching this work for the first time, I wrote an article about the experience for *English Journal* ("Auto/Biography"). When Menchú won the Nobel Prize in 1992, I realized that a book for teachers about her testimony might be worth writing. Her story had affected a number of classrooms, yet students and teachers needed more information. Despite the prize, Menchú herself remained relatively unknown, both in her person and in her testimony. Many teachers were doing interesting things with Menchú's story but they were often unaware of what was happening in other classrooms. Another professor and I advertised in professional journals to find teachers who had taught Menchú's story and would be willing to write about their experiences. Instructors from a variety of levels and disciplines responded, and eventually we published a twenty-eight chapter book, *Teaching and Testimony: Rigoberta Menchú and the North American Classroom.*

Reflecting on *I, Rigoberta Menchú* with students and teachers through these experiences has helped me recognize that there are still worlds of experience I have yet to bring into my teaching. Menchú's story is only one of a whole genre of works potentially useful to cultural studies curriculums. Her story provides fresh perspectives on traditional literary approaches and generates new possibilities for developing and deepening the writing I ask my students to do.

One term frequently used to describe works like Menchú's is "testimonial." John Beverley defines testimonials as edited oral narratives collected from people who are not able to write about their own experience. Testimonials are not exactly biographies, because the subject speaks for himself or herself. Nor are they autobiographies, because they are recorded and transcribed by a second person. They differ from traditional oral histories as they emphasize the experience of the group rather than the perspective of an individual. Indeed, testimonials bring to the center of attention the perspective and experience of previously unheard and marginalized people. The power of a testimonial comes from the immediacy of the social situations it recounts and from its strong individual voice. Acts of memory situated in time, testimonials help us learn about history, revealing connections between personal experience and collective reality. As in the case of Menchú, the recording of testimony may have urgent, real-life consequences. The very activity of testifying can turn victims into survivors, witnesses into agents of change.

Anthropologists write ethnographies, systematic narratives about the cultural practices of the people they investigate. When a group of people seek to describe themselves and, perhaps, speak back to the way others have defined them, what they write might be called "autoethnography"—another term used to describe Menchú's story. Thus the author of an autoethnography recognizes herself or himself as part of a social system and seeks to explain the cultural group in which he or she lives, though perhaps in a more personal way than an anthropologist does. Addressed by a Quiché Indian woman to outsiders, Menchú's testimony responds to those who think of Latin American Indians either as lazy and dirty or as clones of Juan Valdez with white clothes and burro, the mythical figure of coffee corporation advertising. As autoethnography, her testimony defines native Guatemalan experience differently, repudiating these stereotypes and images.

Mary Louise Pratt considers autoethnography to be the literary art of the contact zone where one finds cultural "copresence, interaction, interlocking understandings and practices often within radically asymmetrical relations of power" (*Imperial* 7). These cultural struggles make autoethnographic writing resonate with more than individual significance. Yet, generalizing from one person's testimony or experience is always complicated. Testimony and autoethnography raise age-old questions about how we both distinguish and connect personal stories and collective experience. They urge us toward cultural studies projects that combine a variety of texts, materials, and viewpoints as we try to locate and understand individual voices.

Direct narration, everyday vocabulary, and an emphasis on communication over artistry make testimonials or autoethnographies accessible to a wide variety of students. The ways in which these works try to speak back to stereotypes and established ideas make them especially useful to a cultural studies classroom. A testimonial can engage perspectives offered in traditional literary works, in history textbooks, or in the mass media. While perhaps not "literary" in the sense that a New Critic would define the term, testimonials are ideal texts for students and teachers alike to attempt to hear the voice of the voiceless, to investigate cultural and social differences, and to explore questions about what it means to be "culturally literate."

The relation of individual expression to social experience has always been important in literary study. As more minority and women's voices are being heard in literature classes, in part through autobiographies, memoirs, testimonies, and autoethnographies, we find ourselves increasingly concerned with the interplay between the social and personal aspects of identity. Past generalizations about "human nature" become suspect when they are seen to be based on a limited range of authors and works. Sanctified individual expression is shown to be located in time and reflective of cultural bias. It is not surprising that a great deal of recent social theory has been focused on just the sort of individual/social distinctions that testimonial and autoethnographic works foreground. Under the somewhat indigestible term "poststructuralism," an important school of thought has arisen, that, in its various permutations, is beginning to have a significant impact on the study and teaching of literature.

Poststructuralism

Drawing on linguistics, anthropology, and social theory, an influential form of criticism arose in the 1970s that challenges basic assumptions of traditional literature study and teaching. Poststructuralism begins with the assertion that "consciousness" as we experience it resides in language and that language is always a social phenomenon, created by an interactive community of speakers. Thus no one has an isolated, complete, or "unified" consciousness separate from the language and culture in which we all live. Individuals are cultural beings, and language, texts, institutions, and social

▶

practices script the way we think and act. In this view, rather than being universal, human nature is particular and depends on culture, social codes, and the historical moment.

Unlike New Critics, who focus on a literary work as a closed artistic system, a poststructuralist typically compares the codes and roles found in a literary text with those in other kinds of "texts" in order to recognize established patterns, or "discourses," that shape human behavior. Poststructuralists use the term "text" to encompass things as varied as a popular romance novel, a booklet of school rules, the architectural layout of a suburban tract home, or the rituals of a wrestling match. Indeed, for a poststructuralist, whether or not a work is "literary" in the traditional sense may not be essential. Rather than trying to work out the aesthetic complexity of a great artist, they are interested in broader discourses within which literature plays a part.

While actually drawing on the reader response insight that the meaning of a text is not fixed once and for all time, poststructuralists also tend to see readers and writers not as utterly unique, but as likely to produce texts or make readings that will be, in fundamental ways, familiar, given the social or cultural context of the reading or writing. While influenced by the recognition of diversity and the different experiences of minorities or genders, poststructuralists are also suspicious of claims about biologically essential or historically original "female" (or "male") or "African American" (or "European American") experience.

We might say that poststructuralists believe it is not really possible to go beyond the stereotype and find the "real thing"; the way we know and understand anything will depend on the cultural glasses we are wearing. Instead of thinking of stereotypes as masking a "real" identity, poststructuralists tend to find that when you remove one stereotype, beneath it will be another stereotype and then another, each perhaps more complex, but all of them intimately expressions of the social nature of identity. (For one thing, poststructuralism invites us to examine stereotypes in a more complex and interesting way.)

Since everyone is seen to be a product of language, the English classroom as seen by a poststructuralist is an important place indeed. Poststructuralism allows us to address the ancient question "Who am I?" in a way that directly relates literature to people's lives. If you believe that you are what you eat (in a cultural sense), then examining culture carefully is part and parcel of understanding oneself. The scripts, roles, codes, and institutions—the discourses—that constitute us are found in canonical and noncanonical literatures alike. They are also found in nonliterary texts and in the organization and arrangement of material objects that can be read like texts.

Poststructuralism need not be seen as determinist or pessimistic. There are several versions of poststructuralism—"deconstruction," "post-Marxism,"

▶

or "postmodernism"—that are alternatively creative, transformative, even playful. These forms of thought help us recognize our ability to alter and even create the language and social structures in which we live.

Without naming the genre, teachers have for a long time tapped into the power of testimonial and autoethnographic narrative. The reaction of my students to Menchú's testimonial reminded me of the seriousness and interest that previous students had shown when I taught Holocaust literature. As I described in Chapter 1, Elie Wiesel's *Night* was effective in the classroom precisely because of its testimonial and autoethnographic qualities. *Night* tells Wiesel's personal story, one that is, at the same time, a story of his people. In outline and detail, his testimony was like that of many others, including the Holocaust survivor who visited my class, Diana Golden. Questioning their very humanity, the Nazis treated the Jews as less than human; in its profound simplicity and humanity, *Night* powerfully refutes Nazi ideology and stereotypes.

Many teachers before me have taught Holocaust literature, slave narratives, and other forms of testimonials. Recognizing testimonial as a genre—though, like the novel, a genre with indistinct borders—allows us to better understand many of the works we teach and can help us recognize valuable new materials. Maya Angelou's autobiography, *I Know Why the Caged Bird Sings*, has testimonial and autoethnographic elements. John Hersey's *Hiroshima* (a staple when I started teaching, but now seen less often) is written as the interweaving of testimonials from the survivors of the atom bomb. Oral histories or ethnographies that represent not just an individual but a group experience, exemplified by the work of Studs Terkel or Oscar Lewis, may be testimonial or autobiographic in focus.

Biographic, autobiographic, testimonial, and autoethnographic forms are especially important to the writing of women, minorities, and Third World people for whom the "high" literary genres have been less accessible and less useful. Many of us may already know of specific examples. As I discussed in Chapter 3, Virginia Woolf's *A Room of One's Own* uses biographic and autobiographic styles to disrupt the male-coded genre of the formal essay. According to Henry Louis Gates Jr., African American writing has its origins in the autobiographical slave narrative—very much an autoethnographic form designed to repudiate stereotypes of slaves as illiterate or accepting of their condition. Twentieth-century African American writers such as Wright, Hurston, Baldwin, Ellison, and Marshall draw on autobiographic and autoethnographic traditions. Many African and Latin American novelists are influenced by testimony and autobiography, with examples including Camara Laye, Cheikh Hamidou Kane, Buchi Emecheta, Manlio Argueta, Carlos Fuentes, and Elena Poniatowska.

As new materials come into the canon, they can lead us to think in different and more complex ways. For example, if the authors of mainstream autobiographies typically attempt to explain what makes their own lives unique or different from the general population, minority autobiographies tend to reverse this approach. While minority autobiographies may examine the alienating effects of dominant society, they also explore the connections within and across minority or oppressed cultures, as well as strategies for hope and collective resistance, and thus they take on an autoethnographic dimension. For poor or minority students in particular, giving testimonials time in the classroom may have a powerful influence on attitudes toward writing and school.

While a unit on testimonial or autoethnographic literature could fit into many different "survey" courses, testimonials or passages from testimonials can also work well as companion pieces to the reading of familiar literary works. In the last chapter, I suggested trying to add to our understanding of Jim in *Huckleberry Finn* by simultaneously reading from Frederick Douglass's slave narrative, Harriet Wilson's autoethnographic novel *Our Nig,* or the testimonial "Confessions of Nat Turner." I described a similar procedure in the chapter on homelessness, combining literary works like *Oliver Twist, Maggie,* and *The Grapes of Wrath* with Orwell's autoethnographic *Down and Out in Paris and London,* Jonathan Kozol's collection of the testimonies of homeless people, and the documentary film *Streetwise.* I used testimonial materials in teaching about youth violence, such as the documentary film *Eyes on the Prize* and Malcolm X's *Autobiography* (actually a testimonial transcribed by Alex Haley). I believe that teachers should not hesitate to use materials selectively, borrowing from sections or chapters as best meets their needs. (For a more complete listing of testimonials and testimonial-like narratives appropriate to English teaching, see the list at the end of this chapter.)

In my experience, teaching testimonial narratives leads students to ask challenging questions about the priorities of literature classes and their everyday schooling experiences. I think such questions should be taken seriously and examined in large-group discussions. As we juxtapose novels and ethnographies, we may begin "deconstructing" generic boundaries. Crossing such boundaries can lead to interesting experiments and insights. Literature itself can be read as if it were ethnography in order to explore cultural codes and practices. Ethnography, supposedly objective and scientific, can be see seen as highly subjective, a creative, even artistic, performance, and thus read as literature. Cultural studies teaching is likely to put generic, disciplinary, and institutional boundaries into discussion. With this purpose in mind, testimonials and autoethnographic narratives are useful to a literature and language arts education at a fundamental level.

Deconstruction

Deconstruction is a probing and intellectually intense version of poststructuralism developed by the avant-garde French philosopher Jacques Derrida. Derrida attempts to demystify Western humanist thought not from the outside, but by examining its internal instabilities, its untenable dualisms, and the porousness of its definitions and boundaries. Derrida's close readings of canonical thinkers of Western philosophy challenge universal ideals, metaphysical certainties, and claims to unchanging truths about the human condition. Instead he considers everything we see, experience, and understand as always and already made for us, embedded in social and historical context. "Truths," when examined closely, when "deconstructed," turn out to be fictions created by language and particular systems of meaning situated in time and place. In the late 1970s and early 1980s, Derrida's methods and conclusions became very interesting to many American literary scholars who began applying them to literature and literary criticism. Their efforts were (and continue to be) disturbing to professors who suddenly found stable truths and institutionalized ways of thinking challenged and undermined.

While a deconstructive pedagogy would, by definition, be impossible to delimit once and for all, deconstruction invites English teachers and students to carefully examine the most basic assumptions of the discipline. How might terms such as "literature," "genre," "national tradition," "writer," "reader"—even "teacher" and "student"—be less precise, more blended into their supposed "other" than they appear to be? (How is the "nonliterary" also like the "literary," the "poem" like the "short story," the "American" like the "European" or the "African," or vice versa, and so on?) How might meaning in works of literature (or visual or institutional "texts") not really be as clear or straightforward as it might seem at first? Deconstructive teaching could be seen as injecting a healthy dose of skepticism into the classroom, thus fostering inquiry, and leading, perhaps, to change and renewal.

Nonetheless, deconstruction lives and works within established knowledge and ways of understanding. Rather than erasing the chalkboard, so to

▷

speak, deconstruction asks us to look carefully into what is already there, and, as well, to see behind, around, above, below, and so on. If the poststructuralist insight is correct that our consciousness is determined by language and social discourses, then deconstruction means the English class-room, rather than being separated from the "real world," is a place where meaning and change take place as we examine, rethink, and play with the texts and roles set up for us.

Working with small-town, working-class students in Massachusetts, June Kuzmeskus describes a high school curriculum that weaves together testimonial narrative and students' writing. Becoming conscious of their own identity by examining others' self-accounts, Kuzmeskus's students engage in a problem-posing form of learning tied to their responsibilities as democratic citizens. They read works like *Incidents in the Life of a Slave Girl, Night, I Know Why the Caged Bird Sings, Woman Warrior,* Tillie Olsen's *Yonnondio: From the Thirties,* Russell Baker's *Growing Up,* Annie Dillard's *An American Childhood,* and *I, Rigoberta Menchú.* As Kuzmeskus explains, their study of testimonial opens the door for students to better understand their own experiences and initiate personal reflection and writing:

> I know many of my students struggle with problems that limit their effectiveness as students and truly mar their lives. They confront problems they feel they can't speak of, that compel them, they think, to suffer silently. The courses I teach provide a forum and an academic validation for consideration of a wide range of expression—painful as well as joyful. Within this approach, testimonial literature has value for my students far beyond the classroom. It provides a much-needed signal not to give up on themselves or on others. It inspires them to reach out and speak for themselves, to generalize from their own experience. Using testimonial as a model teaches students first to name their hardship, to contextualize it, and then to reach out through their writing to activate themselves and others. In this way, my students begin to reduce their isolation and harness the power inherent in the commonalities and compassion to be found both among their classmates and in the world beyond the school doors. (124)

Above all, Kuzmeskus views herself as a writing teacher. She explains:

> Everything we read becomes a starting point for student writing. Since I want students to relate directly to their reading, they keep reader response journals in which they quote and respond to passages that

stand out for them. I ask them to note what the central characters learn, what they want, what they are challenged by, how they react to those challenges, who and what supports them, who and what challenges them, and what makes them different from those around them. These same questions are used in many of my responses to the students' individual pieces of reflective writing, both for purpose of content development and to encourage students to take a step back for a clearer view of their own situation. . . .

Thus the authors we read provide role models for courage in the midst of life's challenges, as well as valuable models of writing. I want students to know that there is a "tradition" of literature that people have created to give voice to individual and collective experience. The tradition we explore gives trouble and sorrow a means of expression that is not self-indulgent or self-destructive. Together, we find that one step in the process of growing, healing, and preventing further suffering is to put it into words and bring those words to others. (125)

As Kuzmeskus indicates, testimonial narrative can invigorate student writing. The informal oral language of testimonials may be closer to student's home language than is that of works found in standard school textbooks or anthologies. As published validations of the lives and experiences of people that might otherwise be unknown, testimonials and autoethnographies send the message to students that all lives are important, that their own experiences are worthy of serious attention and academic analysis. An awareness that the most disempowered can speak out and be heard gives students hope that their voice, too, is valuable.

Many testimonials have life and death consequences for their authors, and the real-world seriousness of testimonials can inspire students to see writing as more than an academic exercise. Since testimonial narrative underscores the importance of historical specificity, of social groups, of race, ethnicity, class, gender, and nationality, surprisingly sophisticated thinking results when students use them as a springboard to their own writing. The collective authorship of many testimonial narratives invites students to consider collaboration in writing, and the genre can offer a model for seeking out stories worth listening to and recording. Students may be stimulated to take part in the making and dissemination of testimonials themselves. The real-world context of testimonials gives them a vitality in the learning process, catalyzing examinations of the relationships between literature and lives.

The power of testimony and autoethnography was clearly utilized by Eliot Wigginton in the 1970s as he pioneered the renowned Foxfire approach. From their rural school in Rabin Gap, Georgia, Wigginton's students collected testimonials, folk wisdom, and survival strategies from the older generation of hill people living in their area. Working through a step-by-step process, Wigginton trained his students in interviewing, write-up, analysis, and publication, and these ethnographic procedures unleashed his students' passion for writing. Collecting testimonials, his students came to value the language, knowledge, and perspectives of people in their community. As autoethnography, the Foxfire magazines and books depict a rich cultural context and speak back to stereotypes about "hillbillies" and the rural poor. Wigginton was clear about the relation of testimonial and cultural study and he explored concepts of stereotyping, cultural difference, cultural change, and the "Appalachian experience" with his students.

> I remind them of the purposes of Foxfire, the fact that every tape and photograph they have made goes into our archive for future use, and the fact that even though we do not advocate a return to the days of outdoor toilets and kerosene lamps, we certainly do advocate the need for an understanding of and pride in the parent culture, and a concomitant respect for and interest in the cultures of others. (379)

> One of my most vital tasks as students begin to wrestle with their own culture is to lead them to objectivity . . . to help them see that some aspects of the Appalachian value systems and beliefs are not necessarily appropriate today . . . to help them, for example, look objectively at the traditional Appalachian conception of the woman's role in the home and community, or the role of education or religion or justice, and evaluate that in light of today's needs. (397)

In the Foxfire experience, cultural literacy became not a static set of facts, but a responsible and ethical process of investigation of self, community, and others.

In a course on the topic of how to teach writing, I have used autoethnographic writing to prepare college students to become middle school and high school English teachers. Rather than study theoretical works about writing pedagogy, I ask my students to read a variety of professional writing teacher "autoethnographies," such as *In the Middle: New Understandings about Writing, Reading, and Learning* (Nancie Atwell), *Sometimes a Shining Moment: The Foxfire Experience* (Eliot Wigginton), *Will My Name be Shouted Out?; Reaching Inner City Students through the Power of Writing* (Stephen O'Connor), and *June Jordan's Poetry for the People: A Revolutionary Blueprint* (edited by Lauren Muller). In these books, writing teachers tell stories about their classroom experiences and their development as teachers. As we draw theory and strategies from these classroom testimonies, we also examine the differing social and cultural contexts these teachers work in (small-town Maine, rural Georgia, inner-city New York, and Berkeley, California). We focus on the contexts in which they teach, the variety of approaches they use, and their own growth as teachers and community leaders. Next, working in literature circles, students read multicultural, testimonial, autoethnographic, and biographical literature, and part of the point is to locate themselves as cultural beings, a process that often takes place by counterpoint. While the students create curriculum projects and make presentations about a variety of issues in the teaching of writing, clearly the highlight of the course is the extensive, multigenre, autoethnographic paper they write about themselves and their own experiences in learning to write.

Developing this project, our class becomes a writing workshop where teachers in training experiment with a variety of forms of writing pertinent to their own experience as students of writing instruction. Drawing on Nancie Atwell, they write memories of writing experiences in grade school, middle school, high school, and college. These stories are shared in response groups, critiqued as pieces of writing, and analyzed as samples of writing pedagogy. Using some of the techniques they learn from Eliot Wigginton, future teachers interview a public school writing instructor, preferably one they had themselves. They also interview students who are, in one way or another, different from themselves. They might interview students from their own districts in separate ability groups or academic tracks, or students from different social or ethnic backgrounds. These comparative pieces help future teachers put their personal experiences into broader contexts. Drawing on the play-writing ideas of Stephen O'Connor, we have a minilesson and workshop on writing dialogue. Then, students recreate dialogues related to their schooling experiences. Other workshops are spent writing poetry that attempts to speak from their personal experience and social situation, as June Jordan suggests.

All of these different genres of writing are woven together as students create a multigenre autoethnography of their experiences as students of writing instruction. As we learn about theories and strategies for teaching writing from the professional autobiographies, students are able to be more analytical about their own education and think more clearly about themselves as teachers. Along with their analyses, my students frequently include samples of their writing, documents, photographs of their families and communities, as well as stories, dialogues, and interviews. Invariably issues emerge that can be used to focus analysis and link their autoethnographies together.

A truly "postmodern" form of writing, multigenre essays are characterized by the juxtaposition of various forms and histories. Multigenre writing allows students to incorporate personal narrative, interview material, and social commentary. Rather like the "I-Search" paper that Ken

Macrorie has written about, multigenre autoethnographies allow my students to reflect on the process of research as well as on the product. They find that the multigenre aspect invites creativity and pastiche.

Postmodernism

Increasingly recognized by intellectuals as the dominant cultural movement of the present time, postmodernism means different things to different people. Perhaps this is fitting since it is the very concept of difference, the jarring, collage-like existence of contemporary life, that postmodernism most directly foregrounds. Postmodernists alternately see the world as a cartoonesque Disneyland, an unremitting play of striking cultural difference, the overflow of an uneven and diverse globalism where African slum dwellers watch the Cosby show, where modern buildings are patterned like gift-wrapped Greek temples, where ancient Native American spiritual beliefs set the pattern for cosmopolitan Latin American novels. If postmodernism is, in the words of a Pico Iyer book title, a "Video Night in Katmandu," then it is also the startlingly heterogeneous student populations that English teachers have in their classrooms every day—a member of the Crips gang, seated next to a Cambodian refugee, seated next to an Internet computer nerd, seated next to a devoutly religious Christian fundamentalist (or maybe all these rolled into one person!). To be aware of the diversity of contemporary American young people—and the startling ways in which these cultural juxtapositions overlay themselves within individuals—is to be aware of a postmodern reality.

A postmodern approach to teaching would freely examine the kaleidoscopic variety of contemporary life. As we have seen with the autoethnographies, it would be multigeneric. Postmodern teaching would invite different voices; it would find the historical in the contemporary, and the contemporary in the historical. It might foreground works of magical realism (now written not only in Latin America), explore the carnivalesque aspects of Chaucer, Rabelais, or Swift, or the strangely altered states of science fiction. It would juxtapose genres, texts, and materials that might not normally be thought of together but whose comparison might illuminate modern life. It would read its texts carefully to find the fragmentation already built into the presumably whole and uniform. Postmodernism is thus the most playful of the poststructuralisms, but, like the others, it refuses to accept any simple separation between the "individual" and "society." In its best version, postmodernist teaching means respect for difference; recognition of compositeness, mixture, blending; and examination of the restrictions that prevent people from creative participation in the making and hybridizing of culture.

Tom Romano has helped me think about multigenre writing with high school students. He describes his discovery of multigenre writing and some of the challenges of teaching it in *Writing with Passion: Life Stories, Multiple Genres,*

> I had never read anything like these multigenre research papers before. Most of them were genuinely interesting in style and content. The visions were complex, the writing versatile. Brian's paper was one of six or seven I found astonishing. All was not glory, though. Three of the papers were disappointing, showing little depth, breadth, or commitment. And rest assured, like Reverend Dimmesdale, I did a requisite amount of self-flogging. What did I do wrong? What could I have done?
>
> In retrospect, I do see things I could have done. The disappointing papers didn't emerge from nowhere. The three students' learning journals had revealed puzzlement or a lack of commitment early on. I could have given those students greater support, feedback, and direction. I could have been a better companion for their words. (127)

Overall, students in my classes have truly enjoyed these multigenre autoethnographic projects. To give a sense of the enthusiasm and learning these autobiographies generate, I will share selections from the electronic conference that my students participated in during the course. An exciting new pedagogical resource, electronic conferences enrich classroom dialogue, often allowing students who are less active in class discussion to blossom. Computer conferences have become a regular feature of my teaching, creating an additional forum for reflection and exchange of ideas. Accessing the "Confer" (this is the name of the software we used for computer conferencing) outside regular class time from computers either on campus or at home, my students write hundreds of pages related to a wide variety of topics in the class. (Teachers who would like to set up electronic threaded discussions for their students can do so for free at www.blackboard.com.) The following comments are from a conference item focused on writing the autoethnography.

Item 18
28-Jan-1998

18:1) Author: Emmy
29-Jan-1998 13:50
The more I have thought about the autoethnography, the more excited I am getting. I am going home in two weeks and am anxious to collect my old poems and stories that I have been writing through the years to add into my autoethnography. I think it is going to be

very interesting to reflect on how I learned to write and who influenced me throughout the years. This is a really cool project.

———————

18:4) Author: Wendy
02-Feb-1998 00:21
I had the chance to interview my Language Arts teacher from 6th and 7th grade. It was SO fun to go back to my old middle school (where my brother is in 7th grade now) and see my old teachers, etc. Things haven't really changed all that much, but I've changed. I think what Toby Fulweiler said at the conference on Friday is so true . . . once students interview a real person, they will gain much more enthusiasm and ownership of their writing. This is certainly true for me . . . I'm excited now to re-read my old poetry, etc. :)

———————

18:8) Author: Jacalyn
06-Feb-1998 14:28
I started to go through old papers last night. They brought back a lot of memories and some made me laugh. My handwriting was horrible in grade school! I am going to include some paper books that I made in second grade and a written report that I did on the presidential election in fifth grade. I am still looking for a paper that I wrote in high school because I won an award for it and I am curious to read it again. I think my mom saved every paper that I ever did!! I am also going to include some papers from my advanced composition class. We had to keep a writing folder for that class and it has all of my drafts in it. I want to do some more work on my interview because I am not happy with it yet. I am excited to put this project together, but I am not sure on the organization.

———————

18:11) Author: Katie
10-Feb-1998 14:44
HELP ME!!! S.O.S!
Please, someone out there, explain the "several pages of re-created dialogue" assignment to me! I would love to do it but don't know how to start.

I did go home this weekend and got some GRRReat stuff for the autoeth. project. I spoke to my honors English 9 and AP English teacher and she had some really valuable insights. My mom and I spent three hours looking through old files and found some old writings of mine. Lots of fun involved in that, I strongly recommend it!

———————

18:12) Author: Jennifer
10-Feb-1998 16:47
This message is to Katie about the re-created dialogue. We missed you in class! I was a little confused about the assignment also but I learned a lot today when I went to class. I simply recreated a dialogue I had that made an impact on my life. However, I learned that it would relate better to our ethno project if we somehow related it to school or a past experience in a class or any writing experience. Or simply something that was important to us that may work into our project. Good luck. It was sort of fun to do. Other people did a narrative with dialogue mixed in with it. I think that's what I'm going to do.

18:13) Author: John
10-Feb-1998 17:48
When I started writing my autobiography, I thought that I hated to write. Then I was typing away and realized how much I have missed creative writing. In my high school years, I only had one writing class I enjoyed and that class was Creative Writing. I never thought too much about how we were able to choose what genre we were going to write or the whole process of peer editing, but after writing this paper I see the benefits of choice and working with peers. I have also realized that I don't hate writing as much as I once thought I did.

Anyone else feel this way? . . .

18:14) Author: Jen
11-Feb-1998 13:40
I think there is a lot of room for creativity in our autoethnographies. The re-created dialogue assign. spooked me too, but I found myself writing it in the way I was comfortable writing it. I chose to recall significant conversations in my life about my writing from grade 2 to college. It really gave me a perspective on the evolution of my own writing. Strange... it had been in my head all this time, and until I wrote it down, I hadn't seen the significant impact these conversations had on me. I think that's supposed to be the point of this assignment. Dig up what is already there and learn what you really already know.

18:15) Author: Ellen
12-Feb-1998 11:12

I got so many ideas about what to do with my autoethnography during the last class. I think that it is very beneficial to talk about it and the ideas we are having. The light bulbs keep popping on in my head. Ever since we started really talking about dialogue and drama, I realized just how much that was an important part of my life. When students have to write dialogue that portrays who a person is or how they might talk, they learn the importance of grammar and description. Just a little plug for theater in the classroom.

18:17) Author: Anna
13-Feb-1998 09:35
At first I was really nervous but these things work themselves out. The most hopeful thing was reading and talking to other students about what they are going to include. It really helped me think of many creative things. This seems to be a project that you just need to jump into and start assembling!

18:18) Author: Allen Carey-Webb
16-Feb-1998 07:28
I am excited about the chance to read these autoethnographies!

18:22) Author: Maria
20-Apr-1998 01:27
As I sat down in the computer lab and began my autoethnography, I found my hands just producing this amazing story that just flowed out of my heart. I was looking at some old pictures, some old writing works, etc. and found myself laughing hysterically out loud at some of the ways I thought and looked. I think that was the most enjoyable 20 page paper I have ever written. It was rather therapeutic.

I worked through many of the feelings of inferiority and insecurity as I wrote about myself and my desire to improve my writing skills. However, I also realized how great my family is and how my education in high school really influenced my writing in college.

In full, I am really glad we had the project and plan on using this project within my classroom someday.

18:23) Author: Callie
20-Apr-1998 07:57
I found while writing my autoethnography, that it would prove to be one of the most valuable assignments I have ever completed. Who

knew that so many feelings would come up during the course of a 20 page paper? I never knew how strongly I felt about tracking and its detrimental effects until I had to sit down and actually think about its impact on me. Through writing down my experiences of being a student, I have learned so much about what kind of teacher I want to be. It was so interesting to think about which teachers made me want to go on and keep up with school and which ones just made me hate it.

As their comments on our computer conference indicate, many revelations come as students sift through their experiences in learning to write. Often they learn about the roles played by people around them, by family, teachers, and communities. Looking at their experiences as students gives insight into teaching—both what to do and what to avoid. These experiences and ideas are shared in response groups, reinforcing their value. Many of my students had been placed in advanced groups and upper tracks and had, for the most part, experienced success in school. For these students, it can be a challenge to see how greatly their experience differs from others and, as Callie mentions, how it is affected by tracking.

For students who have moved between academic levels, it is easier to recognize tracking as a central force shaping the experience of writing and reading. I remember a class listening with rapt attention to Michael, one of the quieter students, as he shared the following paragraphs from his autoethnography:

> I was in no way an over achiever when it came to impressing my guidance counselors. They knew what file to look up when my name surfaced for course assignment—the low speed, low motivation section. Wood shop and drafting, along with auto mechanics and marketing were all classes that I was assigned at one point in time. Not that these classes do not deserve my respect, but college administrators must have looked at them and been ready to chalk up another "no admittance," turning to the nearest trash can with my application.
>
> In high school I was put in some lower level freshman English class along with some other friends; well, I will say that most of them were acquaintances, people I had considered mentally challenged from way back. And there I was sitting in the same classroom with them, learning the same boring lessons. Reality was harsh. It came down on me like a heavy coat that I could not shake off. I was embarrassed for myself—ashamed. *I can do better than this.* The teacher acted as if she had to lead the blind in sign language. This is an almost impossible task, she must have thought. Her attitude toward us was that we were too stupid to help, and we were wasting her precious time with our lack of enthusiasm for the written word.

Part of our weekly assignment was to write short one-page essays on some topic of choice. One day, I got up from my desk and walked to hers to ask her a question about my paper. I pointed out my problem, and, while I was standing there waiting for her advice, she noticed something magical in a sentence I had written, some light that had broken a seam through the darkness she and I shared in that classroom.

The next day I was removed from that class by my guidance counselor and placed in a more advanced English course. I was now somehow completely exempt from taking freshman composition, a course required of all students at Davison High, at least for those who didn't test out of it—which many did not. My new class was called "Novels and Short Stories." The teacher seemed more lively, more involved and enthusiastic about getting in front of the class and speaking to a bunch of upper-classmen and a few advanced students. In my previous English classes the teachers usually sat behind their desks assigning lessons to keep us quiet. There was one teacher who I didn't think left his desk once, except to take me out in the hall and verbally smack me with suspension if I didn't stop doing whatever it was that made his thin neck break out in hives.

At any rate, we were actually assigned books to read in my new class. This was the first time I had ever been told to read a book in school. I have to say I was a little overwhelmed by what Mr. Hardy asked of me. We even had to write a critique. To sit down and read a book, by myself. Man, what was I going to say? Where to start something like that, from the first page or what? *You mean you want me to read the whole thing?*

We read *To Kill a Mocking Bird, Animal Farm, Of Mice and Men,* and for my semester book report I read *The Hobbit.* Well actually I looked at the book and opted to see the movie instead. For short stories we read, "The Secret Life of Walter Mitty," and "To Build a Fire." I can't remember actually getting too involved in the books, working on plot and character development and such, but I finished all of them, and loved most of them—except *The Hobbit.* Maybe I was intimidated by the fact that someone was going to be "judging" my work. Would my ego be bruised if he did not like what I had to say, or if he had to correct my misunderstanding of the novel? On the other hand, maybe I was just too lazy to put that much concentration into a book, then turn around and try to interpret it to any great length. But I can still feel the wonder that floated around in that room. This was literature.

Rereading Michael's autoethnography now, I think of so many students I have known who have had the "heavy coat" of low-track classes weigh down on them, or who have never felt the "wonder" that can "float around" a literature classroom.

As I think about where I want to go next with the autoethnographic concept, I imagine trying to create ways to help students use interview and analysis to deepen their learning about the experience of people who are different from themselves. I am curious about how autoethnographic projects might work not just with aspiring English teachers, but in different classes and at other levels—middle school, high school, and college. I try to imagine how we might invite our students to experiment with ethnographic observation, interview, and writing. I wonder if, for example, high school students in low tracks might visit and interview students in upper tracks and write up their observations and commentary. Perhaps the same thing could be tried at the university level between different institutions or different locations within institutions, such as between remedial composition and honors students, for instance. As June Kuzmeskus indicates, autoethnographic literature may be helpful as students seek to find ways to value their own voice and experience. It is also vital that they connect that experience to larger forms of analysis, so that they can see the points of connection between the story Michael tells and, for instance, a "post-Marxist" analysis of the role of educational tracking and continued social and economic inequality.

Post-Marxism

Like poststructuralists, traditional Marxists believe that the way people think and believe, their "ideology," is not something that they freely choose. For Marxists, ideology is most basically the result of the economic structure of society, and changes in forms of thought derive from changes in fundamental and underlying economic realities. A class-based revolution of workers against owners provides the means by which both the material basis of society and its ideological superstructure can be made, in the Marxist view, truly democratic. For present purposes we do not need to take on either a full critique or defense of Marxist thought. The terrifying tyranny that Marxist revolutionary movements have often led to is self-evident (even if we forget the tyrannies that such revolutions replaced).

Yet by breaking with certain more rigid Marxist ideas such as the necessary determination of a social system by its economic structure, the inevitability of revolution, or the justice of a one-party state, many post-Marxist scholars continue to draw insight and inspiration from socialist thought while rejecting its oppressive aspects. A critique of capitalism and materialism, a focus on class and social inequality, and a recognition of the legitimate aspirations for "power to the people" in political, economic, and cultural spheres are powerful ideas that emerge from Marxist traditions. Drawing on these concerns, poststructuralist Marxists analyze discourses with an orientation

▶

toward exposing those that serve the interests of dominant groups, or "the hegemonic." They seek to develop alternative perspectives that bring forward the voices of marginal or oppressed groups, especially the poor and working class, as the "counter-hegemonic."

A post-Marxist approach to teaching might treat schools themselves as texts and ask students to explore the structure of curriculum and learning. High schools and universities quickly make tracking, textbooks, and literature anthologies appear "normal" and instill doubt, even fear, in those who would question the system. Yet, looking at ways in which literature, art, and the mass media serve the interests of particular social groups and exploring the voices and perspectives of oppressed people are, logically and ethically, central parts of good English language arts teaching. Every day, English teachers are engaged in many academically legitimate schemes along these lines. Projects like Rethinking Schools in Milwaukee help teachers learn about critical literacy and connect with each other. At the college level, there is a Marxist Literary Group within the Modern Language Association.

Teachers interested in this approach might, for example, help students examine the connection between academic tracking and economic classes in our society. In their autoethnographies my students report that students in upper-track high school English courses are given extensive writing assignments, are encouraged to use independent thinking, go beyond the textbook, and become prepared for college success, and that they usually have the most experienced teachers. Students in lower-track classes get worksheets, stick to the textbook, are trained to listen and follow the rules, and rarely go to college. They typically have the least experienced teachers. It might be valuable to use ethnographic projects to try to break down the barriers that limit contact between students in different tracks and try to learn about how life expectations become internalized. This kind of analysis of education often goes under the name "critical pedagogy" (see the suggested reading list at the end of the chapter).

My students' multigenre autoethnographies have wetted my appetite to experiment with the teaching possibilities inherent in different forms of poststructuralist analysis, that is, in postmodernism, deconstruction, and post-Marxism. I want to tease out strategies to combine personal writing with ethnographic projects leading to a richer understanding of self within cross-cultural contexts.

The fact that these questions, issues, and possibilities are the ones that are currently animating my teaching experiments makes me realize that it is appropriate to bring to an end this last chapter of stories about my own classroom.

Testimonials for the Classroom

- *Fire from the Mountain: The Making of a Sandinista,* by Sandinista guerrilla Omar Cabezas, tells a side of the story we don't usually hear. The book sheds light on revolutionary struggles.

- *Let Me Speak!: Testimony of Domitila, a Woman of the Bolivian Mines* by Domitila Barrios de Chungara is the story of the courageous wife of a Bolivian miner who witnesses the labor organization of some of the poorest people of Bolivia and also attends an international women's conference in the 1970s.

- *Life Among the Piutes: Their Wrongs and Claims* by Sarah Winnemucca Hopkins tells the story of the encounter between her people and white settlers in Nevada, Oregon, and Washington during the second half of the nineteenth century.

- *One Day of Life,* a recent novel from El Salvador, in which Manlio Argueta infuses elements of testimonial into the novel form to describe the Civil War from the viewpoint of a peasant family.

- *Rachel and Her Children: Homeless Families in America* by Jonathan Kozol compiles oral testimony from homeless families in New York—see discussion in Chapter 2.

- *To Destroy You Is No Loss: The Odyssey of a Cambodian Family* by Joan Criddle and Teeda Butt Mam is a testimony of an urban Cambodian family driven to the countryside by the Khmer Rouge dictatorship in 1975, where they become survivors of the "killing fields."

- *When Heaven and Earth Changed Places: A Vietnamese Woman's Journey from War to Peace* is the story of Le Ly Hayslip who grew up in a Vietnamese village during the war, fought as a Viet Cong, struggled to survive in Saigon, married an American, and then returned to Vietnam as a Vietnamese American in 1985.

- *Zlata's Diary: A Child's Life in Sarajevo* by Zlata Filipovic is an Anne Frank–like diary account of the war in Yugoslavia in the early 1990s.

- Two texts close to testimonial from South Africa are *Kaffir Boy* by Mark Mathabane, an autobiographical account of growing up under apartheid, and *The Testimony of Steve Biko*, testimony in the most legal sense. The film *Cry Freedom* could be a companion to either book.

- Film often has testimonial or documentary elements. The classic *Salt of the Earth* or the documentaries *Roger and Me; Harlan County, U.S.A.;* and *The Global Assembly Line* would work nicely with Chungara's *Let Me Speak* or Steinbeck's *The Grapes of Wrath.* There are several films available addressing Rigoberta Menchú, including *When the Mountains Tremble.*

- There are several books about testimonial narrative that may be of interest. These include the book Steve Benz and I edited, *Teaching and Testimony: Rigoberta Menchú in the North American Classroom*, Gugelberger's *The Real Thing: Testimonial Discourse and Latin America* (a collection of the most important essays on testimony up to 1996), and Arias's *The Rigoberta Menchú Controversy,* which responds to the questions and debate generated by Stoll's *Rigoberta Menchú and the Story of All Poor Guatemalans.*

Readings from Poststructuralism, Postmodernism, Deconstruction, and Post-Marxism

- *Acts of Literature,* a collection of some of Jacques Derrida's most influential writings, is one place to start with this controversial, famously difficult philosopher and founder of deconstruction.

- Michel Foucault's *Discipline and Punish: The Birth of the Prison* is a powerful and lucid examination of the historical development of social institutions, including the prison and the school, that teach people to be obedient and to internalize authority. The book would be a good introduction to Foucault's thought.

- "Ideology and Ideological State Apparatuses," an essay by Louis Althusser (in his book *Lenin and Philosophy*), elaborates the relationship of individuals to institutions and is an engaging and key text in the development of poststructuralist and post-Marxist thought.

- Sharon Crowley's *A Teacher's Introduction to Deconstruction,* written for composition teachers and focused on the implications of deconstruction for writing pedagogy, offers a lucid overview of Derrida's work. Crowley uses deconstruction to both validate and push the limits of process writing pedagogy.

- Stanley Fish's *Is There a Text in This Class?: The Authority of Interpretive Communities* examines the way in which identity and understanding are shaped by institutions, particularly literary institutions. It contains the wonderful essay "How to Recognize a Poem When You See One."

- Roland Barthes's *Mythologies* is a collection of essays by yet another interesting French philosopher crucial to the various forms of poststructuralist thought. This book addresses semiotics (the interpretation of sign systems) and Marxist ideological critique. It includes his famous essay on popular wrestling matches.

- Jonathan Culler's *On Deconstruction: Theory and Criticism After Structuralism* is an influential introduction to deconstruction and poststructuralist theory. Written fairly early on, the book addresses European theorists, psychoanalysis, linguistics, and reader response critics to consider their perspectives on reading and criticism.

- *Outside Literature* by Tony Bennett is an accessible and extended analysis of literature, aesthetics, and criticism from a post-Marxist perspective.

- *The Postmodern Condition: A Report on Knowledge* by Jean François Lyotard is a famous seventy-five page essay on technology, language games, social bonds, and education—one of the defining texts of postmodern analysis.

- Fredric Jameson's *Postmodernism, Or, The Cultural Logic of Late Capitalism* is an extensive discussion of literature, video, film, and architecture by America's leading Marxist literary critic.

Readings in Critical Pedagogy

Many of these works are not only interesting for teachers but fascinating to students as well; they open up a variety of critical perspectives for classroom analysis of educational practices and institutions.

- *Critical Teaching and Everyday Life* by Ira Shor focuses on his experience of teaching composition in the community college.

- *Critical Teaching and the Idea of Literacy* by Cy Knoblauch and Lil Brannon provides a useful overview of theories of literacy instruction from a critical pedagogy perspective.

- Richard Ohmann's *English in America* is a study of the politics of university English departments. It includes a relevant chapter on high school AP English.

- Henry Giroux, often along with Peter McLaren, Stanley Aronowitz, or Patrick Shannon, has written and edited a series of powerful and increasingly theoretically dense books that critically examine education.

- *I Won't Learn from You* by Herbert Kohl is a persuasive essay on school failure.

- *Keeping Track: How Schools Structure Inequality* by Jeannie Oakes is a wonderfully readable analysis of what is wrong with ability grouping and tracking.

- Paulo Freire's *Pedagogy of the Oppressed*, an internationally influential analysis of the relation of classroom and society, is also an attempt by a Christian leftist in the 1970s to instruct Latin American revolutionaries on how not to impose politically correct ideas.

- *Rethinking Schools* is a newspaper written by and for teachers emphasizing social justice and antiracist approaches. The Rethinking Schools Collective in Milwaukee also has a variety of publications in the same vein, including *Rethinking Columbus* and *Rethinking Classrooms*.

- *Schooling in Capitalist America: Educational Reform and the Contradictions of Economic Life* by Samuel Bowles and Herbert

Gintis is a persuasive history of American education from a socialist perspective.

- Michael Apple's *Teachers and Texts: A Political Economy of Class and Gender Relations in Education* includes an analysis of the effect of the textbook industry on the English curriculum.

- bell hooks's *Teaching to Transgress: Education as the Practice of Freedom* draws on Freire's work and uses powerful personal stories to examine the influence of race relations and feminism in the college classroom.

Web Sites to Support Critical Pedagogy and Progressive Teaching

- The Critical Project is a collection of online materials and links to other Web sites. Its URL is http://www.wvu.edu/~lawfac/jelkins/critproj/opening.html.

- The Web site of the Gay, Lesbian, and Straight Education Network is located at http://www.glstn.org/.

- The online *Journal of Critical Pedagogy* maintains a Web site at http://www.lib.wmc.edu/pub/jcp/jcp.html.

- The National Education Association has a large site: http://www.nea.org/index.html.

- The Network of Educators on the Americas publishes a catalog of multicultural, antiracist materials for teachers titled "Teaching for Change." See http://www.teachingforchange.org/.

- The Paulo Freire Institute Web site can be found at http://www.paulofreire.org/principal-i.htm.

- The Rethinking Schools Online site offers publications, links to other sites, and the text of the current issue of *Rethinking Schools*. See http://www.rethinkingschools.org/.

- The Web site for *Teaching Tolerance* magazine, published by the Southern Poverty Law Center, can be found at http://www.splcenter.org/cgi-bin/goframe.pl?refname=/teachingtolerance/tt-1.html.

- A Web site titled Critical Pedagogy offers a bibliography of online critical pedagogy essays: http://www.cudenver.edu/~mryder/itc_data/crit_ped.html.

English Teacher Professional Autobiographies

- Tom Romano's books, *Clearing the Way: Working with Teenage Writers* and *Writing with Passion: Life Stories, Multiple Genres*, are inspiring and highly readable narratives of a classroom writing teacher helping students find their voices.

- *The Freedom Writers Diary: How a Teacher and 150 Teens Used Writing to Change Themselves and the World Around Them* is a collection of journal entries by Erin Gruwell, a dynamic new teacher, and her students, "The Freedom Writers." Inner-city "at-risk" students in Long Beach, California, are inspired and transformed by connecting the diaries of Anne Frank and Zlata Filipovic and other autobiographical works to their own lives.

- *In the Middle* by Nancie Atwell is a testimony to the writing workshop as a teaching method. Set in a small town in Maine, Atwell's book clearly explains how she sets up and runs workshops with middle school students. First published in 1987, it was substantially rewritten in 1998.

- *It's Never Too Late: Leading Adolescents to Lifelong Literacy* by Janet Allen tells the story of her low-track ninth-grade classroom in a small town in Maine and her efforts to incorporate whole language principles into the teaching of reading.

- *June Jordan's Poetry for the People: A Revolutionary Blueprint,* edited by Lauren Muller, documents the dynamic, multicultural, and community-based poetry writing program at the University of California at Berkeley.

- *Just Teach Me, Mrs. K.: Talking, Reading and Writing with Resistant Adolescent Learners* by Mary Mercer Krogness tells the story of an experienced elementary teacher who takes on at-risk and largely minority seventh- and eighth-grade students in Shaker Heights, Ohio. The book features classroom strategies including speaking, drama, literature, writing, and assessment.

- *Lives on the Boundary: A Moving Account of the Struggles and Achievements of America's Educational Underclass* tells Mike Rose's personal and deeply committed story of teaching poor and working-class students in secondary school, night school, and college.

- Linda Rief's *Seeking Diversity: Language Arts with Adolescents* documents the middle school classroom of a New Hampshire writing project teacher; it includes lots of student writing and art.

- Samuel Freedman's *Small Victories: The Real World of a Teacher, Her Students, and Their High School* tells the story of Jessica Siegel, an outstanding high school English teacher whom Freedman, a journalist, followed during the 1987–1988 school year. The book chronicles the struggles and successes of her diverse, inner-city students.

- *Sometimes a Shining Moment: The Foxfire Experience* by Eliot Wigginton is one of the best books about teaching English. Wigginton and his rural Georgia students pioneered the *Foxfire* magazine, a community-based, student-written publication (with cultural studies aspects) that continues to affect the profession.

Readers must learn about Wigginton's criminal behavior (see "A Trust Betrayed" by Debra Viadero, *Education Week*, November 17, 1993). In short, Wigginton was found to have molested some of his students—a terrible crime, and his rising star quickly crashed. Yet his work with *Foxfire* was most admirable, and I encourage teachers to look at *Sometimes a Shining Moment* for themselves.

- *Will My Name be Shouted Out?* by Stephen O'Connor tells the story of a powerful year spent as a playwright and author-in-the-schools at an inner-city New York middle school.

8 Conclusion

Cultural studies provides the opportunity for educators and other cultural workers to rethink and transform how schools, teachers, and students define themselves as political subjects capable of exhibiting critical sensibilities, civic courage, and forms of solidarity rooted in a strong commitment to freedom and democracy.

Henry Giroux, *Border Crossings: Cultural Workers and the Politics of Education*

The idea of changing the curriculum or of learning about literary scholarship and theory is intimidating because we are, already, too busy. There is never enough time to cover the material *already* in the textbook or anthology. There is never enough time to cover all the skills that students need to learn. There is never enough time, money, or flexibility to add new books to the curriculum. There is never enough time to plan teaching, grade papers, and meet with colleagues. There is never enough time to take graduate courses, to attend conferences, to read and write on one's own.

Literature and Lives does not seek to add to the time drain on us or to represent the last word about what literature teaching is all about. Nor do I think that the new ideas, materials, or cutting-edge teaching described in this book can or should be put in place in one swoop. Each of us must examine our own values and beliefs, and, working within the context in which we find ourselves, we must evolve and make changes with the materials that come to hand. Large effects come from small changes. Alterations add up and eventually become whole new ways of doing things. A different conception of goals and purposes changes the way that books are read. New fields of interest suddenly allow students and teachers to link familiar works in vivid and surprising ways. A relatively small amount of supplemental material may cause whole new paradigms to emerge and may create new bridges between literature and student lives.

As my own approach to teaching has developed and changed, the process has actually ended up giving energy rather than draining it away. I am convinced that an awareness of the dramatic developments in literary theory and scholarship will be revitalizing for others as well.

While literature teaching in the new century will be significantly different from that of the past, I want to state clearly that the changes we are currently undergoing represent an evolutionary process rather than a radical break from a static tradition. Change in our profession has been continuous and ongoing. The way we teach and think about literature in the present is significantly different from how it was in the past—more different, perhaps, than many of us realize. American literature and even English literature are themselves relatively new as school subjects, becoming literatures of instruction only 80 and 150 years ago, respectively. The content of the so-called "canon" has always been in flux.

Moreover, even when they explicitly declare themselves alternatives to past traditions, new scholarly and pedagogical approaches build on those that came before, sometimes more deeply than they acknowledge. And rather than traditional authors such as Homer, Shakespeare, or Twain being jettisoned in favor of more contemporary ones, the future of English studies, I expect, will not so much abandon today's canon but pluralize and complexify it. Rather than a simple "adding on," the pluralizing of the tradition not only introduces new materials and approaches, but also asks us to significantly change the way in which "great works" themselves are taught and understood, and thus to help our students become more conscious of the way knowledge and authority come into being. It is not so much that our students need to be entertained—though some have seen it this way—but that they need to understand the purpose and meaning of what they are doing if we are going to succeed at keeping them engaged.

I am convinced that Henry Giroux is right (in the passage above) not just about cultural studies, but more profoundly in the notion that the very perpetuation of democracy depends significantly on what we do in English classrooms. The new developments in literary theory and literature study have the potential to make English teaching more relevant to students both individually, in their quest to understand the world, and collectively, as they fulfill responsibilities as national and global citizens. As we have seen in this book, the developments in literature study over the last few decades promise to expand the canon, enlarge the objects of our attention, and transform what we do and how we think about it. In this sense, all of the new forms of literary criticism that we have explored in the context of my own teaching contribute to developing our students' "cultural literacy" in a way that is deeper and more meaningful than any abstracted list of "great books" or "important facts."

The new approaches open many doors, making our jobs as English teachers both more complex and more interesting—and of potentially greater impact. Perhaps it is this very potential for impact that has generated some of the public controversies about the new literary theories and texts. While controversy is not always productive, these recent debates over the content and purposes of English can serve to energize our teaching. If invited in, controversy can become, under the direction of a good teacher, an animating and motivating force for dialogue and continued learning. Gerald Graff suggests that the best way to respond to different approaches to literature is to "teach the conflicts." Yet the conflicts we need to teach are not only about approaches to scholarship, but also about the many and deep conflicts in our society that touch our students' and our own lives.

You have seen how I am trying to integrate the developments in literature criticism and theory into my English teaching. The ways in which your students will engage the conflicts of our time is significantly in your hands.

Appendix A: Letter Exchange with a First-Year Teacher

Subject: Are you there?
Date: Fri, 20 Nov 1998 06:35:49-0500 (EST)
From: Jjoh114213@aol.com
To: allen.careywebb@wmich.edu

Dear Allen,

I don't know if you're still at this email address. Or, you may be on sabbatical leave, if I remember correctly. Nevertheless, I figured I'd try to reach you anyway.

I hope you haven't forgotten me! Jackie Johnson. (Tall, confused black girl!) :) I intern taught at Loy Norrix High School? Yeah, me! How are you?

I'm not doing so well. I'm down here in Greensboro, North Carolina, teaching at Lincoln Middle School. I have seventh graders. I teach Language Arts and Social Studies (yes, they stuck me with an area I know absolutely nothing about!).

I got my wish . . . I'm teaching in the inner city. The school is in one of the worst areas in the city. Our student population is 97% minority. The faculty is 98% minority. I enjoy working with my students and I love my colleagues. The principal is okay. He's a push-over, but he loves people . . . especially our "exceptional" children at Lincoln.

Despite the fact that I enjoy living here in the South where it's nice and warm, I hate teaching. I don't like using that word but I do feel that strongly about my career choice. It's too much work. I was not prepared for this workload. I'm up late every night grading papers and getting lesson plans together. Then I'm up early the next morning meeting with parents before school. Then there are the boring, pointless staff meetings, which are really "bitch sessions." I have no time for myself.

I realize I'm overwhelmed since it's my first year teaching, but my mentor teacher, Janet, who has been teaching for eleven years now, says my situation may or may not change, depending on how much I put into my career. She told me she hasn't read a book or written in her journal in ten years!

I'm considering resigning at the end of the school year and going back to school to find a different career. My once passionate love for teaching has dwindled down to mere survival.

If you receive this message, please give me some words of encouragement so that I have a prayer of making it to Christmas.

Please tell me it gets better!

Sincerely,
Jackie Johnson

Subject: RE: Are you there?
Date: Mon, 23 Nov 1998 04:28:33-2300
From: allen.careywebb@wmich.edu
To: JJoh817194@aol.com

Dear Jackie,

Thanks so much for writing.

I know something of what you must be going through. After the second month of my first year I also decided I wasn't coming back. The next August I think the only reason I signed the contract again was that I was so disappointed in my performance that I wanted to prove to myself that I didn't have to be a complete failure.

Not much of a reason to stick with it, was it?

You talk about being overwhelmed with work. I know what you mean. Five classes a day, some of them in subjects I didn't know well, students with tremendous needs bombarding me every moment—some of the students outright hostile—papers to grade, almost no time to reflect on what I was doing, let alone time for myself . . . yes, teaching middle school or high school English is an awesome undertaking.

In a way I agree with Janet. There are teachers, some of them very fine teachers, who work so hard at teaching that it swallows them up entirely. It is also true that often these same people can come out of balance and, in the long run, that can hurt their teaching, not to mention their private lives.

There are also teachers who are basically burned out, do the minimum amount of work, and stick with poor methods just because they are easier. (We both know a teacher like that; I don't need to mention her name.) It is hard for me to believe that this burnout doesn't carry over into their private lives as well . . .

Where I disagree with Janet is that I believe there are ways to lead a balanced life, not be overwhelmed with work, and also be a great teacher.

Though it is true that such a goal is hardest to achieve in the first year, even in the first year you have to have some kind of balance.

You said that the word "survival" is replacing your "passion for teaching." You know what? In my opinion your own survival is a perfectly good goal to aim at this year. Survival is enough for right now.

You have survived the semester so far and now just take it a week, a day, even, one class period at a time and try to hold on till Christmas. Don't think about whether or not you will teach again next year; you can make that decision later. Don't try to be the world's greatest teacher—save that for the future. For now, just survive.

If you have a good moment in your class even just once a week or with just one student that is really something to celebrate and to tell other people about—no matter that the rest of the time seems like chaos and disappointment. Find those good moments and give yourself credit for them. You deserve it, and as you clearly recognize, you are working hard to make those moments happen.

I think it is a good sign that you can still enjoy your students and that you like your colleagues. I remember when I was new I found it difficult to talk with my fellow teachers about my frustrations; I didn't want to give them the impression that I was doing a bad job and I didn't know exactly who I should trust.

Bob Hamm, the teacher whose room was next to mine, occasionally invited me out after school for a beer and a talk. I wonder if he knows to this day how precious those conversations were to me.

My poor family and friends must have been sick of hearing about school and my students! It seemed like that was all I could talk about—and that I couldn't stop talking. I realize now how much I needed them to simply listen.

The main thing you mention in your letter is the amount of work. There are no magical answers. Here are four suggestions:

1) You mention staying up every night grading papers. I suggest that you don't read all, or even most, of your student's writing. Just as a good track coach does not have to comment every time a javelin thrower practices tossing a javelin, a good teacher doesn't have to read all of her student's writing. Writing takes practice and not all of that practice can or should be closely scrutinized. Many assignments can just be checked off.

When you do read student writing, remember responding to what they are saying is more important than correcting their errors. Just a few words of human response and good listening on an occasional assignment can do a great deal to encourage students to keep writing—and that is the real goal, isn't it?

I imagine that your students have many problems in their writing, right? Remember the research that shows that writing lots of comments on their papers or doing whole class grammar exercises is not very helpful. Mini-lessons, carefully targeted comments, and writing practice are likely to be the most important—and these don't have to take up a great deal of your preparation time.

Remember also that students are more likely to have homework done if you collect it from them personally and individually at the beginning of the period (rather than picking it up after class or just having them pass papers to the front).

2) Borrow lesson plans, worksheets, activities from other teachers even if they might not be the greatest or especially relevant to what you are doing. A perfectly reasonable question to ask a colleague is: do you have any worksheets, assignments, or activities that you have used that I could try? Experimenting in this way doesn't require much preparation time either and is a good way to get ideas. It helps you develop rapport with other teachers as well.

In my first year I felt like I was going through a dark tunnel. I didn't know what was coming next or how it related to what came before. I didn't know where I was going and I didn't have any clue about whether there was light at the end or not. Developing materials, and building a really good thematically integrated cultural studies curriculum at the right level for your students takes years of experience; don't feel you have to be there already.

3) Allow yourself to have some classes that don't require much planning on your part. Sometimes such classes are more valuable than those you slave over.

One of the best things you can do as a new teacher is just have a few class periods where you and students talk with each other in an open way about things that are on your mind or theirs. Issues in the news, in their lives, or at school, for example. Telling stories about yourself, your experiences in high school and college can be very valuable to your students. Whether they admit it or not, they are looking to you as a role model. These conversations may be equally or more important than the official curriculum; they can also create jumping off points for important writing and learning.

Reading aloud to students is a good way to spend a class period. Most students enjoy being read to and they learn about written language in this way. If you can find the right book, you might even set up a regular schedule for reading it a chapter at a time. Short stories work well. Remember having students spend time in class simply reading on their own is a good utilization of the period. Writing in class and writing workshops are also important and a perfectly valid way to put class time to use. (Of course, as I am sure you have already found out, these activities do require classroom management, students to bring their materials, etc. . . .) Nancie Atwell's book *In the Middle* is a great resource for using writing workshops in middle school, and it is a quick read.

There is no shame in showing the occasional movie, especially if you can integrate it into what you are doing. Many educational films are not all that great, but when I was a new teacher I tried them all. I don't know if your school has a computer lab or language arts software; if so, experimenting with computers might be interesting. I found word processing programs a great help for kids with writing difficulties.

But don't get involved in activities or lessons that will eat up your time. I learned, for example, that while I thought guest speakers or field trips might take some of the pressure off, it was a lot more work to have someone come to my class or try to arrange a trip than to hold class as usual.

4) Jackie, above all, take time for yourself. Keeping yourself physically, mentally, and emotionally healthy is vital to maintaining your poise, energy, and attentiveness as a teacher. One of the most important things you can do, in my opinion, is to bring some of your own joy in life to your students. It is pretty hard to do this when you are stressed out, isn't it?

The topic of your own reading and writing is one point where I disagree with your colleague Janet. I have found it very important to keep reading and writing. I think it has been more valuable to my students that I do this— and that I talk with them about my reading and writing—than that I spend the same time grading their papers or, even preparing lessons. Students will pay more attention to what you do than what you say.

I know it is hard to carve out the time, but your own sanity must be your number one priority.

I don't know if it is any comfort, but whether or not you leave the profession, I suspect that the time you are in right now, the last couple of months of your first semester, is likely to be the absolute bottom. It was for me.

I don't really have any magic story about myself or any "silver bullets" that will make teaching easy.

I can tell you, Jackie, that I know you well and that I have tremendous faith in you. Of the many, many teachers I know, I am completely confident that Jackie Johnson has exactly what it takes to become, in time, one of the truly greats.

I imagine it doesn't feel like that now.

You might be interested in some educational research that shows that it is often the most sensitive, imaginative, and intelligent new teachers who have the greatest frustration and disappointment at the beginning of their careers. Do you know why?

To me the answer is clear: it is because these teachers can visualize what really good teaching ought to be like, and they can also, at the same time, see very clearly how far short of this goal their own teaching is falling.

Ironically, it is the potentially best teachers who are often the ones to leave the profession. Should you leave, Jackie, you would be in this category.

I think this is what really killed me and made me want to quit when I was at your point in teaching.

At times it felt like it was the amount of work, but, deep down, it really wasn't the overwhelming work or the stress on my personal life. It was the just plain fact staring me in the face every day and almost every class period: I was not a good teacher.

Hard as it was, I could survive the work (barely), but what was I to make of the fact that even with my incredible efforts I was not only not helping my students, I was, indeed, at times, actually damaging them?

I had started teaching because I wanted to help kids, but the truth was, and no one knew this better than I—even my colleagues and friends who tried to encourage me—my classes were, very often, a true disaster. The students didn't seem to want to learn. They wouldn't do the work and I was lucky to even get them to sit down and listen every once in a while.

My classes were a disaster and, not only that, I couldn't be myself. I was turning into just the kind of rigid, unfeeling, and uptight teacher that I precisely dreaded. At times I hated myself for not being able to control the class, for losing my cool, for demanding too much (or not enough) from my students, for not being able to respond to students as a person because I was too busy trying to figure out how to take the damn attendance. I found myself trying to force students to jump through the hoops of a boring, irrelevant curriculum that, to tell the truth, I didn't even believe in.

I saw that I was starting to blame the students for my own failure. Yet I couldn't see any way to do it differently given the situation I was in. All I could see ahead of me in this teaching career that I had wanted so much was work, frustration, and a sense that I was, at some profound level, a failure.

Since you know me now and have been my student, I hope you agree that it didn't turn out that way. The joy and meaning that teaching has brought me, in time, is something that I could barely have guessed at in those dark days of the first year. I realize now that eighteen years ago I was awfully young to try to confront the monumental challenge of teaching.

Learning about my students, the classroom, and myself that first year was like trying to drink out of a fire hydrant, with the full force of the water hitting me in the face.

Now it is almost too easy for me to say that there was also something wonderful about that first year, even about the way I was overwhelmed and frustrated. I learned so much, including a solid dose of humility. I did some wonderful and good things despite my shortcomings, and, I am still around to tell the story. In the years that have followed I have kept learning, growing, and changing. The story is still far from over; I guess in my own writing about teaching I am still trying to tell it.

Jackie, I am sorry that I have written so long a letter to you. I realize you will barely have time to read it. But I want you to know that you are important to me and that you are having impacts on your students this year that you can't yet begin to appreciate. Should you stay in teaching your influence will be beyond measure.

Yours,
Allen

Subject: Thanks, so much!
Date: Sun, 06 Dec 1998 21:58:41 -0500 (EST)
From: JJoh817194@aol.com
To: careywebb@wmich.edu

I'm so glad I was able to get in touch with you. Thank you for writing back.

I can't begin to thank you enough for the positive messages and the suggestions. I needed to hear those things.

I appreciate you sharing your past experiences with me. I can't believe you faced some of the difficulties I am! I look at you now as Allen, the awesome professor, and find it hard to picture you as a struggling teacher like me.

I guess it does take work, huh? I am too hard on myself. I want to be the best NOW.

I've tried some of your suggestions. For one, I've checked homework at the beginning of class. I went around the room with my grade book and gave credit to those who did the assignment. That worked well. I checked journal entries on Friday during my plan period instead of taking them all home with me over the weekend. I have three plan periods, so I was able to still read them thoroughly. That's one of my highlights of the week . . . reading their daily entries. Their ways of thinking are of great interest to me.

I can't believe I didn't have any work to take home with me over the weekend! I did all of my lesson plans for the upcoming week during my plan periods, too, so I'm all set to go tomorrow. I set time aside just for me this weekend. I went to dinner with my teacher buddies and we went to one of the college basketball games last night. Today we caught a movie. I even wrote in my journal this morning after breakfast! I was so excited! I must have written ten pages. The last entry was dated September 10th!!!! I had a lot of catching up to do! I feel so much better now!

Despite the very positive week I've had, I'm still feeling uneasy. I know things won't happen overnight, but I'm still doubting my decision to become a teacher. Something just doesn't feel right. I can't put my finger on it, but I'm still not happy about going to work in the morning. I chose a career so that I could enjoy going to work everyday . . . maybe even look forward to it. I don't feel that with this teaching job.

I don't want to give up on my dream just yet, but I can't help but feel that this just isn't my niche in life.

I've been checking out graduate programs around here in Greensboro. I want to keep my options open. I don't want to trap myself into a profession I don't like, but at the same time, I don't want to throw in the towel too soon.

Hmmm. . . .

Well, thanks again for listening. I hope things are going well for you.

Where are you now? How's your family? Please keep in touch. Take care.

With thanks,

Jackie

Postscript: Later in the year, Jackie Johnson left her position in North Carolina, but she did not abandon her ambition to teach English. She has subsequently accepted employment as a high school English teacher in a school near Chicago.

Appendix B: A Note to Teachers on the Truth of Rigoberta Menchú's Testimonial

In 1999, David Stoll, in *Rigoberta Menchú and the Story of All Poor Guatemalans,* claimed that Rigoberta Menchú, winner of the 1992 Nobel Peace Prize, falsified facts about herself in her 1983 testimony, the account that first brought her to world attention. Moreover, Stoll argued that liberal university professors who supported the Guatemalan resistance movement had embraced Menchú's story without question. When Stoll's book was published, *The New York Times* ran a front page article questioning Menchú's integrity, and the controversy entered the popular press. Although many editorial writers picked up the tone of Stoll's criticism, a collection of essays by established experts on Guatemala and Menchú's testimony was published a year later; edited by Arturo Arias and titled *The Rigoberta Menchú Controversy,* it seriously challenged Stoll's data, inferences, and conclusions. (I wrote a chapter in that book describing the skepticism, difficulties, and critical reflections that Menchú's testimony often evokes in the classroom.)

David Stoll is a professional anthropologist who, over the course of ten years, interviewed Guatemalans and undertook archival research focused on identifying errors, exaggerations, shortcomings, and bias in Menchú's testimony. In contrast, Menchú gave her testimony without notes in twenty-four hours of taped conversation over an eight-day period when she was twenty-three years old, not long after the murder of her father, mother, and brother, and her escape to Mexico. Her testimony was recorded, transcribed, reorganized, and published by Elizabeth Burgos-Debray, another anthropologist, who is the book's legal author (and who receives the substantial royalties the testimony has generated). In the course of his research, Stoll never interviewed Menchú herself.

In considering the controversy it is important to carefully examine the charges David Stoll has actually made. An attentive reading of Stoll's book, *Rigoberta Menchú and the Story of All Poor Guatemalans,* makes it clear that the initial press reports on his research were sensationalistic.

While the *New York Times* claimed that Rigoberta Menchú "fabricated," "seriously exaggerated," and told "one lie after another" in her testimonial, the surprising fact is that Stoll's research, on the contrary, serves to affirm the truth of Menchú's story on all of its major points, and certainly on those points that are most relevant to the vast majority of American teachers and students who have worked with Menchú's testimonial.

Stoll prefaces his book by asserting that there is "no doubt about the most important points" Menchú makes (viii). Moreover, despite press reports about requests to the Nobel Prize Committee to rescind Menchú's Peace Prize after the *Times* article, Stoll states that awarding the Nobel Prize to Rigoberta Menchú was a "good idea" and that "she has been the first to acknowledge that she received it, not for her own accomplishments but because she stands for a wider group of people who deserve international support" (ix). (The prize was awarded to Menchú not for her testimony but for her subsequent political work and peace organizing.)

Specifically, Stoll's research leads him to corroborate the following information in Menchú's 1983 testimony:

1. Rigoberta Menchú's father was burned alive when the army attacked the Spanish Embassy he was occupying to protest human rights abuses, an occurrence that is widely known in Guatemala. Stoll believes Menchú's account of the events at the embassy is more balanced than most others (Stoll 80).

2. Rigoberta Menchú's mother was detained, raped, tortured, and killed, and her body was mutilated by the Guatemalan army. Rigoberta Menchú's gruesome description of what happened to her mother is corroborated by independent sources (127).

3. Rigoberta Menchú's sixteen-year-old brother Petrocino was seized, tortured, and shot by the army, and his mutilated body was left in the street of the town of Chajul. Rigoberta Menchú reports that her brother was burned alive; Stoll argues he may have been burned after he was killed, but that it "was not rare" for the army to humiliate, torture, and burn people alive in front of their families (70).

4. Rigoberta Menchú's village, Chimel, was attacked by the army, and the villagers used self-defense strategies to protect themselves, much as Menchú describes (129).

5. Rigoberta Menchú's two younger sisters did join the guerrillas after the murder of their mother (130).

6. Ladinos in the highlands near Menchú's village were, at least during the war, closely associated with the army and with attacks on indigenous people and on Menchú's family (136).

7. Guatemalans regard Menchú's testimonial as a "truthful portrayal of their country" (246).

David Stoll's research also adds information that Menchú does not include in her testimony:

1. The military coup in Guatemala in 1954 was "organized" by the U.S. government, through the CIA, to overthrow a popularly elected government. This military coup can be held directly responsible for a loss of political development, for the country's economic collapse and military violence, and for the revolutionary movement. Had the coup not taken place, Stoll believes Guatemala "could have evolved in the direction of Costa Rica, which leads Latin America in per capita income and political stability" (46).

2. Rigoberta Menchú's village was completely destroyed by the Guatemalan army not long after her testimony was recorded.

3. Rigoberta Menchú's brother Victor was shot and killed by the army after peacefully turning himself in (135).

4. Rigoberta Menchú's sister-in-law was killed and her nieces, aged three and five, were starved to death while in army custody (134–136).

5. Rigoberta Menchú's closest friend at school, Bernadina Us Hernández, was killed by the army, as were Bernadina's father, her brother (in front of the family), and six other male family members (46).

6. Stoll documents many other murders of innocent indigenous people in the region Menchú comes from, using words such as "slaughter," "massacre," and "Holocaust."

7. The international pressure that Menchú and her testimony created led, eventually, to negotiation between the guerrillas and the government and to a reduction in the power of the army—in Stoll's words, "quite an achievement" (278).

8. In the 1990s, Rigoberta Menchú had become a powerful leader for reconciliation between a wide cross section of constituencies in Guatemala and was considered a possible candidate for presidency of the country.

There are several points on which Stoll continues to dispute with Menchú's 1983 testimonial. Menchú herself has responded to several of these points:

1. Testimonies from other Guatemalans indicate that Rigoberta Menchú's brother was not burned alive (after being tortured and before being killed) and that Menchú herself was not present when his body was dumped in the street outside Chajul. Menchú responds that her testimony repeats the firsthand account her

mother gave her and that, until she is presented with the evidence of her brother's body itself, she will continue to believe her mother. Independent human rights records do record the public burning of indigenous people by the army in Chajul at roughly the same period. (See *Guatemala!: The Horror and the Hope* [1982], edited by Rarihokwats.)

2. Based on conversations with neighbors and on archives in the national land office, Stoll argues that Rigoberta Menchú's father was involved in a land dispute not with Ladinos but with relatives of Rigoberta Menchú's mother, the Tums. Rigoberta Menchú responds that her family believed that Ladinos had secretly bought the land from some members of the Tum family and were using their Quiché names in the dispute as a front. While Stoll elaborates disputes between indigenous Guatemalans over land, he does not mention that the vast majority of land in Guatemala is in the hands of a tiny minority of Ladino elite and that only 10% of rural families have enough land to live on (Pratt 62).

3. Stoll argues that Rigoberta Menchú was a student in a junior high boarding school for three years, an experience she does not mention in her 1982 account. Menchú responds that she did not speak about the school in 1982 because she wanted to protect it from reprisals by the army. (Stoll mentions that the school was surrounded at various times by the army, that students were interrogated, and that Menchú's best friend at the school was killed by the army—thus making credible Menchú's stated reason for not mentioning it.) Menchú also explains that she was on a charity scholarship at the school that only allowed her three hours of classes per day and the rest of her time was spent cleaning the school as a servant.

4. Stoll claims that Rigoberta Menchú's brother Nicholas could not have died from malnutrition as she claims in her testimonial because he met her brother Nicholas alive and well in Guatemala. Rigoberta explains that her father was married twice and named two different sons "Nicholas," a common tradition among native Guatemalans. She maintains that it was the first Nicholas who did, indeed, die of malnutrition.

5. Stoll can find no evidence of the death of Petrona Chona on the coffee plantation where he believes Rigoberta Menchú might have worked (Menchú reports Petrona Chona's killing by the landowner's son when she refuses his amorous advances). Stoll does find evidence of the death of a "Pascuala Xoná Chomo," whose husband was accused of killing her based on rumors of a relationship with the landowner's son.

6. Stoll can find no specific evidence supporting Rigoberta Menchú's claim of having worked on coffee and sugar plantations or as a maid in the capital. Aside from wondering how Menchú could have fit these activities in with everything else she was doing,

Stoll offers no evidence to refute Menchú's account. He corroborates that many indigenous Guatemalans do work on these plantations and that Menchú's description of working conditions is accurate. Menchú describes these conditions as abject, exploitative, abusive, and violent.

7. Stoll blames the revolutionary guerrillas for the violence of the army. He cites several instances where the Guatemalan army was helpful to native Guatemalans, yet he doesn't dispute human rights reports that blame the army for the murder of 100,000 innocent indigenous Guatemalans.

8. Stoll believes that Rigoberta Menchú's testimonial portrays indigenous Guatemalans as more sympathetic to the guerrilla movement than they actually were. He bases his belief on interviews nearly ten years after the events Menchú describes. This is a point of contention that scholars more qualified than I am respond to in *The Rigoberta Menchú Controversy*. Yet, it seems obvious to me that after ten years of unbelievably harsh repression of indigenous people by the Guatemalan army—a period during which any mention of sympathy or support for guerrillas lead to almost certain death not just of individuals, but also of entire families and villages—it is not surprising that Stoll does not find many indigenous Guatemalans who tell him of their support for armed rebellion.

In conclusion, though David Stoll argues that Rigoberta Menchú "romanced" her story to favor the guerrillas, an examination of his book and of the evidence on this question reveals Stoll's position as a matter of narrow, unbalanced, and even bizarre interpretation. While Stoll raises issues that may be appropriate to take up in particular classroom contexts, it is, frankly—given Menchú's and other scholars' responses to his arguments, and the minor points of factual disagreement that remain—hard for me to see how David Stoll's book could have relevance to the vast majority of American teachers and students. An examination of the controversy it stirred up might, perhaps, be useful as a study of the mass media's fascination with personalities, its penchant for character assassination, and its failure to address fundamental social, political, historical, and economic issues. In contrast stands Rigoberta Menchú's testimony itself, still a most valuable classroom text and resource for encountering and exploring some of the most profound and disturbing realities of our time.

Appendix C: Philology

Both before and during the heyday of New Criticism, there were many other rich and pedagogically relevant schools of scholarship. Perhaps the founding approach to the study of literature is the tradition called philology ("love of language") which emphasized the study of European and Classical (Latin and Greek) languages and literatures within and across national and ethnic perspectives. Philologists might be less interested in, say, metaphor or irony and more interested in the relationship of language to cultural identity, the development of literary cultures from oral and folk traditions, and the evolution of Modern forms from Classical antecedents. There are interesting points of contact between traditional philology and contemporary multiculturalism. While philologists took interest in myths, folk literature, drama, and especially epics, they also came to concern themselves with all forms of literary expression within the rich European literary heritage.

Enormously learned scholars like Friedrich von Schlegel (1772–1829) developed German Romanticism and pioneered literary interpretation and criticism in the Greek, German, Italian, Spanish, Portuguese, Nordic, English, and French languages. The Frenchman Hippolyte Taine (1828–1893) demonstrated how texts reflect national and individual identities and particular periods. More contemporary philologists such as Erich Auerbach (1892–1957) and Leo Spitzer (1887–1960) combine an encyclopedic knowledge of languages and literatures with interests in political philosophy, psychology, aesthetic theory, and linguistics. If philology typically strove for a comparative and internationalist perspective, it also lent itself too easily, as it became institutionalized during the period of late nineteenth-century nation building and colonialism, to chauvinistic nationalism, to the creation of mythic ethnic pasts, "unified" linguistic cultures, and European racial superiority. Edward Said's book *Orientalism* explores the ways in which this older tradition of cultural scholarship, along with other disciplines such as anthropology, tended to accept and perpetuate derogatory conceptions of non-Europeans.

The influence of philology continues to be felt, however, in literature curriculums. Courses that focus on mythology and folk tales, and textbooks that include epics like *The Odyssey* and *Beowulf,* are indebted to a philological tradition, not to New Criticism. A philological approach to teaching literature, then, emphasizes a knowledge of linguistic and national origins, cultural traditions, and the development of genres rather than literary skill in close reading of complex texts. While much broader than New Criticism in its range of interests, it tends, like New Criticism, to have a White, Eurocentric, nationalistic, and highly traditional bias in its choice of texts—and an unself-critical acceptance of categories of literature and nation. Are nations ever as culturally unified or self-contained as "national literary traditions" represent them to be? Does it really make sense, for example, to consider Old English oral poetry as a starting point for English literary traditions, when such poetry remained virtually unknown until the end of the nineteenth century? Or to do the same in American literature for Puritan religious texts, when the Puritans themselves were all but gone by the 1700s? Must an author be an American to have made a significant contribution to American culture? How have these same traditions, all along, been international, cross-cultural? And so on . . .

Appendix D: Readings in Literary Theory for English Teachers

- Arthur Applebee's book *Tradition and Reform in the Teaching of English: A History* (1974) is an examination of the history of the public school English curriculum, and his more recent book *Curriculum as Conversation: Transforming Traditions of Teaching and Learning* (1996) is in many ways compatible with the reader-response cultural studies approach put forward in this book.

- *Beginning Theory: An Introduction to Literary and Cultural Theory* (1995) by Peter Barry is an accessible introduction.

- *Literary Theory: A Very Short Introduction* (1997) by Jonathan Culler is an easy, clear, and insightful quick overview of contemporary theory and its relation to literary study. It includes a chapter on cultural studies and an appendix that provides an overview of specific theoretical approaches.

- Terry Eagleton's book *Literary Theory: An Introduction* (1983) is a sound and intellectually challenging way to try to sort out some of the major strands of contemporary theory and criticism. His discussion of reader response comes out of the European reception theory, and the chapters on psychoanalytic and structuralist approaches cover ground not addressed in *Literature and Lives*. The more recent edition (1996) includes a final chapter that touches on newer approaches.

- A good way for English teachers to gain an understanding of schools of criticism and their role in influencing teaching would be to read *Professing Literature: An Institutional History* (1989) by Gerald Graff. This book narrates the history of literary studies in the United States from the early nineteenth century to the present. Graff's *Beyond the Culture Wars: How Teaching the Conflicts Can Revitalize American Education* (1992) examines ways in which literature teachers can foster their students' exploration of conflicting approaches to literature study.

- English teachers wanting to update their knowledge on current approaches to literature scholarship will find *Redrawing the Boundaries: The Transformation of English and American Literary Studies* (1992) an attractive and comprehensive book. The essays collected here by Stephen Greenblatt and Giles Gunn are lucid pieces by leading scholars covering historical periods as well as schools of criticism. Literature teachers can obtain an overview of approaches to composition studies, feminist criticism, American literary studies, and African American, psychoanalytic, and Marxist criticism, or any other of a host of fields that might interest them.

- Vincent Leitch's *American Literary Criticism from the Thirties to the Eighties* (1988) provides a lucid decade-by-decade summary of the major approaches to literary criticism.

- *Critical Terms for Literary Study* (1995) is a fine and approachable introduction to literary theory edited by Frank Lentricchia and Thomas McLaughlin and includes chapters by well-reputed scholars on specific topics such as author, narrative, gender, race, history, interpretation, and ethics.

- *Literary Terms: A Practical Glossary* (1999) by Brian Moon offers an entertaining and easy introduction to theory for a wide range of audiences, from high school to graduate school. Literary theories and terms are described in a few paragraphs, beginning with a simple puzzle or problem that brings the term into focus and followed by a practice activity that involves application of the concept in a textual context.

- *Interpreting Young Adult Literature: Literary Theory in the Secondary Classroom* (1997) by John Noell Moore is an introduction to literary theory through the examination of particular works of young adult literature.

- NCTE has a growing series of books introducing theory and scholarship to teachers, and several of the volumes in this series are listed elsewhere in this book. It now includes *A Teacher's Introduction to Postmodernism* (1996) by Ray Linn, *A Teacher's Introduction to Deconstruction* (1989) by Sharon Crowley, *A Teacher's Introduction to Reader-Response Theories* (1993) by Richard Beach, *A Teacher's Introduction to Composition in the Rhetorical Tradition* (1994) by W. Ross Winterowd with Jack Blum, and *A Teacher's Introduction to Philosophical Hermeneutics* (1991) by Timothy Crusius.

- Robert Scholes's *Textual Power: Literary Theory and the Teaching of English* (1985) explores theoretical approaches including deconstruction, semiotics, and Marxism to argue that literature teaching at the college level should move away from a New Critical focus on literary texts and toward a more inclusive and response-oriented kind of textual study.

- A rich resource for teachers interested in learning more about traditional approaches to literary scholarship and criticism is René Wellek's *A History of Modern Criticism 1750–1950*. Published in eight volumes from the 1950s to the 1980s, these books form a monument of scholarship that is easy to read and refer to. Elmer Borklund's *Contemporary Literary Critics* (1982) is another encyclopedia of critics and their views.

Appendix E: Web Sites for Exploring Literary Theory and Cultural Studies

- The Internet Public Library Literary Criticism collection "contains 3,624 critical and biographical Web sites about authors and their works that can be browsed by author, by title, or by nationality and literary period": http://www.ipl.org/ref/litcrit/guide.html.

- The Johns Hopkins Guide to Literary Theory and Criticism: http://www.press.jhu.edu/books/hopkins_guide_to_literary_theory/.

- *Jouvert* is an online academic journal in postcolonial studies: http://152.1.96.5/jouvert/.

- Professor Mary Kloges has posted her helpful lecture notes on a variety of aspects of contemporary literary theory: http://www.colorado.edu/English/ENGL2012Klages/lecturelinks.html.

- George P. Landow, professor at Brown University and at the National University of Singapore, offers a site providing an introduction to contemporary postcolonial literature and theory: http://landow.stg.brown.edu/post/misc/postov.html. Landow is also the driving force behind The Victorian Web, which includes a page examining the idea of literary canonicity and feminist responses: http://landow.stg.brown.edu/victorian/canon/litcan.html.

- The Literary Theory site offers good information and links: http://www.hull.ac.uk/php/elplnr/.

- Michael Terry has created an introduction to literary theory that describes the work of individual theorists in various historical periods: http://members.home.com/mikencarrie/critcont.htm.

- The Voice of the Shuttle Web Page for the Humanities is a comprehensive guide to literary theory resources on the Web: http://vos.ucsb.edu/shuttle/theory.html. Voice of the Shuttle also has a comprehensive guide to cultural studies resources on the Web: http://vos.ucsb.edu/shuttle/cultural.html.

- Sara Zupkho's Cultural Studies Center has an enormous number of links to journals, theorists, listservs, and newsgroups: http://www.popcultures.com/.

Appendix F: Web Sites to Support Literature Teaching

There is an enormous number of Web sites to support literature and English teaching. Those listed below are barely a starting point!

Professional Organizations for English Teachers

- Educational Theater Association: http://www.etassoc.org/.
- The International Reading Association: http://www.reading.org/.
- The Modern Language Association: http://www.mla.org/.
- The National Council of Teachers of English: http://www.ncte.org/.
- The National Forensics League: http://debate.uvm.edu/nfl.html.
- The National Middle School Association: http://www.nmsa.org/.
- The National Scholastic Press Association: http://www.student press.org/nspa/index.html.
- The National Writing Project: http://www.writingproject.org/.

Online Literature Archives:

- The Bartleby Project at the University of Columbia: http://www.bartleby.com/.
- The Electronic Text Center at the University of Virginia: http://etext.lib.virginia.edu/.
- The English Server at Carnegie Mellon University: http://eng.hss.cmu.edu/.
- The Humanities Text Initiative at the University of Michigan: http://www.hti.umich.edu/.
- The University of Toronto English Library: http://www.library.utoronto.ca/utel/.

Lesson Plan Archives

- Cyber Guides: Teacher guides and student activities for specific literary works: http://www.sdcoe.k12.ca.us/score/cyberguide.html.

- Encarta Language Arts: http://encarta.msn.com/schoolhouse/menus/menulangarts.asp.

- ERIC Language Arts Plans: http://ericir.syr.edu/Virtual/Lessons/Lang_arts/index.html.

- NCTE *NOTES Plus*: http://www.ncte.org/notesplus/.

- Outta Ray's Head: http://www3.sympatico.ca/ray.saitz/lessons3.htm.

- The University of Illinois Collaborative Lesson Archive: http://faldo.atmos.uiuc.edu/CLA/.

Sites for Integrating the Internet into English Teaching

- Beyond Books offers Internet support for a wide variety of secondary courses in English, history, mathematics, science, foreign language, and other subjects. The fee is $1 per student per year. Go to http://www.beyondbooks.com.

- The bigchalk.com site is a rich offering that includes, among other things, lesson plan archives, technology resources for teachers, and ways of connecting with teachers online: http://www.bigchalk.com.

- Blackboard.com allows teachers to post syllabi; create threaded discussions, chats, and bulletin boards for student work; maintain grades; and so on: http://www.blackboard.com.

- Chapbooks.com offers an easy, inexpensive, and attractive way for students or classes to publish their writing: http://www.chapbooks.com. You might also try this site: http://www.writetogether.com/.

- Cyber English is a course created by Ted Nellen to assist English teachers in using the Web. The site has sample English teacher Web pages and resources: http://www.tnellen.com/cybereng/.

- The eGroups.com site can help you set up electronic discussions: http://www.egroups.com/.

- The ePALS site is a resource for connecting classes and students to other parts of the country or world: http://www.epals.com.

- The Filamentality site helps teachers build Web sites into classroom learning projects: http://www.kn.pacbell.com/wired/fil.

- Kiko helps teachers develop Web quests and do Internet teaching: http://www.kiko.com.

- The Online Writing Center Consortium supports the teaching of writing electronically: http://owcc.colostate.edu/.

- Schoolnotes is a site where teachers can post class information, homework, and other materials for students and parents: http://www.schoolnotes.com.

- Secondary English offers a new online journal especially for secondary English teachers: http://secondaryenglish.com.

- TaskStream is an asset for creating lesson plans, rubrics, and curriculum plans: http://www.taskstream.com.

- ThinkQuest has an outstanding library of content-area learning sites created by international student teams: http://www.thinkquest.org/.

- Several sites are available to assist teachers in developing Web sites, including TechTrekkers, located at http://www.techtrekkers.com, and The Webquest Page, located at http://edweb.sdsu.edu/webquest/webquest.html. The webTeacher site offers a tutorial to help you or your students learn to use the Web and make your own Web pages: http://www.webteacher.org. Surfette's Pages for Teachers (for Developing Educational Web Pages) is another useful resource: http://www.members.home.net/surfette/.

General English Teaching Sites

- Robert Barsanti is one of the pioneers in online secondary English teaching: http://www.capecod.net/~bbarsant/class/.

- This site, titled English Literature on the Web, offers links to primary texts, criticism, and theory: http://lang.nagoya-u.ac.jp/~matsuoka/EngLit.html.

- Literary Resources on the Web, maintained by Jack Lynch, is a good resource: http://andromeda.rutgers.edu/~jlynch/Lit/.

- The Middle and Secondary Literature page of the School Library Media Center can be found at http://falcon.jmu.edu/~ramseyil/yalit.htm.

- The Site on Shakespeare and the Renaissance is a fine gateway to the many Web materials on these topics: http://web.uvic.ca/shakespeare/Annex/ShakSites1.html.

- English and American literature resources maintained by the University of Connecticut are offered at http://www.lib.uconn.edu/subjectareas/engweb.html.

- English education links and resources posted by Mary Ellen Van Camp at Ball State University can be found at http://nova.bsuvc.bsu.edu/~00mevancamp/enged.html.

- My own Web site has professional information I have developed for secondary English teachers, course materials, and links to English teaching organizations, as well as Web sites of special interest: http://vms.cc.wmich.edu/~careywebb/.

Appendix G: Web Sites to Support New Teachers

- The NCTE TEACH*2000* Web site is designed to support new English teachers: http://www.ncte.org/teach2000/.

- The New Teacher Resources page is a gateway to sites of interest: http://www.teachersfirst.com/new-tch.htm.

- New-Teacher.com includes articles and materials by and about new teachers: http://www.peaklearn.com/newteach/default.html.

- A "survival guide" created by a classroom teacher for her new colleagues can be found at http://www.dun.org/sulan/teacher/.

- An annotated list of books recommended for beginning teachers is offered at http://www.datasync.com/~teachers/teacher_books.html.

- Another gateway to resources for new teachers is located at http://hometown.aol.com/sskufca/teachtps.htm.

- My Web site also has suggestions for student teaching, job searching, substituting, addressing classroom discipline, and other concerns of new teachers: http://vms.cc.wmich.edu/~careywebb.

References

Print Materials

Abelove, Henry, Michèle Barale, and David Halperin, eds. *The Lesbian and Gay Studies Reader.* New York: Routledge, 1993.

Achebe, Chinua. *Anthills of the Savannah.* New York: Doubleday, 1989.

———. *Arrow of God.* 2nd ed. London: Heinemann, 1995.

———. "An Image of Africa: Racism in Conrad's *Heart of Darkness. Heart of Darkness: An Authoritative Text, Backgrounds and Sources, Criticism.* 3rd ed. Ed. Robert Kimbrough. New York: Norton, 1988. 251–262.

———. *A Man of the People.* London: Heinemann, 1972.

———. *No Longer at Ease.* London: Heinemann, 1989.

———. *Things Fall Apart.* Portsmouth, NH: Heinemann, 1986.

Acuña, Rodolfo. *Occupied America: The Chicano's Struggle Toward Liberation.* San Francisco: Canfield P, 1972.

Addams, Jane. *Twenty Years at Hull House.* New York: Macmillan, 1938.

Allen, Janet. *It's Never Too Late: Leading Adolescents into Lifelong Literacy.* Portsmouth, NH: Heinemann, 1995.

Allen, Paula Gunn. *The Sacred Hoop: Recovering the Feminine in American Indian Traditions.* Boston: Beacon P, 1992.

———, ed. *Spider Woman's Granddaughters: Traditional Tales and Contemporary Writing by Native American Women.* New York: Fawcett Columbine, 1989.

Althusser, Louis. *Lenin and Philosophy, and Other Essays.* Trans. Ben Brewster. London: New Left, 1971.

Anaya, Rudolfo, and Francisco Lomelí, eds. *Aztlán: Essays on the Chicano Homeland.* Albuquerque: U of New Mexico P, 1989.

Anderson, Elijah. "The Code of the Streets." *Atlantic Monthly* May 1994: 80–94.

Angelou, Maya. *I Know Why the Caged Bird Sings.* New York: Random House, 1970.

Anzaldúa, Gloria. *Borderlands = La Frontera.* 2nd ed. San Francisco: Aunt Lute, 1999.

Apple, Michael. *Teachers and Texts: A Political Economy of Class and Gender Relations in Education.* New York: Routledge, 1988.

Applebee, Arthur. *Literature in the Secondary School: Studies of Curriculum and Instruction in the United States.* Urbana, IL: NCTE, 1993.

————. "Stability and Change in the High School Canon." *English Journal* 81.5 (1992): 27–32.

Arac, Jonathan. *Huckleberry Finn as Idol and Target: The Functions of Criticism in our Time*. Madison: U of Wisconsin P, 1997.

Argueta, Manlio. *One Day of Life*. Trans. Bill Brow. New York: Vintage, 1983.

Arias, Arturo, ed. *The Rigoberta Menchú Controversy*. Minneapolis: U of Minnesota P, in press.

Armah, Ayi Kwei. *The Beautyful Ones Are Not Yet Born: A Novel*. New York: Collier, 1973.

Ashcroft, Bill, Gareth Griffiths, and Helen Tiffin. *The Empire Strikes Back*. New York: Routledge, 1989.

Associated Press. "Gap grows between prices, incomes." *Eugene Register-Guard* 29 July 1990.

Atwell, Nancie. *In the Middle: New Understandings about Writing, Reading, and Learning*. 2nd ed. Portsmouth: Boynton/Cook, 1998.

Aufderheide, Patricia, ed. *Beyond PC: Toward a Politics of Understanding*. Saint Paul: Greywolf, 1992.

Baker, Houston. *The Journey Back: Issues in Black Literature and Criticism*. Chicago: U of Chicago P, 1980.

Bakhtin, M. M. *The Dialogic Imagination: Four Essays*. Ed. Michael Holquist. Trans. Caryl Emerson and Michael Holquist. Austin: U of Texas P, 1981.

Baldwin, James. *If Beale Street Could Talk*. Dell: New York, 1974.

Ballantyne, R. M. *The Coral Island*. New York: Penguin, 1995.

Bambara, Toni Cade. *Gorilla My Love*. New York: Random, 1972.

Barry, Peter. *Beginning Theory: An Introduction to Literary and Cultural Theory*. New York: Manchester U P, 1995.

Barthes, Roland. *Mythologies*. New York: Noonday, 1993.

Baudelaire, Charles. *Twenty Prose Poems*. Trans. Michael Hamburger. San Francisco: City Lights, 1988.

Bauer, Marion, ed. *Am I Blue?: Coming Out from the Silence*. New York: HarperCollins, 1995.

Beach, Richard. *A Teacher's Introduction to Reader-Response Theories*. Urbana, IL: NCTE, 1993.

Behn, Aphra. *Oroonoko, or, The Royal Slave*. Boston: Bedford/St. Martin's, 2000.

Beier, A. L. *Masterless Men: The Vagrancy Problem in England 1560–1640*. New York: Methuen, 1985.

Belenky, Mary. *Women's Ways of Knowing: The Development of Self, Voice, and Mind*. New York: Basic, 1997.

Bell, Bernard. "Twain's 'Nigger Jim': The Tragic Face Behind the Minstrel Mask." *Satire or Evasion?: Black Perspectives on Huckleberry Finn*. Ed. James S.

Leonard, Thomas A. Tenney, and Thadious M. Davis. Durham: Duke U P, 1992. 124–140.

Bennett, Tony. *Outside Literature*. New York: Routledge, 1990.

Bercovitch, Sacvan, ed. *The Cambridge History of American Literature*. 5 vols. Cambridge: Cambridge U P, 1994–98.

Berlin, James, and Michael J. Vivion. *Cultural Studies in the English Classroom*. Portsmouth, NH: Boynton/Cook Heinemann, 1992.

Beverley, John. *Against Literature*. Minneapolis: U of Minnesota P, 1993.

Bigelow, Bill, and Bob Peterson. *Rethinking Columbus: The Next 500 Years*. 2nd ed. Milwaukee: Rethinking Schools, 1998.

Bigelow, Bill, et al., eds. *Rethinking Our Classrooms: Teaching for Equity and Justice*. Milwaukee: Rethinking Schools, 1994.

Blake, William. *Songs of Innocence; and, Songs of Experience*. New York: Dover, 1992.

Booth, Wayne. *The Company We Keep: An Ethics of Fiction*. Berkeley: U of California P, 1988.

Borklund, Elmer. *Contemporary Literary Critics*. Detroit: Gale, 1982.

Bowles, Samuel, and Herbert Gintis. *Schooling in Capitalist America: Educational Reform and the Contradictions of Economic Life*. London: Routledge, 1977.

Brantlinger, Patrick. *Crusoe's Footprints: Cultural Studies in Britain and America*. New York: Routledge, 1990.

Breight, Curtis. *Surveillance, Militarism, and Drama in the Elizabethan Era*. New York: St. Martin's, 1996.

Brill de Ramírez, Susan Berry. *Contemporary American Indian Literatures and the Oral Tradition*. Tucson: U of Arizona P, 1999.

Brinkley, Ellen. *Caught Off Guard: Teachers Rethinking Censorship and Controversy*. Boston: Allyn, 1999.

Brontë, Charlotte. *Jane Eyre*. New York: New American Library, 1960.

Bruchac, Joseph. "Thoughts on Teaching Native American Literature." *Rethinking Our Classrooms: Teaching for Equity and Justice*. Ed. Bill Bigelow et al. Milwaukee: Rethinking Schools, 1994.

Brutus, Dennis. *A Simple Lust: Selected Poems*. London: Heinemann, 1973.

Burnett, Mark. *Masters and Servants in English Renaissance Drama and Culture: Authority and Obedience*. New York: St. Martin's, 1997.

Burress, Lee. *Battle of the Books: Literary Censorship in the Public Schools 1950–1985*. Metuchen, New Jersey: Scarecrow, 1989.

Burress, Lee, and Edward Jenkinson. *The Students' Right to Know*. Urbana, IL: NCTE, 1982.

Butler, Judith. *Gender Trouble: Feminism and the Subversion of Identity*. New York: Routledge, 1990.

Carey-Webb, Allen. "Auto/Biography of the Oppressed: The Power of Testimonial." *English Journal* 80.4 (1991): 44–47.

———. *Making Subject(s): Literature and the Emergence of National Identity.* New York: Garland, 1998.

———. "Representing the Homeless." *American Literary History* 4.4 (1992): 697–708.

———. "Tarzan, Kurtz, and the 'Third World': Canons and Encounters in World Literature, English 109." *Order and Partialities: Theory, Pedagogy, and the "Postcolonial."* Ed. Kostas Myrsiades and Jerry McGuire. Albany: State U of New York P, 1995.

Carey-Webb, Allen, and Stephen Benz, eds. *Teaching and Testimony: Rigoberta Menchú and the North American Classroom.* Albany: State U of New York P, 1996.

Césaire, Aimé. *A Tempest: Based on Shakespeare's* The Tempest: *Adaptation for a Black Theater.* Trans. Richard Miller. New York: Ubu Repertory Theater, 1992.

Charvat, William. *The Profession of Authorship in America, 1800–1870: The Papers of William Charvat.* Ed. Matthew Bruccoli. Columbus: Ohio State U P, 1968.

Chaucer, Geoffrey. *The Canterbury Tales.* New York: Barnes and Noble, 1994.

Cheung, King-Kok. *An Interethnic Companion to Asian American Literature.* Cambridge: Cambridge U P, 1997.

Chin, Frank, Jeffrey Paul Chan, Lawson Fusao Inada, and Sharon Wong. *Aiiieeeee!: An Anthology of Asian-American Writers.* Washington: Howard U P, 1974.

Chopin, Kate. *The Awakening.* New York: Avon, 1972.

Christensen, Linda. "Building Community From Chaos." *Rethinking Our Classrooms: Teaching for Equity and Justice.* Ed. Bill Bigelow et al. Milwaukee: Rethinking Schools, 1994. 50–55.

Christian, Barbara. *Black Feminist Criticism: Perspectives on Black Women Writers.* New York: Pergamon, 1985.

Cisneros, Sandra. *The House on Mango Street.* New York: Vintage, 1989.

Cliff, Michelle. *Abeng.* New York: Plume, 1995.

———. *No Telephone To Heaven.* New York: Vintage, 1987.

Clise, Michele Durkson. *Stop the Violence Please.* Seattle: Allied Arts Foundation in association with U of Washington P, 1994.

Coetzee, J. M. *Foe.* New York: Penguin, 1986.

———. *Waiting for the Barbarians.* New York: Penguin, 1999.

Cofer, Judith Ortiz. *The Line of the Sun.* Athens: U of Georgia P, 1989.

Conrad, Joseph. *Heart of Darkness.* New York: Signet, 1997.

Cox News Service. "Income of richest 20% equals income of everyone else." *Eugene Register-Guard* 24 July 1990.

Crane, Stephen. *Maggie, A Girl of the Streets, and Other Tales of New York*. New York: Penguin, 2000.

———. "New York City Sketches." In *The University of Virginia Edition of the Works of Stephen Crane*. Vol. 8. Charlottesville: U of Virginia P, 1973.

Criddle, Joan, and Teeda Butt Mam. *To Destroy You Is No Loss: The Odyssey of a Cambodian Family*. New York: Anchor, 1987.

Crowley, Sharon. *A Teacher's Introduction to Deconstruction*. Urbana, IL: NCTE, 1989.

Crusius, Timothy. *A Teacher's Introduction to Philosophical Hermeneutics*. Urbana, IL: NCTE, 1991.

Culler, Jonathan. *Literary Theory: A Very Short Introduction*. New York: Oxford U P, 1997.

———. *On Deconstruction: Theory and Criticism After Structuralism*. Ithaca: Cornell U P, 1982.

D'Amico, Jack. *The Moor in English Renaissance Drama*. Gainesville: U of South Florida P, 1991.

Dangarembga, Tsitsi. *Nervous Conditions: A Novel*. Seattle: Seal, 1988.

Dates, Jannette, and William Barlow. *Split Image: African Americans in the Mass Media*. Washington: Howard U P, 1993.

Defoe, Daniel. *Robinson Crusoe*. New York: Doubleday, 1959.

Desai, Anita. *Bye-bye Blackbird*. New Delhi: Orient, 1985.

Dickens, Charles. *Oliver Twist*. New York: Bantam, 1982.

Dillard, Annie. *An American Childhood*. New York: Perennial, 1988.

Dollimore, Jonathan, and Alan Sinfield. *Political Shakespeare: New Essays in Cultural Materialism*. Ithaca: Cornell U P, 1985.

Dorfman, Ariel. *The Empire's Old Clothes: What the Lone Ranger, Babar, and Other Innocent Heroes Do to Our Minds*. New York: Pantheon, 1983.

Dorfman, Ariel, and Armand Mattelart. *How to Read Donald Duck: Imperialist Ideology in the Disney Comic*. Trans. David Kunzle. New York: International General, 1984.

Dorris, Michael. *Morning Girl*. New York: Hyperion, 1992.

Douglas, Susan. *Where the Girls Are: Growing Up Female with the Mass Media*. New York: Times, 1994.

D'Souza, Dinesh. *Illiberal Education: The Politics of Race and Sex on Campus*. New York: Free, 1991.

Duncan, Barry. *Mass Media and Popular Culture* (Version 2). Toronto: Harcourt, 1996.

Dusinberre, Juliet. *Shakespeare and the Nature of Women*. New York: St. Martin's, 1996.

Eagleton, Terry. *Ideology.* New York: Longman, 1994.

———. *Literary Theory: An Introduction.* 2nd ed. Oxford: Blackwell, 1996.

———. *Marxism and Literary Criticism.* Berkeley: U of California P, 1976.

Easthope, Antony. *Literary into Cultural Studies.* New York: Routledge, 1991.

Edgerton, Susan Huddleston. *Translating the Curriculum: Multiculturalism into Cultural Studies.* New York: Routledge, 1996.

Eliot, T. S. *Selected Essays, 1917–1932.* New York: Harcourt, 1932.

Ellison, Ralph. *Shadow and Act.* New York: Random House, 1964.

Emecheta, Buchi. *In the Ditch.* Portsmouth, NH: Heinemann, 1994.

———. *Joys of Motherhood.* New York: George Braziller, 1979.

———. *Second-Class Citizen.* Portsmouth, NH: Heinemann, 1994.

Empson, William. *Seven Types of Ambiguity.* London: New Directions, 1947.

Equiano, Olaudah. *The Life of Olaudah Equiano, or, Gustavus Vassa, the African.* Mineola, NY: Dover, 1999.

Ervin, Hazel Arnett, ed. *African American Literary Criticism, 1773 to 2000.* New York: Twayne, 1999.

Fall, Aminata Sow. *The Beggars' Strike, Or, The Dregs of Society.* Trans. Dorothy Blair. Harlow, Essex: Longman, 1981.

Fang, Irving. *A History of Mass Communication: Six Information Revolutions.* Boston: Focal, 1997.

Fanon, Frantz. *The Wretched of the Earth.* London: Penguin, 1990.

Ferguson, Robert. *Representing "Race": Ideology, Identity, and the Media.* New York: Arnold, 1998.

Filipovic, Zlata. *Zlata's Diary: A Child's Life in Sarajevo.* New York: Scholastic, 1994.

Fish, Stanley. *Is There a Text in This Class?: The Authority of Interpretive Communities.* Cambridge: Harvard U P, 1980.

Fishkin, Shelley Fisher. *Was Huck Black?: Mark Twain and African-American Voices.* New York: Oxford U P, 1993.

Foerstel, Herbert. *Banned in the U.S.A.: A Reference Guide to Book Censorship in Schools and Public Libraries.* Westport, CT: Greenwood, 1994.

Forster, E. M. *A Passage to India.* London: Penguin, 2000.

Foucault, Michel. *Discipline and Punish: The Birth of the Prison.* Trans. Alan Sheridan. New York: Vintage, 1979.

———. *The History of Sexuality, Volume 1: An Introduction.* New York: Vintage, 1980.

———. *The History of Sexuality, Volume 2: The Use of Pleasure.* New York: Vintage, 1986.

Frank, Anne. *The Diary of a Young Girl: The Definitive Edition*. London: Puffin, 1997.

Fredrickson, George. *The Black Image in the White Mind: The Debate on Afro-American Character and Destiny, 1817–1914*. New York: Harper, 1971.

Freedman, Samuel. *Small Victories: The Real World of a Teacher, Her Students, and Their High School*. New York, HarperPerennial, 1991.

Freire, Paulo. *Pedagogy of the Oppressed*. New York: Continuum, 1987.

Garbarino, James, Kathleen Kostelny, and Nancy Dubrow. *No Place to Be a Child: Growing Up in a War Zone*. Lexington, MA: Lexington, 1991.

Gardner, John. *Grendel*. New York: Vintage Books, 1989.

Gaskell, Elizabeth. *The Life of Charlotte Brontë*. Ed. Temple Scott and B. W. Willett. London: Downey, 1901.

Gates, Henry Louis, Jr. *Loose Canons: Notes on the Culture Wars*. New York: Oxford U P, 1993.

———. *The Signifying Monkey: A Theory of African-American Literary Criticism*. New York: Oxford U P, 1988.

Gilbert, Sandra, and Susan Gubar. *The Madwoman in the Attic: The Woman Writer and the Nineteenth-Century Literary Imagination*. New Haven: Yale U P, 1979.

———, eds. *The Norton Anthology of Literature by Women: The Tradition in English*. New York: Norton, 1985.

Gilligan, Carol. *In a Different Voice: Psychological Theory and Women's Development*. Cambridge, MA: Harvard U P, 1982.

Gilman, Charlotte Perkins. *Herland, The Yellow Wall-paper, and Selected Writings*. New York: Penguin, 1999.

Giroux, Henry. *Border Crossings: Cultural Workers and the Politics of Education*. London: Routledge, 1992.

Glassman, Bernard. *Anti-Semitic Stereotypes without Jews: Images of the Jews in England, 1290–1700*. Detroit: Wayne State U P, 1975.

Golding, William. *Lord of the Flies: A Novel*. New York: Penguin, 1999.

Goodwillie, Susan, ed. *Voices from the Future: Our Children Tell Us about Violence in America*. New York: Crown, 1993.

Gordimer, Nadine. *Something Out There*. London: Bloomsbury, 1994.

Gordon, Lyndall. *Charlotte Brontë: A Passionate Life*. New York: Norton, 1995.

Gordon, W. Terrence. *McLuhan for Beginners*. New York: Writers and Readers, 1997.

Graff, Gerald. *Beyond the Culture Wars: How Teaching the Conflicts Can Revitalize American Education*. New York: Norton, 1992.

Gray, Mary. *In Your Face: Stories from the Lives of Queer Youth*. New York: Haworth, 1999.

Greenblatt, Stephen. *Learning to Curse: Essays in Early Modern Culture.* New York: Routledge, 1990.

———. *Marvelous Possessions: The Wonder of the New World.* Chicago: U of Chicago P, 1991.

———, ed. *The Power of Forms in the English Renaissance.* Norman, OK: Pilgrim, 1982.

———. *Shakespearean Negotiations: The Circulation of Social Energy in Renaissance England.* Berkeley: U of California P, 1988.

Greenblatt, Stephen, and Giles Gunn, eds. *Redrawing the Boundaries: The Transformation of English and American Literary Studies.* New York: MLA, 1992.

Greene, Bette. *The Drowning of Stephan Jones.* New York: Bantam, 1996.

Grossberg, Lawrence, Cary Nelson, and Paula Treichler, eds. *Cultural Studies.* New York: Routledge, 1992.

Gugelberger, Georg M., ed. *The Real Thing: Testimonial Discourse and Latin America.* Durham, NC: Duke U P, 1996.

Guy, Rosa. *Ruby.* New York: Viking, 1976.

Hallberg, Robert Von, ed. *Canons.* Chicago: U of Chicago P, 1983.

Harris, Wilson. *Palace of the Peacock.* Boston: Faber, 1998.

Henderson, Katherine Usher, and Barbara F. McManus. *Half Humankind: Contexts and Texts of the Controversy about Women in England, 1540–1640.* Urbana: U of Illinois P, 1985.

Henry, Peaches. "The Struggle for Tolerance: Race and Censorship in *Huckleberry Finn.*" *Satire or Evasion?: Black Perspectives on Huckleberry Finn.* Ed. James S. Leonard, Thomas A. Tenney, and Thadious M. Davis. Durham, NC: Duke U P, 1992. 25–48.

Hentoff, Nat. *The Day They Came to Arrest the Book: A Novel.* New York: Dell, 1982.

Hersey, John. *Hiroshima.* London: Penguin, 1986.

Hicks, Granville. *The Great Tradition: An Interpretation of American Literature Since the Civil War.* New York: Macmillan, 1935.

Hinton, S. E. *The Outsiders.* Oxford: Heinemann, 1996.

Hirsch, E. D. *Cultural Literacy: What Every American Needs To Know.* New York: Vintage, 1988.

Hirsch, Kathleen. *Songs from the Alley.* New York: Ticknor, 1989.

Hoch, Charles, and Robert A. Slayton. *New Homeless and Old: Community and the Skid Row Hotel.* Philadelphia: Temple U P, 1989.

hooks, bell. *Teaching to Transgress: Education as the Practice of Freedom.* New York: Routledge, 1994.

Hope, Marjorie, and James Young. *The Faces of Homelessness.* Lexington, MA: Lexington, 1986.

Hopkins, Sara Winnemucca. [Reproduction of] *Life Among the Piutes: Their Wrongs and Claims*. 1883. Ed. Mrs. Horace Mann. Bishop, CA: Chalfant, 1969.

Hosain, Attia. *Sunlight on a Broken Column*. New York: Penguin, 1988.

Hubbard, Jim. *American Refugees*. Minneapolis: U of Minnesota P, 1991.

Hulme, Peter. *Colonial Encounters: Europe and the Native Caribbean, 1492–1797*. New York: Methuen, 1986.

Hurston, Zora Neale. *Their Eyes Were Watching God: A Novel*. Urbana: U of Illinois P, 1978.

Hymes, Dell. *"In Vain I Tried to Tell You": Essays in Native American Ethnopoetics*. Philadelphia: U of Pennsylvania P, 1981.

Jameson, Fredric. *Postmodernism, Or, The Cultural Logic of Late Capitalism*. Durham, NC: Duke U P, 1991.

Jawitz, William. *Understanding Mass Media*. 5th ed. Lincolnwood, IL: National Textbook, 1996.

Jay, Gregory. *American Literature and the Culture Wars*. Ithaca, NY: Cornell U P, 1997.

Jiménez, Francisco. *The Identification and Analysis of Chicano Literature*. New York: Bilingual, 1979.

Johnson, Samuel. *Johnson's Lives of the Poets*. London: Bell, 1900.

Jones, Rhett. "Nigger and Knowledge: White Double Consciousness in *Adventures of Huckleberry Finn*." *Satire or Evasion?: Black Perspectives on Huckleberry Finn*. Ed. James S. Leonard, Thomas A. Tenney, and Thadious M. Davis. Durham, NC: Duke U P, 1992. 173–198.

Kalamazoo Gazette. Staff article. "Teachers Protest *Huck Finn* Ban." 26 Nov. 1991.

Kane, Cheikh Hamidou. *Ambiguous Adventure*. Trans. Katherine Woods. London: Heinemann, 1972.

Kazin, Alfred. *On Native Ground: An Interpretation of American Prose Literature*. New York: Harcourt, 1942.

Kellner, Douglas. *Media Culture: Cultural Studies, Identity, and Politics between the Modern and the Postmodern*. New York: Routledge, 1995.

Kenyon, Thomas, and Justin Blau. *What You Can Do to Help the Homeless*. New York: Simon, 1991.

Kim, Elaine. *Asian American Literature: An Introduction to the Writings and Their Social Context*. Philadelphia: Temple UP, 1982.

King, Martin Luther, Jr. "Letter from a Birmingham Jail." *Why We Can't Wait*. New York: Harper, 1963.

Kipling, Rudyard. *Kim*. New York: TOR, 1999.

Kissen, Rita. *The Last Closet: The Real Lives of Lesbian and Gay Teachers*. Portsmouth, NH: Heinemann, 1997.

Knoblauch, Cy, and Lil Brannon. *Critical Teaching and the Idea of Literacy.* Portsmouth, NH: Boynton/Cook, 1993.

Kohl, Herbert. *I Won't Learn from You: And Other Thoughts on Creative Maladjustment.* New York: New, 1994.

Kozol, Jonathan. *Rachel and Her Children: Homeless Families in America.* New York: Crown, 1988.

Krogness, Mary Mercer. *Just Teach Me, Mrs. K.: Talking, Reading and Writing with Resistant Adolescent Learners.* Portsmouth, NH: Heinemann, 1995.

Kuzmeskus, June. "Writing Their Way to Compassionate Citizenship: Rigoberta Menchú and Activating High School Learners." *Teaching and Testimony: Rigoberta Menchú and the North American Classroom.* Ed. Allen Carey-Webb and Stephen Benz. Albany: State U of New York P, 1996.

Lamming, George. *The Pleasures of Exile.* London: Allison & Busby, 1984.

Lauter, Paul. *Canons and Contexts.* New York: Oxford U P, 1991.

Lawrence, Karen. *Decolonizing Tradition: New Views of Twentieth-Century "British" Literary Canons.* Urbana: U of Illinois P, 1992.

Laye, Camara. *Dark Child.* New York: Noonday, 1994.

Leitch, Vincent. *American Literary Criticism from the Thirties to the Eighties.* New York: Columbia U P, 1988.

Leonard, James S., Thomas A. Tenney, and Thadious M. Davis, Eds. *Satire or Evasion?: Black Perspectives on Huckleberry Finn.* Durham, NC: Duke U P, 1992.

Lester, Julius. "Morality and *The Adventures of Huckleberry Finn.*" *Satire or Evasion?: Black Perspectives on Huckleberry Finn.* Ed. James S. Leonard, Thomas A. Tenney, and Thadious M. Davis. Durham, NC: Duke U P, 1992. 199–207.

Levi, Primo. *Survival in Auschwitz: The Nazi Assault on Humanity.* New York: Simon, 1996.

Levinson, Marjorie. *Wordsworth's Great Period Poems: Four Essays.* New York: Cambridge U P, 1986.

Lewis, Oscar. *The Children of Sánchez: Autobiography of a Mexican Family.* New York: Modern, 1969.

Li, David Leiwei. *Imagining the Nation: Asian American Literature and Cultural Consent.* Stanford, CA: Stanford U P, 1998.

Linn, Ray. *A Teacher's Introduction to Postmodernism.* Urbana, IL: NCTE, 1996.

Lyotard, Jean François. *The Postmodern Condition: A Report on Knowledge.* Trans. Geoff Bennington and Brian Massum. Minneapolis: U of Minnesota P, 1984.

Macrorie, Ken. *The I-Search Paper.* Portsmouth, NH: Boynton/Cook Heinemann, 1988.

Mander, Jerry. *Four Arguments for the Elimination of Television.* New York: Morrow, 1978.

Mannoni, Octave. *Prospero and Caliban: The Psychology of Colonization.* Trans. Pamela Powesland. New York: Praeger, 1964.

Maran, René. *Batouala.* Portsmouth, NH: Heinemann, 1987.

Markandaya, Kamala. *Nectar in a Sieve: A Novel.* New York: New American, 1982.

Marshall, Paule. *Brown Girl, Brownstones.* New York: Random, 1959.

———. *Praisesong for the Widow.* New York: Dutton, 1983.

Masterman, Len. *Teaching about Television.* London: Macmillan, 1980.

Mathabane, Mark. *Kaffir Boy: The True Story of a Black Youth's Coming of Age in Apartheid South Africa.* New York: New American, 1987.

Mayhew, Henry. *London Labour and the London Poor.* New York: Penguin, 1985.

McCall, Nathan. *Makes Me Wanna Holler: A Young Black Man in America.* New York: Random, 1994.

McKenna, Teresa. *Migrant Song: Politics and Process in Contemporary Chicano Literature.* Austin: U of Texas P, 1997.

McLuhan, Marshall. *The Medium is the Massage.* New York: Penguin, 1967.

———. *Understanding Media: The Extensions of Man.* London: Routledge, 1994.

Menand, Louis, ed. *The Future of Academic Freedom.* Chicago: U of Chicago P, 1996.

Menchú, Rigoberta, with Elisabeth Burgos-Debray. *I, Rigoberta Menchú: An Indian Woman in Guatemala.* Trans. Ann Wright. London: Verso, 1984.

Michaels, Walter Benn, and Donald Pease, eds. *The American Renaissance Reconsidered.* Baltimore: Johns Hopkins U P, 1985.

Moon, Brian. *Literary Terms: A Practical Glossary.* Urbana, IL: NCTE, 1999.

Moore, John Noell. *Interpreting Young Adult Literature: Literary Theory in the Secondary Classroom.* Portsmouth, NH: Boynton/Cook, 1997.

Moraga, Cherríe, and Gloria Anzaldúa. *This Bridge Called My Back: Writings by Radical Women of Color.* New York: Kitchen Table, Women of Color, 1983.

More, Sir Thomas. *Utopia.* Boston: Bedford, 1999.

Morrison, Toni. *Beloved.* New York: Penguin, 1987.

———. *The Bluest Eye.* New York: Knopf, 1997.

———. *Playing in the Dark: Whiteness and the Literary Imagination.* Cambridge: Harvard U P, 1992.

———. *Tar Baby.* New York: Knopf, 1981.

Muller, Lauren, ed. *June Jordan's Poetry for the People: A Revolutionary Blueprint.* New York: Routledge, 1995.

Myers, Walter Dean. *Scorpions.* New York: Harper, 1988.

Nabokov, Peter. *Native American Testimony: An Anthology of Indian and White Relations; first encounter to dispossession.* New York: Harper, 1978.

Narayan, R. K. *The Guide: A Novel.* New York: Penguin, 1988.

———. *The Man-Eater of Malgudi.* London: Penguin, 1983.

———. *The Painter of Signs.* Harmondsworth, Middlesex: Penguin, 1982.

Ngugi Wa Thiong'o. *Decolonising the Mind: The Politics of Language in African Literature.* London: Currey, 1986.

———. *Weep Not, Child.* London: Heinemann, 1976.

Nwapa, Flora. *Efuru.* London: Heinemann, 1978.

Oakes, Jeannie. *Keeping Track: How Schools Structure Inequality.* New Haven: Yale U P, 1986.

Ochoa, Anna, ed. *Academic Freedom to Teach and to Learn: Every Teacher's Issue.* Washington: NEA, 1990.

O'Connor, Stephen. *Will My Name be Shouted Out?: Reaching Inner City Students Through the Power of Writing.* New York: Simon and Schuster, 1996.

Ohmann, Richard. *English in America: A Radical View of the Profession.* Middleton, CT: Wesleyan U P, 1996.

Olsen, Tillie. *Tell Me a Riddle.* New York: Delacorte, 1956.

Ondaatje, Michael. *Running in the Family.* New York: Norton, 1982.

Orwell, George. *Down and Out in Paris and London.* New York: Harcourt, 1961.

———. *1984: A Novel.* New York: Harcourt, 1983.

———. "Shooting an Elephant." *Shooting an Elephant and Other Essays.* San Diego: Harcourt, 1984.

Owens, Robert E. *Queer Kids: The Challenges and Promise for Lesbian, Gay, and Bisexual Youth.* New York: Haworth, 1998.

Paredes, Américo. *"With His Pistol in His Hand": A Border Ballad and Its Hero.* Austin: U of Texas P, 1971.

Parrington, Vernon L. *Main Currents in American Thought: An Interpretation of American Literature from the Beginnings to 1920.* 3 vols. New York: Harcourt, 1927.

Paton, Alan. *Cry, the Beloved Country.* New York: Macmillan, 1987.

Pipher, Mary. *Reviving Ophelia: Saving the Selves of Adolescent Girls.* New York: Putnam, 1994.

Pirie, Bruce. *Reshaping High School English.* Urbana, IL: NCTE, 1997.

Plath, Sylvia. *The Bell Jar.* New York: Bantam, 1971.

Ploeg, Jan van der, and Evert Scholte. *Homeless Youth.* London: Sage, 1999.

Postman, Neil. *Amusing Ourselves to Death: Public Discourse in the Age of Show Business.* New York: Viking, 1985.

Power, Brenda Miller, Jeffrey D. Wilhelm, and Kelly Chandler, eds. *Reading Stephen King: Issues of Censorship, Student Choice, and Popular Literature*. Urbana, IL: NCTE, 1997.

Pradl, Gordon. *Literature for Democracy: Reading as a Social Act*. Portsmouth, NH: Boynton/Cook, 1996.

Pratt, Mary Louise. "Daring to Dream: Re-Visioning Culture and Citizenship." *Critical Theory and the Teaching of Literature: Politics, Curriculum, Pedagogy*. Ed. James Slevin and Art Young. Urbana, IL: NCTE, 1996.

———. *Imperial Eyes: Travel Writing and Transculturation*. New York: Routledge, 1992.

———. "'Me llamo Rigoberta Menchú': Authoethnography and the Recoding of Citizenship." *Teaching and Testimony: Rigoberta Menchú and the North American Classroom*. Ed. Allen Carey-Webb and Stephen Benz. Albany: State U of New York P, 1996.

Prothrow-Stith, Deborah, with Michaele Weissman. *Deadly Consequences: How Violence Is Destroying Our Teenage Population and a Plan to Begin Solving the Problem*. New York: Harper, 1991.

Pryse, Marjorie, and Hortense Spillers. *Conjuring: Black Women, Fiction, and Literary Tradition*. Bloomington: Indiana U P, 1985.

Purves, Alan, Theresa Rogers, and Anna Soter. *How Porcupines Make Love III: Readers, Texts, Cultures in the Response-Based Literature Classroom*. Rev. ed. White Plains, NY: Longman, 1995.

Rampersad, Arnold. "*Adventures of Huckleberry Finn* and African American Literature." *Satire or Evasion?: Black Perspectives on Huckleberry Finn*. Ed. James S. Leonard, Thomas A. Tenney, and Thadious M. Davis. Durham, NC: Duke U P, 1992. 216–227.

———. *The Life of Langston Hughes*. New York: Oxford U P, 1986.

Rarihokwats, ed. *Guatemala!: The Horror and the Hope*. York, PA: Four Arrows, 1982.

Rationales for Challenged Books. CD-ROM. Urbana, IL: NCTE in partnership with IRA, 1998.

Retamar, Roberto Fernández. *Caliban and Other Essays*. Minneapolis: U of Minnesota P, 1989.

Reynolds, David. *Walt Whitman's America: A Cultural Biography*. New York: Knopf, 1995.

Rhys, Jean. *Wide Sargasso Sea*. New York: Norton, 1982.

Rich, Adrienne. *On Lies, Secrets, and Silence: Selected Prose, 1966–1978*. New York: Norton, 1979.

Richardson, Robert D. *Emerson: The Mind on Fire: A Biography*. Berkeley: U of California P, 1995.

———. *Henry Thoreau: A Life of the Mind*. Berkeley: U of California P, 1986.

Rief, Linda. *Seeking Diversity: Language Arts with Adolescents.* Portsmouth, NH: Heinemann, 1992.

Rius. *Marx for Beginners.* New York: Pantheon, 1989.

Rodó, José Enrique. *Ariel.* Ed. Gordon Brotherston. Trans. Margaret Sayers Peden. Cambridge: Cambridge U P, 1967.

Rodriguez, Luis J. *Always Running: La Vida Loca, Gang Days in L.A.* Willimantic, CT: Curbstone, 1993.

Romano, Tom. *Clearing the Way: Working with Teenage Writers.* Portsmouth, NH: Heinemann, 1987.

———. *Writing with Passion: Life Stories, Multiple Genres.* Portsmouth, NH: Boynton/Cook, 1995.

Rose, Mike. *Lives on the Boundary: A Moving Account of the Struggles and Achievements of America's Educational Underclass.* New York: Penguin, 1989.

Rosenblatt, Louise. *Literature as Exploration,* 5th ed. New York: MLA, 1995.

Ruoff, A. LaVonne Brown. *American Indian Literatures: An Introduction, Bibliographic Review, and Selected Bibliography.* New York: MLA, 1990.

Rushdie, Salman. "Chekov and Zulu." *East, West: Stories.* Toronto: Vintage, 1996.

Said, Edward. *Culture and Imperialism.* New York: Knopf, 1993.

———. *Orientalism.* New York: Vintage, 1979.

Saldívar, Ramón. *Chicano Narrative: The Dialectics of Difference.* Madison: U of Wisconsin P, 1990.

Salih, Tayeb. *Season of Migration to the North.* Portsmouth, NH: Heinemann, 1991.

Sanders, Andrew. *The Short Oxford History of English Literature.* New York: Clarendon Press, 1994.

Scholes, Robert. *Textual Power: Literary Theory and the Teaching of English.* New Haven: Yale U P, 1985.

Sedgwick, Eve Kosofsky. *Epistemology of the Closet.* Berkeley: U of California P, 1990.

Sembène, Ousmane. *God's Bits of Wood.* Trans. Frances Price. London: Heinemann, 1982.

———. *Tribal Scars and Other Stories.* Trans. Len Ortzen. London: Heinemann, 1974.

———. *Xala.* Trans. Clive Wake. Westport, CT: Lawrence Hill, 1976.

Semonin, Paul. "Monsters in the Marketplace: The Exhibition of Human Oddities in Early Modern England." *Freakery: Cultural Spectacles of the Extraordinary Body.* Ed. Rosemarie Garland Thomson. New York: New York U P, 1996. 69–81.

Sergel, Sherman L., Roma Connable, and Alfred Connable. *Twelve Angry Men: A Play in Three Acts* (adapted from the television show by Reginald Rose). New York: Washington Square, 1973.

Shakespeare, William. *Complete Works*. New York: Viking, 1969.

Shakur, Sanyika. *Monster: Autobiography of an L.A. Gang Member*. New York: Penguin, 1994.

Shakur, Tupac. *2pacalypse Now*. Interscope, 1991.

Shapiro, James. *Shakespeare and the Jews*. New York: Columbia U P, 1996.

Shirer, William L. *The Rise and Fall of the Third Reich: A History of Nazi Germany*. New York: Simon, 1960.

Shor, Ira. *Critical Teaching and Everyday Life*. Chicago: U of Chicago P, 1987.

Showalter, Elaine. *A Literature of Their Own: British Women Novelists from Brontë to Lessing*. Princeton: Princeton U P, 1977.

Sinclair, Upton. *The Jungle*. New York: New American, 1990.

Slotkin, Richard. *Regeneration Through Violence: The Mythology of the American Frontier, 1600–1860*. Middletown: Wesleyan U P, 1973.

Smith, David. "Huck, Jim, and American Racial Discourse." *Satire or Evasion?: Black Perspectives on Huckleberry Finn*. Ed. James S. Leonard, Thomas A. Tenney, and Thadious M. Davis. Durham, NC: Duke U P, 1992. 103–123.

Speer, Albert. *Inside the Third Reich*. 1970. London: Phoenix, 1995.

Spiegelman, Art. *Maus: A Survivor's Tale*. New York: Pantheon Books, 1986.

Spiller, Robert, et al., eds. *Literary History of the United States*. 4th ed., rev. New York: Macmillan, 1974.

Spivak, Gayatri. *The Post-Colonial Critic: Interviews, Strategies, Dialogues*. Ed. Sarah Harasym. New York: Routledge, 1990.

Spring, Joel. *Images of American Life: A History of Ideological Management in Schools, Movies, Radio, and Television*. Albany: State U of New York P, 1992.

Stoll, David. *Rigoberta Menchú and the Story of All Poor Guatemalans*. Boulder: Westview, 1999.

Strasser, Todd. *The Wave: The Classroom Experiment That Went Too Far*. New York: Dell, 1981.

Sundquist, Eric. *To Wake the Nations: Race in the Making of American Literature*. Cambridge: Harvard U P, 1993.

Susag, Dorothea. *Roots and Branches: A Resource of Native American Literature—Themes, Lessons, and Bibliographies*. Urbana, IL: NCTE, 1998.

Swann, Brian, ed. *Coming to Light: Contemporary Translations of the Native Literatures of North America*. New York: Random House, 1994.

Swift, Jonathan. "A Modest Proposal." *The Portable Swift*. Ed. Carl Van Doren. New York: Penguin, 1977.

Terkel, Studs. *Working: People Talk About What They Do All Day and How They Feel About What They Do.* New York: New, 1974.

Thomas, Anika. *Life in the Ghetto.* Kansas City, MO: Landmark, 1991.

Thomas, Cal. *Book Burning.* Westchester, IL: Crossway, 1983.

Todorov, Tzvetan. *The Conquest of America: The Question of the Other.* Trans. Richard Howard. New York: Harper, 1984.

VanderStaay, Steven. *Street Lives: An Oral History of Homeless Americans.* Philadelphia: New Society, 1992.

Vaughan, Alden T., and Virginia Mason Vaughan. *Shakespeare's Caliban: A Cultural History.* Cambridge: Cambridge U P, 1991.

Veeser, Aram. *The New Historicism.* New York: Routledge, 1989.

———, ed. *The New Historicism Reader.* New York: Routledge, 1994.

Viadero, Debra. "A Trust Betrayed." *Education Week* 17 Nov. 1993:. 18–25.

Volavková, Hana. *I Never Saw Another Butterfly: Children's Drawings and Poems from Terezín Concentration Camp 1942–1944.* New York: McGraw, 1966.

Welch, James. *Fools Crow: A Novel.* New York: Viking, 1986.

Wells, H. G. *The Island of Dr. Moreau.* London: Orion, 1996.

Whaley, Liz, and Liz Dodge. *Weaving in the Women: Transforming the High School English Curriculum.* Portsmouth, NH: Boynton/Cook, 1993.

Wideman, John Edgar. *Philadelphia Fire.* London: Picador, 1995.

Wiesel, Elie. *Night.* New York: Bantam, 1982.

Wiget, Andrew. *Handbook of Native American Literature.* New York: Garland, 1996.

———. *Native American Literature.* Boston: Twayne, 1985.

Wiggins, Marianne. *John Dollar: A Novel.* New York: Washington Square, 1999.

Wigginton, Eliot. *Sometimes a Shining Moment: The Foxfire Experience.* Garden City, NY: Anchor/Doubleday, 1985.

Wilhelm, Jeffrey D. *"You Gotta BE the Book": Teaching Engaged and Reflective Reading with Adolescents.* New York: NCTE and Teachers College Press, 1997.

Wilson, Harriet E. *Our Nig, or, Sketches from the Life of a Free Black.* New York: Random House, 1983.

Wilson, Richard, and Richard Dutton. *New Historicism and Renaissance Drama.* New York: Longman, 1992.

Winterowd, W. Ross, and Jack Blum. *A Teacher's Introduction to Composition in the Rhetorical Tradition.* Urbana, IL: NCTE, 1994.

Wolf, Naomi. *The Beauty Myth: How Images of Beauty Are Used Against Women.* New York: Morrow, 1991.

Woolf, Virginia. *A Room of One's Own.* New York: Harcourt, 1957.

———. *Three Guineas*. New York: Harcourt, 1966.

Worsnop, Chris. *Screening Images: Ideas for Media Education*. Mississauga, Ontario: Wright, 1994.

Wright, Richard. *Black Boy: A Record of Childhood and Youth*. New York: Harper, 1966.

———. *Native Son*. New York: Harper, 1940.

X, Malcolm, and Alex Haley. *The Autobiography of Malcolm X*. New York: Ballantine, 1965.

Zinn, Howard. *A People's History of the United States*. New York: Harper, 1980.

Films and Videos

Anne Frank Remembered. Dir. Jon Blair. SonyPictures Classics, 1996.

Beyond Killing Us Softly: The Strength to Resist. Dir. Margaret Lazarus and Renner Wunderlich. Cambridge Documentary Films, 2000.

Boyz 'n the Hood. Dir. John Singleton. Columbia Pictures, 1991.

Down and Out in America. Dir. Lee Grant. MPI Home Video, 1986.

Home Less Home. Dir. Bill Brand. Parabola Arts Foundation, 1991.

Inside the Third Reich. Dir. Marvin J. Chomsky. Starmaker Entertainment, 1982, 1994.

Juice. Dir. Ernest Dickerson. Paramount Pictures, 1992.

Killing Us Softly. Advertising's Image of Women. Dir. Margaret Lazarus and Renner Wunderlich. Cambridge Documentary Films, 1979.

Menace II Society. Dir. Allen Hughes and Albert Hughes. New Line Cinema, 1993.

Modern Times. Dir. Charlie Chaplin. Magnetic Video, 1936.

Night and Fog. Dir. by Alain Resnais. International Historic Films, 1955.

Promises to Keep. Dir. Ginny Durrin. Durrin Productions, 1988.

Roger and Me. Dir. Michael Moore. Warner Home Video, 1989.

Salaam Bombay! Dir. Mira Nair. Virgin Vision, 1988.

Schindler's List. Dir. Steven Spielberg. Universal Pictures, 1993.

Shoah. Dir. Claude Lanzmann. New Yorker Films, 1985.

South Central. Dir. Steve Anderson. Warner Home Video, 1992.

Still Killing Us Softly: Advertising's Image of Women. Dir. Margaret Lazarus and Renner Wunderlich. Cambridge Documentary Films, 1987.

Strapped. Dir. Forest Whitaker. Home Box Office, Osiris Films, 1993.

Streetwise. Dir. Martin Bell. New World, 1984.

Sugar Cane Alley. Dir. Euzhan Palcy. Image Entertainment, 1984.

Takeover. Dir. Pamela Yates and Peter Kinoy. Skylight Pictures, 1991.

West Side Story. Dir. Jerome Robbins. United Artists, 1961.

Index

Author

Allen Carey-Webb, a former high school English teacher, is currently professor of English at Western Michigan University. His Ph.D. is in comparative literature (University of Oregon, 1992), and his areas of teaching and research include English education and postcolonial and American minority literatures. Carey-Webb is the author of *Making Subject(s): Literature and the Emergence of National Identity* (1998) and the co-editor of *Teaching and Testimony: Rigoberta Menchú in the North American Classroom* (1997). His articles have been published in a variety of journals, including *English Journal, College Literature, Early Modern Literary Studies, Hispanic Issues,* and *American Literary History.* He maintains a Web site for English teachers at http://vms.cc.wmich.edu/~careywebb.

This book was typeset in Avant Garde and Garamond by Electronic Imaging.
The typeface used on the cover was Triplex.
Cover calligraphy by Barbara Yale-Read.
The book was printed on 60-lb. Lynx Opaque by Versa Press, Inc.